An HONEST PRESIDENT

Also by H. Paul Jeffers

An HONEST PRESIDENT

The Life and Presidencies of

GROVER CLEVELAND

H. PAUL JEFFERS

WILLIAM MORROW
An Imprint of HarperCollins*Publishers*

HarperCollins books may be purchased for educational, business, or sales promotional use. For information please write: Special Markets Department, HarperCollins Publishers Inc., 10 East 53rd Street, New York, NY 10022.

FIRST EDITION

Designed by IPA

Printed on acid-free paper

Library of Congress Cataloging-in-Publication Data has been applied for.

ISBN 0-380-97746-X

00   01   02   03   04   QW   10   9   8   7   6   5   4   3   2   1

For Stanley Gordon

What is the use of being elected or re-elected
unless you stand for something?

— GROVER CLEVELAND

Contents

Prologue

The Big One
and the Dude

In the parlor of the graceful old house in Princeton, New Jersey, on Friday, June 26, 1908, no one spoke a eulogy. Not a word was offered in recital of who Grover Cleveland was or what he had done. Ministers of the religion into which he had been born read the simple Presbyterian ritual of burial. An old friend, the Reverend Dr. Van Dyke, read part of poet William Wordsworth's "The Character of the Happy Warrior." Then friends and distinguished men who had come to do him this last honor followed the widow and the coffin to the graveside. Among them went the twenty-sixth president of the United States.

Two days earlier, in a proclamation officially announcing the passing of the man who had been the twenty-second and twenty-fourth president, Theodore Roosevelt had said of Grover Cleveland, "As mayor of his city, as governor of his state, and twice as president, he showed signal powers as an administrator, coupled with entire devotion to the country's good, and a courage that quailed before no hostility once he was convinced where his duty lay." They were qualities he had personally witnessed.

Theodore Roosevelt had met Grover Cleveland a quarter of a century before in the New York state capital, Roosevelt a native of the Empire State, Cleveland a transplant from New Jersey. For different reasons each had been regarded as a political phenomenon.

After training himself as a lawyer, Cleveland had served as Erie County assistant district attorney and a sheriff and had made a name for himself in the rough-and-tumble of politics as an honest and fearless mayor of Buffalo. Living a happy-go-lucky bachelor's life of hunting, fishing, and frequenting saloons and the best places to eat, he won from the people a landslide election for governor and from the reporters who covered him a nickname. And when Roosevelt first laid eyes on "the Big One" in Albany at his January 1, 1883, inauguration, he understood the sobriquet immediately, for he beheld a lushly mustached, fat man who weighed at least three hundred pounds.

As a brash young Republican political novice with pince-nez glasses, a much more modest mustache, a mouthful of awesome teeth, a penchant for Brooks Brothers suits, and a flamboyant manner, Roosevelt had been stuck with a nickname of his own. Veteran Assembly members referred to him, though never to his face, as "the Dude." A twenty-four-year-old beginning his second term, he'd boasted that since being elected he had "risen like a rocket" to become Minority Leader of the Assembly. But he could not overlook the fact that the Big One had gone from obscure upstate lawyer to mayor of Buffalo, the third largest city in New York, nor that Grover Cleveland had been elected governor with the largest plurality in state history. He had even carried Roosevelt's district.

Faced with a Democrat in the governor's mansion and Democrats in the majority in the Assembly, there was little Roosevelt could do but raise his tinny, sometimes ear-grating voice and offer such colorful assertions as "The difference between your party and ours is that your bad men throw the good ones out, while with us the good throw out the bad."

There would be considerable Roosevelt ridiculing and Democratic rough-riding over Republicans whom Roosevelt called "my men." But while February waned, Roosevelt was abandoning partisanship to back a Democratic bill requiring the state to break its contract with the Manhattan Elevated Railroad by compelling reduction in fares from ten to five cents. Roosevelt viewed this as a boon for the working classes and a blow against financier Jay Gould and others who, despite Roosevelt's own wealth, were his enemies.

If someone else had not introduced the bill, he declared, he would have done so himself. Passed handily, Assembly Bill No. 58 went to Grover Cleveland on March 1.

Before signing it into law, the governor followed a policy he had exhibited as mayor of Buffalo. He settled his considerable girth into a commodious chair to read a bill in its entirety, but as he did so and the hands of the clock passed midnight, he recognized that he was being asked to put his name to a measure that flew in the face of a clause of the Constitution of the United States which prohibited passage of a law by any state that would impair obligations of contracts. While states had authority to alter or repeal charters of corporations, they were compelled not to interfere in legal commercial contracts. In his review of the performance of the company covered by the bill, he found the firm had fulfilled all its contractual obligations.

Acutely aware of the popularity of the bill, he gambled with his future in politics by vetoing it. Going to bed, he said out loud,

"Grover Cleveland, you've done the business for yourself tonight."

The next day his veto message to the legislature said, "The state should not only be strictly just, but scrupulously fair."

He later told a friend, Richard Watson Gilder, that he went to bed that night expecting to be "the most unpopular man in the state of New York." The next morning as he went down to the Executive Office he was, he would recall, "feeling pretty blue, but putting a smiling face on it." Going through the morning's mail, he asked his secretary, Dan Lamont, "What have the morning papers got to say about me, anything?"

"Why, yes," said Lamont enthusiastically, "they are all praising your political courage."

While the question was floating as to whether Cleveland's surprising veto would be overridden, Theodore Roosevelt instead engaged in some political soul-searching. To the astonishment of Democrats and Republicans, he leapt to his feet in the Assembly to announce that he had come to the conclusion the governor was right. "I have to say with shame that when I voted for this bill," he confessed on the Assembly floor, "I did not act as I think I ought to have acted."

He said he had "weakly yielded, partly in a vindictive spirit toward the infernal thieves" of the Elevated Railroad and "partly in answer to the popular voice of New York." Condemning "the wealthy criminal class," he said he would rather leave politics having the feeling he had done what was right than win approval by acting "as I ought not to."

Without the assent of Roosevelt and those who followed his lead, there were not enough votes to override, and the Republican found himself cited in one newspaper for having demonstrated "characteristic manliness," but denounced by downstate editors who favored the fare reduction bill. He was also branded a weakling, a hoodlum, a "bogus reformer," and "The Chief of the Dudes."

Hailed for an act of political courage, the Big One could not overlook Roosevelt's equally brave act. Grateful and admiring, he invited Roosevelt to discuss a subject "of mutual interest."

Eager to learn what the Big One had in mind, Roosevelt went.

The topic was dear to both men's hearts and the centerpiece of a growing national movement: civil service reform. Indeed, Roosevelt had introduced a bill intended to reduce political patronage in the state. Unfortunately, on orders from the bosses of both political parties, the measure was blocked in the Judiciary Committee of the Assembly.

With ally Isaac Hunt at his side, Roosevelt sat in the Executive Chamber as the Democrat Grover Cleveland devoted an hour to expressing support for Roosevelt's stalled bill and consulting with the two Republicans on how to wrench it from committee so a bipartisan coalition could be hammered together to pass it.

Leaving the conference, Roosevelt was "dee-lighted," as he was wont to say, that he had won such powerful support.

But it was a fluke of timing which provided the breakthrough. Presiding over a meeting of the Judiciary Committee, Hunt looked around and noticed that some of the bill's opponents were not in their chairs. Grasping the moment, he called for a vote, and the bill was approved and sent to the Assembly.

"My object in pushing this measure," declared Roosevelt as the measure was debated, "is to take out of politics the vast band of hired mercenaries whose very existence depends on their success, and who can almost always in the end overcome the efforts of them whose only care is to secure pure and honest government." Despite cries of "No! No!" and "Nonsense!" on the part of the opposition, Roosevelt Republicans and Cleveland Democrats carried the day. Both the Big One and the Dude basked in the praise that followed.

Consequently, several times during the legislative sessions of 1883 and 1884 both Cleveland and Roosevelt fired the public's imagination by battling leaders of their respective party machines, Tammany Hall's Roscoe Conkling and the Republican "Easy Boss," Thomas Platt. This impression of an alliance between the governor and the feisty legislator was soon reinforced by newspapers. One cartoonist depicted them linking arms and surveying a disintegrating Tammany Hall tiger. Thomas Nast's work in *Harper's Weekly* showed them conferring amicably on reform legislation.

As fate would have it, both men would leave Albany to carry their campaigns for good government into "a larger kingdom," as Roosevelt's mentor Senator Henry Cabot Lodge would call it. Cleveland got there fourteen years before Roosevelt. But by a couple of twists of fate, he preceded Roosevelt in the presidency by only nine months. When Cleveland died in June 1908, the man who had come into that larger kingdom as the result of the assassination of William McKinley was in his last year of national governance.

★   ★   ★

Elihu Root, a towering presence in the politics of Roosevelt and Cleveland's time, wrote in the introduction to a two-volume biography of the only man elected to two nonconsecutive presidencies, "Biography makes a period interesting by throwing a highlight on a central figure and establishing a relation between all the conditions and incidents of the time with that figure."

In a period of dramatic and lasting changes in America, what a central figure Grover Cleveland had proved to be. He presided in years history calls the Gilded Age. His second term would span half the decade known as the Gay Nineties. Yet beneath gilding and gaiety, millions of Americans lived with poverty, disease, government corruption, and brutal indifference on the part of a ruling class of Wall Street tycoons and robber barons who controlled industry: railroads, steel, coal, and almost everything else.

Seeking better lives and a brighter future, the people looked to a nationwide movement for reform led by enlightened members of an educated class and firebrands of a fledgling labor movement the likes of which no president had ever confronted.

Yet it is not these events and personal traits for which Grover Cleveland is remembered. Rather than being recalled for honesty; for setting records as mayor, governor, and president in vetoing bills he considered blatant raids on the Treasury; for his achievements in governmental reform; for a vigorous defense of the Monroe Doctrine without resort to war; and for resisting a wave of American imperialism by refusing to approve annexation of Hawaii, he is known primarily as the only president to win the popular vote for a second term but lose the election in the Electoral College, then come back and win four years later.

What also sticks to pages of history books are these hallmarks of his presidency: the first president to get married in the White House; father of the first child born there; and the fact that years before he became president he admitted he had fathered a child out of wedlock.

Consequently, when presidential sexuality burst into headlines following accusations that President Bill Clinton had an adulterous relationship with a young intern in the White House, Americans were made vividly aware by the news media that Cleveland had exhibited an honesty in his paternity scandal which seemed astonishing in contrast to Clinton and many other public officials whose reaction to scandal was to look for ways to "spin" their image. Instead of attempting a cover-up of the paternity revelation, Cleveland admitted it. Similarly, in the heat of his 1884 presidential campaign, he owned up to taking advantage of a law that allowed him to avoid military service during the Civil War by paying another man to go in his place.

As for the judgment of posterity, the man who weathered these campaign tempests and became the twenty-second president of the United States, and then the twenty-fourth, said of his life in politics and eight years in the White House as he lay dying at the age of seventy-one, "I have tried so hard to do right."

★　★　★

The first Democrat elected to the presidency since the Civil War, Cleveland had come into an office still overshadowed by Abraham Lincoln and diminished by the scandals of the Grant administration. He also confronted a period of national readjustment in the bitter and divisive wake of Reconstruction. The challenge before him involved not only a recovery from the enormous losses of the war, including the abolition of slavery, but reconciliation of North and South. This was not an easy task for a New York Democrat.

It was a time, as a contemporary observer of events saw it, requiring a leader possessing strong common sense, simplicity and directness without subtlety, instinctive and immobile integrity, courage, a kindly nature with a great capacity for friendship, and a great capacity for wrath that made him a dangerous man to trifle with.

The country did not need a visionary or fanatic, or a man who was self-seeking. Above all, he had to be honest.

An assessment of whether the twenty-second and twenty-fourth president of the United States had met these needs and succeeded in his desire "to do right" was remanded to the judgment of anyone who might tackle writing his biography. The English essayist Thomas Carlyle opined in 1830, "History is the essence of innumerable biographies." Ralph Waldo Emerson was even more emphatic. "There is properly no history," he declared, "only biography."

In that spirit, and mindful of Elihu Root's admonition to throw a highlight on a central figure by establishing a relation between that figure and conditions and incidents of the figure's time, this recounting of the life of Grover Cleveland endeavors not only to present a fresh assessment of him, but also to provide, from the perspective of an America on the cusp of both a new century and a new millennium, an evaluation of a remarkable life and political career that brimmed with achievements and foreshadowed issues and controversies confronting the nation and its political leadership more than a century later.

Theodore Roosevelt labored to secure an honored place in history by leaving posterity an autobiography and numerous other self-laudatory writings, along with a treasure trove of saved letters, memorandums, and other missives to inform those who would write his life story.

Cleveland, however, was so unconcerned about trumpeting himself that his official and personal papers were left in what an early Cleveland biographer, Robert McElroy, described as an enormous mass in "chaotic condition."

Although Grover Cleveland wrote retrospective articles on a few aspects of his presidency, there is no autobiography. While in office he gave no thought to plans for a repository in a library with an attached museum of the kind enthusiastically erected for every chief executive since Franklin D. Roosevelt and paid for in perpetuity by taxpayers. Upward of 50,000 documents, letters, and final copies of many of Cleveland's presidential messages brought from Washington at the end of his public life were stored in a friend's New York country house.

"He apparently made no attempt to keep his files complete," Professor McElroy wrote in 1923, "and frequently the only copy of an important document was given to some friend who wished a specimen of his handwriting."

Since publication of McElroy's two-volume *Grover Cleveland: The Man and the Statesman*, full biographies of him have been few and far between. They include versions by Horace Samuel Merrill (1957) and Rexford Guy Tugwell (1968), an analysis of his presidency by Richard E. Welch Jr. (1988), and a massive *Grover Cleveland: A Study in Courage* (1932), by Allan Nevins.

With so little material available to consult, it was understandable that a writer in the 1990s seeking comparisons for President Clinton's possible place in history observed, "Being down there with Grover Cleveland and James K. Polk is not an inviting prospect."

These were mistaken parallels. Hardly any student of presidents places Cleveland and Polk "down there" in significance. Arthur M. Schlesinger Jr.'s 1966 poll of historians ranked Polk highly and rated Cleveland as "high average," along with John Adams, James Monroe, William McKinley, Dwight D. Eisenhower, John F. Kennedy, and Lyndon B. Johnson.

A rationale for a perception of Cleveland's status as low was proposed in 1997 when the *Los Angeles Times* observed that service in "uneventful times means a minor reputation."

That Cleveland's times were uneventful is not true.

During his eight years in the Executive Mansion, as the White House was formally titled, he opposed political bossism by fighting the spoils system and seeking civil service reforms, vetoed Civil War veterans' pension bills as a fraud for pillaging public coffers, contended with the first "march on Washington," restrained the doctrine of "manifest destiny" by blocking a plan to annex Hawaii, sent out the army to keep Western railroads in operation during the first national strike, wrestled with the effects of a financial panic and subsequent economic depression, championed the gold standard, invoked "executive privilege" in a wrangle with Congress, carried on a campaign denouncing a "lying" and "mean" press, threatened Great Britain with war in defense of the Monroe Doctrine, battled the nation's first "populist" political movement, sought to lower tariffs, authorized a cover-up of a secret operation for cancer, proposed to a woman more than thirty years his junior, and married her in the East Room.

Yet, more than a century after these events, the adjectives applied to Cleveland are "long-forgotten" and "less celebrated," and he is often incorrectly catalogued with such presidential failures as Millard Fillmore, Ulysses S. Grant, and Warren G. Harding.

One American who evidently did not relegate Cleveland to the backwaters of historical significance was President Bill Clinton. An article in *U.S. News & World Report* observed on November 4, 1997, that Clinton had favorably compared himself at various times to Franklin Roosevelt, Harry Truman, John Kennedy, and Theodore Roosevelt. The article went on to note that Clinton had recently become fascinated "with one of his less-celebrated predecessors,

Grover Cleveland" and found in him something of "a soul mate," a Democratic president who struck Clinton as a reformer, futurist, and "vastly underappreciated leader." In the maelstrom of a sex scandal involving President Clinton and a White House intern in 1998, others would compare Clinton to Cleveland and find the parallel inappropriate.

Drawing upon Cleveland's papers, letters, and speeches and on the accounts of contemporary observers, including newspapers and magazines, as well as Cleveland biographies and other histories of his times, this book attempts not only to reconstruct for a general readership the life and presidency of Grover Cleveland, but to show that in important respects he represents a model for anyone seeking or in public office in our time, and that what he said then is still a guide to how the American people should measure their public servants:

Unswerving loyalty to duty, constant devotion to truth, and a clear conscience will overcome every discouragement and surely lead the way to usefulness and high achievement.

1

❋

Happy Bachelor

No one who happened to be on Buffalo's Washington Street one evening in 1873 could recall what triggered the fistfight between the lawyers. It probably was an issue of Democratic Party politics. What everyone vividly remembered was that at some point leading up to the battle Mike Falvey called Grover Cleveland a liar. The next thing Falvey knew, he'd been banged into a gutter near Seneca Street. The combatants then raged as far as Swan Street, where an armistice was mutually proposed and promptly sealed by bellying up to the bar in Gillick's saloon.

Except for politics and the practice of law, Grover relished nothing more than downing large steins of pale lager, especially when accompanied by heaping plates of sausages and sauerkraut and culminating with the smoking of a good cigar, in one of Buffalo's numerous beer gardens and saloons. The thirty-six-year-old bachelor enjoyed the roistering atmosphere of sand-covered floors, flickering gaslights, laughter, loud singing, card games, swapping tales of fishing and hunting, and, being a bachelor, the company of pretty women.

"He was not a great talker," a friend recalled. "Once in a while something would start him going, and he would run on for half an evening, but for the most part he let others do the talking; he listened." His voice was "a little higher than expected from such a large man . . . somewhat nasal, though not unpleasant [with] tenderness in it."

At the time of the fisticuffs with Falvey, Grover had been a Buffalo resident for eighteen years. Man and place proved to be a good match. Bustling, uncouth, materialistic, hardworking Buffalo stood on the cusp of the rugged Western frontier and the conservative, refined East. It offered little in the way of surface graces but brimmed with people of common sense, tenacity, and stubborn character. These traits harmonized with Grover Cleveland's spirit of independence, conscientiousness, efficiency, and, above all, honesty, which had been handed down to him by ancestors, starting in New England.

The first, Moses, for whom the city of Cleveland, Ohio, would be named, had left Ipswich, England, as an indentured apprentice and had landed in Massachusetts in 1635. The family name was of Saxon origin and taken from a region around Whitby, England, known for "clefts or cleves which abound there." It was variously spelled Cliveland, Cleivland, Clifland, Cleffland, and Cleaveland. The "a" was dropped in 1770 by Grover's grandfather, William, whose son Richard was born in Norwich, Connecticut, in 1804.

A brilliant student, Richard Cleveland garnered high honors in Yale's class of 1824 and immediately began studying for the Protestant ministry in Baltimore. There he fell in love with twenty-two-year-old Ann Neal, daughter of a lawbook publisher. After

The fifth child of Rev. Richard and Ann Neal Cleveland, Stephen Grover Cleveland was born on March 18, 1837, in this house called "The Manse" in Caldwell, New Jersey.

continuing his studies at Princeton Theological Seminary, he was ordained in 1828 and accepted the pastorate of the First Congregational Church in Windham, Connecticut. He married Ann the following year. After four years in Connecticut and the births of Anna and William, they moved to Portsmouth, Virginia, where Mary Allen was born. Two years later, Richard accepted a pastorate in New Jersey and the couple settled in Caldwell in time for the arrival of their second son, Richard Jr.

When a fifth child and third boy was born on March 18, 1837, he was named in honor of Richard's predecessor in Caldwell's Presbyterian pulpit, the Reverend Stephen Grover. Over the next few years the Cleveland children would total nine, each of whom would learn filial reverence, strict obedience, unquestioning belief in parental wisdom, and all the other tenets of the Holy Bible and Westminster Catechism. These verities and absolutes were intended to produce a keen sense of responsibility, ethical behavior, and trustworthy character. The effect on Grover was expressed in an essay he wrote at the age of nine. Its central point was that time was not to be wasted. Citing the examples of George Washington and Andrew Jackson, Grover wrote, "If we expect to become great and good men and be respected and esteemed by our friends we must improve our time when we are young. If we wish to become great and useful in the world we must improve our time in school."

When Grover penned these thoughts, the Clevelands were no longer living in Caldwell but in Fayetteville, New York, a village near Syracuse, where Grover was enrolled in a school called the Fayetteville Academy. They remained nine years in a spot to which President Grover Cleveland would return for a brief visit some forty years later. Speaking then of his boyhood in "this pretty village," he cited "the many estimable benefits I received—my early education, the training of Sunday school, the religious advantages, the advantages of your social life. These are the things which have gone with me every step in life. And so, when in short intervals of freedom from the cares and duties of my office, my mind revels in retrospection, these early recollections are the truest, pleasantest, and brightest spots on which my memory lights."

Always large for his age, Grover was during nine years in Fayetteville, in his sister Susan's eyes, "a little round-faced, blue-eyed boy," and in the view of Grover's schoolmates, "chuck full of fun." They found the youth they called Big Steve to be a prankster who was fond of sports, swimming, and tramping up the hills and around in the woods, and crazy about fishing. The latter would be such a lifelong passion that in 1902 he wrote a book on that subject and another of his joys, game shooting. "No man can be a completely good fisherman unless he is generous, sympathetic and honest," he wrote. "The manifestation of littleness and crowding selfishness in other quarters, and the over-reaching conduct so generally permitted in business circles, are unpardonable crimes in the true fisherman's code."

Much of the central code and governing reality of Grover's approach to fishing and all other aspects of life had been instilled by his father. Considered a handsome man, the Reverend Richard Cleveland was large of frame with genial blue eyes, a diminishing hairline, a prominent Roman nose, and a firm mouth. His flock found him kindly, expansive, and somewhat of a charmer who was studious but not brilliant. A colleague in the clergy described Richard Cleveland as distinguished not for one outstanding trait, but for "the happy union and equal development of his virtues" and combining the "tastes and habits of the Christian scholar with practical wisdom and efficiency."

If these characteristics did not result in a great preacher and minister, they proved to be ideal traits in a father. Combining insistence on sound religious training with a commitment to the education of his children, he appreciated that when the fundamental obligations of the day had been met, there had to be room in the lives of children for play. After chores and study they were permitted outdoor fun and evening games involving the entire family. The only thing he could not provide his wife and offspring was an abundance of money. The most he ever earned as a man of the cloth was never as much as a thousand dollars a year. This proved an inadequate sum to sustain such a large family. Consequently, Grover and his brothers were required to find jobs to supplement the coffers. For Grover and the others this meant working on the Erie Canal, directing barges and boats to spots where they could be loaded with the area's chief export, rock lime. Success in coupling boat to shipper earned Grover ten cents.

"Looking back over my life," President Cleveland would say, "nothing seems to me to have in it more both of pathos and interest of the spectacle of my father, a hard-working country clergyman, bringing up acceptably a family of nine children, educating each member so that, in after life, none suffered any deprivation in this respect."

No wonder, then, that late in 1850, when Grover was thirteen years of age, Richard Cleveland welcomed the offer of a new job with not only an annual salary of one thousand dollars, but considerably more prestige than that of a village pastor. The post was district secretary of the Central New York Agency of the American Home Missionary Society, located in Clinton, New York, site of Hamilton College.

As the Clevelands ended their nine-year stay in Fayetteville and settled in Clinton, Grover received an invitation to visit an uncle, Lewis F. Allen. A breeder of short-horned cattle, he had a farm at Black Rock, on the outskirts of Buffalo. Writing to his sister Mary at their new address, Grover recorded that his westward journey via an Erie Canal boat had been slow, that he had "a great many adventures" to relate, and that he hoped to visit Niagara Falls the next day. He found his relatives delightful and wished he could "stay the longest allotted time."

Dated October 29, 1850, the letter is the earliest piece of correspondence to be preserved and was signed "Stephen G. Cleveland."

Rejoining the family in Clinton, he plunged into studies at Clinton Liberal Institute, a small school with only two teachers, and dreamed of following his brother William in attending Hamilton. But scholarliness did not emerge as his strong suit. He would look back on those days and admit that he "foundered through four books of the *Aeneid*." His sister Margaret would recall "a lad of rather unusual good sense, who did not yield to impulses—he considered well, and was resourceful—but as a student Grover did not shine."

While frustrated with his performance in school and concerned about a decline in his father's health, the fourteen-year-old found life in Clinton a time in which "our family circle entire, parents and children, lived day after day in loving and affectionate converse."

Unfortunately, this idyllic existence soon grounded on shoals of continuing financial hardship. As the ailing reverend's thousand-a-year wages again proved to be inadequate to the needs of the family, it became imperative that Grover leave school and find a job. He did so, thanks to a family friend back in Fayetteville. The deacon of Rev. Richard Cleveland's former church, John McVicar, owned a general store and, fortuitously, needed a clerk. The job would pay Grover $50 the first year and $100 the next, with free room and board.

Another clerk in Deacon McVicar's employ, F. G. Tibbits, provided this account of his and Grover's average day: "It was our duty to wait on customers, sweep and clean up, open and close the place, run errands, and do a turn for neighbors at odd times . . . Our room was large with a plain pine bed, with cords upon it to lay the tick . . . In that room, without carpet, without wallpaper, without pictures, bare, drear, and desolate, we two lived together one whole year. In the winter we fairly froze sometimes. There was no stove in the room, heat coming up from a pipe leading to the store below . . . Grover used to rise, in those days, at about five o'clock in the summer and half-past five in the winter. He would go out to an old green pump that then stood in the square, used for watering horses, and make his morning toilet in the trough, then back to the store; open up; sweep out; build the fire; dust up; lay out the goods. By and by, about seven o'clock, along would come Mr. McVicar."

Mrs. McVicar took the greatest interest in Grover and concluded from his integrity and correctness that it was foreordained, as she advised Grover, that he should follow his father (and brother William) into the ministry.

A clue to what Grover Cleveland might do in his future presented itself when he and other former students of the Fayetteville Academy formed a debating society, known as a "gymnasium." Elected vice-archon, Grover served as judge of a debate on whether Roman Catholic institutions were a menace to the interests of the Union. Grover ruled the negative side winner. When he joined a debate as to whether an attorney would be justified in defending a man whom the lawyer knew to be guilty, he argued no. Many years later, both questions would be raised again in the context of the career Grover Cleveland ultimately chose. The latter would arise when he was a lawyer, prosecutor, and sheriff in Buffalo. The place of Catholicism in American politics would come up in a sensational, and arguably decisive, manner during the presidential campaign of 1884.

That thirty-two years after toiling as Deacon McVicar's store clerk Grover Cleveland would run for president of the United States, and be elected, certainly never entered his mind, or anyone else's. Indeed, Grover exhibited no sign of peering farther into the future than returning to Clinton and pursuing an education at Hamilton. Whether Grover expected it to lead to the fulfillment of Mrs. McVicar's prognostication that he would follow his father's footsteps into a lifetime in the clergy, he offered no hint.

When he left Deacon McVicar's employ after a year and returned to Clinton in March 1853, his purpose was to attend the wedding of his eldest sister, Anna, to Rev. Eurotas Hastings, a missionary just back from years of service in Ceylon, and to resume his studies. Upon arriving in Clinton, Grover learned that his father's illness had been attributed to a gastric ulcer. If Richard Cleveland were to have any chance of improvement in his health, the doctor advised, he would have to abandon his post with the Missionary Society and find a less demanding position. When he reluctantly resigned to accept the Presbyterian pulpit in the nearby hamlet of Holland Patent, the New York *Evangelist* judged his mission work "successful and much approved."

When the forty-nine-year-old reverend gave his first sermon to the Holland Patent congregants in September 1853, Grover was sixteen and a half and looking forward to the wedding of another sister, Mary. On October 1, having been asked to accompany her on a shopping trip to Utica, ten miles away, Grover arose early, looked briefly into his father's room, and found him sleeping peacefully. Waiting in the carriage several hours later while Mary shopped, he heard a paperboy shouting the news that Rev. Richard Cleveland was dead. He had passed away minutes after Grover had looked in on him. The cause was peritonitis.

In old age and facing the imminence of his own death, Grover Cleveland would say to a friend and former colleague in government and one of his biographers, George F. Parker, that it was impossible to exaggerate his father's strength of character. "It emphasizes," he said, "the qualities of pluck and endurance which have made our people [Americans] what they are."

As the patriarch of the Cleveland family was laid to rest on October 4, 1853, Grover faced the disappointing reality that his dream of going to Hamilton College had been dashed. Upon him had fallen the responsibility of providing for not only his virtually destitute mother, but four younger brothers and sisters.

As to what to do to shoulder the burden, the oldest of the Cleveland children offered Grover a suggestion. Having taken a job in New York City at the Institution for the Blind, William proposed that Grover go along with him and apply for a position as assistant teacher. With no other prospects on the horizon, Grover went and was hired.

A young pupil named Fanny Crosby discerned in the seventeen-year-old newcomer who had just lost his father "an air of pensive sadness." She discovered his mind "unusually well developed for his years; so well in fact that he might be called a marvel of precocity." She and Grover quickly became friends, and remained so until his death. Surviving him by many years, she was interviewed by Professor Robert McElroy for his 1923 Cleveland biography.

She left this portrait of the teenage Grover. Physically, he was "nearly full grown as to height, but slender." Intellectually, he struck Fanny as having reached maturity "many years earlier than your average man." He was a persistent reader of history, she continued, and appeared to be developing "something of a bent for the law." But he did not confine his reading entirely to history and law. Many times he favored Fanny and other students with readings of the poets. So concerned was Fanny about the youth's studiousness that she warned him, "Take care that you do not study too much and injure yourself."

Thus began a year which Grover Cleveland would remember with none of the nostalgia he felt for his nine years in Fayetteville. Assigned to the literary department in a huge, cold, and bleak building which filled the block between Eight and Ninth avenues and Thirty-third and Thirty-fourth streets, he helped supervise and teach from nine in the morning to half-past four in the afternoon. Along with his brother, he was in charge of the boys' dormitory at night. More prison than school, the Institution for the Blind was under the strict control of a martinet-superintendent whose name seemed to have been taken from a Charles Dickens tale, T. Colden Cooper.

According to Fanny Crosby, when Cooper meted out extremely severe punishment to a blind boy, Grover "could not, of course, in his position, take steps to resent it by a physical demonstration, but he showed it in every word and action that he would like to punish [Cooper] in the most effective way."

After a year of increasing frustration and distress over conditions which he was powerless to change, Grover handed in his resignation, said good-bye to colleagues, students, and his brother, and returned to Holland Patent. When efforts to find employment failed, he joined forces with another Holland Patent youth and set out for a burgeoning city with a name which to Grover "seemed like an inspiration." But en route to Cleveland, Ohio, he paused in Buffalo to visit his uncle, Lewis Allen, and found him poring over paperwork related to his cattle business. After hearing his nephew's plans and hopes for a future in law in Cleveland, Allen cautioned that going to a strange city, with no money and no prospects for a situation, was a "precarious" undertaking. A wiser idea, he suggested, was for Grover to extend his visit for five months. During that period, Allen would endeavor to find a law firm willing to employ him while Grover completed his law studies. Grover accepted the offer.

There is no way of knowing how often the course of history has pivoted on such a spur-of-the-moment decision, but, as Cleveland biographer Allan Nevins noted, "Had Cleveland embarked upon the law in an older city like Boston or New York his lack of intellectual distinction would have militated against his advancement, while if he had begun his work farther west, in the still rough-and-tumble city like Chicago or Milwaukee of that day, his quintessential traits of character and courage would have counted for less than they did."

Just how rough-and-tumble Buffalo, New York, was in 1855, Grover promptly learned. It was in many ways still a frontier town. Dotted with saloons, brothels, and gambling houses, it had a reputation as one of the most dangerous towns in America, so perilous that the police patrolled only in daylight, and always in pairs. Nor was the waterfront city which linked the East with the West pleas-

Cleveland's uncle, Lewis F. Allen, persuaded him to settle in Buffalo in 1855 and begin a career in law.

ing to eyes or nostrils. Lacking a sewage system and always be-clouded by smoke from factories, it was architecturally bleak, bar-ren of parks, and deficient in artistically or culturally uplifting institutions such as museums and concert halls. The few graces to be found were in its church edifices and houses of leading citizens, such as that maintained by Lewis Allen on Niagara Street.

"It was a pleasant home in which young Cleveland found him-self," wrote Charles H. Armitage in *Grover Cleveland, as Buffalo* *Knew Him,* published by the *Buffalo Evening News* in 1926. "The house was of stone, roughly stuccoed; square and solid like its new inmate. It had something of a history itself, having been built in 1817 by General Peter B. Porter, of a family long prominent along the Niagara Frontier. Since 1836 it had been the residence of Mr.

Allen. Henry Clay and Daniel Webster has been entertained there. So had General Winfield Scott and Millard Fillmore and William H. Seward and Horace Greeley."

A man of considerable substance, Lewis Allen also owned five hundred acres at Black Rock, site of his cattle farm. Because of his prominent status in the city he was a familiar and welcome figure in the downtown business district with its stores and blocks of suites, including offices in the most distinguished edifice—the Weed Block—of Buffalo's most prestigious and busy law firms, with a register of clients stretching back to Millard Fillmore. And so it was to the senior member of Rogers, Bowen and Rogers that Grover was presented by his uncle in December 1855. Informed that the young man desired to study law, Henry W. Rogers plunked onto his desk a copy of the thick, weighty bible of the legal profession, Blackstone's commentaries on law. Pointing to it, he declared, "There's where you begin."

Sometime later, Allen asked Grover, "How are you getting on at the office?"

"Pretty well, sir, only they won't tell me anything."

When Allen reported this to Rogers, he was answered, "If the boy has brains he'll find out for himself without anybody telling him."

Between December 3, 1855, and June 27, 1856, while reading Blackstone and finding out what was going on in the firm, Grover was being paid $152.75 in sixteen small installments, ranging from two to twenty dollars. This income was apparently enough to permit him to take a vacation and to move out of his uncle's home and into a boardinghouse.

Grover provided an insight into his state of mind at this time in letters to his sister Anna. At the end of 1856 he wrote, "I am still living alone as I have always done, maintaining life and energies by means of eating, drinking, and sleeping. Indeed, I am so addicted to these habits that I find it impossible to forego them for any length of time. I must have my *provender* three times a day and eat and drink in proportion. It's lamentable, isn't it? I am boarding at a second-class hotel and paying at the rate of $4 a week. I am not very much pleased with my situation in this respect and contemplate a change soon. My employers are very kind to me, and all things taken into consideration, I try to be happy, though sometimes I find it pretty hard."

Two months later he wrote to Anna, "I still live," and proceeded to report he was "doing well." He added, "I flatter myself, and my employers assure me, that if I keep on I'll make a lawyer."

Toward that goal he worked hard, and evidently very quietly. Early in his studies he was reading in the law library at the office's closing time. Only when he decided to allow himself a respite did he look up from Blackstone to discover that he was alone—locked in by the departed partners and clerks. Bemused, he vowed to himself, "Some day I will be better remembered."

At age nineteen he was three years shy of being able to vote in that year's presidential election. But he wasn't too young to work on behalf of the Democratic Party's candidate for president, James Buchanan, claiming that he was "repelled" by the candidacy of Republican John C. Fremont, which he regarded as "having a good deal of fuss and feathers about it." Whether he decided then that the Democratic Party would remain his affiliation for the rest of us life, we have no way of knowing. It seems reasonable to suppose that as he labored to help elect Buchanan, he could not have anticipated that the next Democrat elected president of the United States would be himself.

At the beginning of the last year of Buchanan's single term as president, Grover's law studies ended and he applied for admission to the New York State Bar. Granted his law license in May 1860, he was empowered to hang out his own shingle. Instead, he remained with the firm of Rogers, Bowen and Rogers and made slow but steady advancement, beginning with promotion to the post of managing clerk. Now old enough to vote, he began taking on a larger role in the Democratic Party in Buffalo and Erie County. In 1862, at age twenty-five, he won his first elective office, supervisor of the Second Ward. That November, partly in recognition of his work for the party and in part because the Democrat who had been elected district attorney was quite elderly, he was appointed assistant district attorney. The result, he would later tell an interviewer, was to make him de facto D.A. During his three years in the office, he noted, he'd attended all of the twelve grand juries and presented the majority of the cases. Nearly all indictments had been drawn by him, and about half of the trials he'd handled personally. On more than one occasion he had conducted four jury trials a day and won them all. Then he went to his office and worked from eight o'clock in the evening to three in the morning to prepare for the next day's work, only to be back at his desk five hours later, ready to joust with "some of the best criminal practitioners in the county."

Of this fresh face in the political arena an editorial in the Buffalo *Courier* said, "Mr. Cleveland is one of the most promising young members of the bar, is a thoroughly read lawyer, and possesses talent of a high order. He will have an opportunity of demonstrating this and 'more too,' and, our word for it, he will prove himself equal to the occasion."

*Cleveland at age twenty-seven as assistant
district attorney of Erie County.*

While this praise and an impressive record as assistant district attorney signaled possibly greater things for him should he continue in politics, Grover's being a prosecutor came at a financial cost. The job paid half what he earned annually in private practice at a time when he was shouldering the burden of providing for his mother and two unmarried younger sisters: Susan, age eighteen, and the youngest of Richard and Ann Cleveland's children, fourteen-year-old Rose.

Help could not be realistically expected from his brother William, who was newly married and earning meager wages as a Presbyterian minister in Southampton, Long Island. The two other Cleveland boys, Lewis Frederick (called Fred) and Richard Cecil (who also went by his middle name), had gone off to fight for the Union in the Civil War. Neither could afford to send money home. What might happen in terms of the financial support for their mother and sisters should Grover be conscripted was an unthinkable prospect and unanswerable question—until Abraham Lincoln took up a pen to sign into law the Conscription Act of March 3, 1863.

Its provisions allowed draft-eligible men to buy their way out of serving by paying $300 for a "commutation," or by furnishing a suitable substitute. When the conscription procedure began with drawings of names in May, Grover's was chosen on the first day. But he was ready. He had found a substitute in the person of a Great Lakes seaman named George Brinske, also known as Benninsky. Had Grover wished, as assistant district attorney he could have found an almost limitless roster of substitutes among discharged convicts or friendless men accused of a crime who would have gladly chosen army life over imprisonment.

Satisfied with the financial arrangement offered him ($150),

Benninsky was sworn into the army at Fort Porter on July 6, 1863. Serving with the Seventy-sixth New York Regiment on the Rappahannock River in Virginia, he injured his back (not in combat) and served as an orderly in a military hospital in Washington, D.C., for the remainder of the war.

During the approximately two years of Benninsky's army service, Grover continued as assistant district attorney and in his life as a bachelor with a reputation for lacking the social graces and not mixing with Buffalo's young society. A contemporary recalled, "He never attended Cobleigh's dancing academy, where the young men and maidens received instruction in the polka, lancers and other popular dances. Outside of a few cronies he didn't have the reputation of being a good mixer. Once, and only once, is it of record that he attended Buffalo's chief social function, the charity ball."

When another local election loomed in 1865, he offered himself to Buffalo voters as the Democratic candidate for Erie County district attorney. His declaration was promptly hailed by the *Courier*. It depicted a public official whose gentlemanly deportment and conceded ability had given him a standing at the bar which had seldom been gained by one of his years. "He is a young man," the newspaper added, "who, by his unaided exertions, has gained a high position at the bar, and whose character is above reproach."

His Republican opponent, Lyman K. Bass, who happened to be his roommate, beat him by barely 600 votes in a predominantly Republican county. Out of public office and no longer in the firm of Rogers, Bowen and Rogers, Grover formed a partnership with Isaac K. Vanderpoel that lasted three years. This was succeeded in 1869 by a partnership with Albert P. Laning and Oscar Folsom. A genial young graduate of Rochester University, Oscar proved to be one of the rare friends of Grover who found favor with Grover's uncle and aunt, the latter of whom referred to Grover's associates in the city's saloons as "queer people."

There were, in fact, two Grover Clevelands. The one who garnered approval from Mrs. Lewis Allen was the serious, hardworking lawyer who toiled at his desk until two in the morning. The second left the office at that hour and made his way to cafés and saloons for drinks and games of cards with a rough crowd who greeted him as one of their kind and called him "Big Steve." The nickname was fitting. Since arriving in Buffalo in 1855, he had grown in girth by about a hundred pounds. A beard which had been added soon after he settled in Buffalo was ultimately trimmed to a lush mustache which remained part of his profile for the rest of his life.

During the law partnership with Laning and Folsom, Grover was recognized as the one who got the work done, but only in civil litigation. True to his stated belief in the Fayetteville debate that a lawyer was justified in refusing to defend a client he knew to be guilty, he refused to take cases in which the case against the defendant was provable beyond a reasonable doubt.

He cautioned clients against haste in bringing civil litigation. "A lawsuit, like a gun," he counseled, "is a dangerous thing without lock, stock or barrel."

Hung on a wall in his office was a plaque representing the allegorical figures of Life, Duty, and Death. Beneath them was a motto: "As thy days are, so shall thy strength be."

His days as a lawyer certainly were busy, as his late father's days as a clergyman had been filled with activity, but the income of a lawyer often proved as insufficient as the wages of a minister. Consequently, when leaders of the Erie County Democratic Party approached him to run for sheriff—a position whose salary was based on a collection of fees which could easily total $40,000 in three years—he sought advice from a friend. "I know that it is not usual for lawyers to be sheriffs," he said to William Dorsheimer, "but there are some reasons why I should consider the latter carefully. I have been compelled to earn my living since I was seventeen. I have never had time for reading, nor for thorough professional study. The sheriff's office would take me out of practice, but it would keep me about the courts, and in professional relations. It would give me considerable leisure, which I could devote to self-improvement. Besides, it would enable me to save a modest competency, and give me the pecuniary independence which otherwise I may never have. I have come for your advice. What would you do in my place?"

Dorsheimer said he would seek the position. When Grover did so, the *Courier* again rallied behind him. Referring to him as "*facile princeps* among the younger members of the Bar of Buffalo," the newspaper saw him as "at the same time so true a gentleman, so generous, modest, and lovable a man, that we have never heard of anybody's envying him. He will rally the utmost strength of the Democracy to the polls, and afterwards make one of the best sheriffs Erie County ever had."

Despite such praise for him and impressive pluralities in Erie County by the Democratic candidates for governor and congressman, Grover squeaked by with an edge of only 303 votes. When he took office on New Year's Day 1871 for a two-year term, he was less than three months away from his thirty-fourth birthday and in charge of an office with a reputation for corruption and official skulduggery in a county whose chief city was as lawless, vice-ridden, and governmentally corrupt as any spot with a waterfront on the east or west coast of the United States. Buffalo offered one saloon for every 220 residents (150,000 people, 673 bars), scores of gambling dens whose doors never shut, and dozens of brothels. Not listed among these statistics was the number of individuals in city and county government offices with greedy hands outstretched for any amount of graft being offered, or eager to look the other way (for a price) if anyone who had a government contract found a means to cheat on it. But as one supplier of cordwood who had always come up short by several board feet discovered, Sheriff Grover Cleveland not only was determined to expose such shady practices but possessed a tape measure. Suppliers of grain and other foodstuff for county prisons quickly learned that the practice of short-weighting goods was also expected to cease forthwith.

Two men who discovered that Sheriff Cleveland was not a man to shirk his duty had the opportunity to witness his mettle from a misfortunate vantage point. The first was a waterfront drunkard named Patrick Morrissey who had been convicted of stabbing his mother to death with a bread knife because she refused to give him money. He was sentenced to die by public hanging on September 6, 1872. As in the case of virtually every such hanging in history, the event was eagerly anticipated by a bloodthirsty crowd. But as they gathered at the prison on the appointed date, they were shocked and outraged to discover that screens had been erected to block their view. Even more amazing, the disappointed sightseers would learn, the sheriff had been so troubled by the prospect of executing Morrissey that he had discussed with his mother whether it was right to take advantage of the law by paying someone a ten-dollar fee to carry out the gruesome task. Ann Cleveland assured him that it was all right. In a rare case of disobedience to his mother, he carried out the task of dispatching Morrissey by springing the trap himself.

Several months later, he found himself troubled by the case of Jack Gaffney, convicted for the murder of a friend during a bar-room brawl. After an unprecedented address to the jury at Jack's trial on the question of his dubious mental stability, Grover heard the jury reject the insanity plea. Once again refusing to delegate the responsibility for the hanging, he did it himself.

In assessing Grover's record at this time, biographer Allan Nevins wrote, "In every way Cleveland made a conscientious and effective sheriff. He worked well with the public prosecutors [and he] was resolute with lawbreakers, kept the jail in excellent order, and served writs promptly." Although he was earning more money than at any time in his life, his younger brothers had relieved him of the pressure of taking care of their mother and shouldered the burden themselves. Fred had turned the Fairfield House hotel in Fairfield, Connecticut, into a thriving summer resort. In association with Cecil, he was in the process of planning the opening of another hotel venture, the Royal Victoria, in Nassau, Bahamas. To further that objective, they sailed from New York City on the steamer *Missouri* on October 17, 1872. Five days later and twenty-five miles off the coast of the Bahamian island of Great Abaco, the ship caught fire.

Informed by telegram that Fred and Cecil, along with some eighty other passengers, had perished, Grover rushed to his mother's home in Holland Patent. In the midst of comforting her, he learned that while the executorship of Lewis's substantial estate had fallen to him and Lewis's New York attorney, the actual responsibility would be his. This involved becoming active in the details of management of the hotel properties and other financial aspects of the estate during the monetary panic of 1873, while at the same time carrying out his duties as sheriff.

When Grover returned to private law practice in partnership with Lyman K. Bass and Wilson S. Bissell, his friend William Dorsheimer felt that Grover had emerged a stronger man and better man. He had also become notably larger. Thanks to large quantities of lager and good German food and a sedentary lifestyle, he would continue to do so, prompting nieces and nephews to bestow upon him the nickname Uncle Jumbo. Yet two other friends, Timothy Mahoney and H. M. Gerrans, found him to be nonetheless vigorous and energetic, as his Washington Street brawl with Mike Falvey convincingly demonstrated.

Another friend, John G. Milburn, provided this portrait:

> He was a prominent citizen, deeply respected for his independence, force of character, and inbred integrity. He was genial and companionable, with his intimacies mainly among men . . . He was more inclined to circumscribe his professional work than to extend it; but he did his work with extraordinary thoroughness . . . [working] all through the night and [resuming] the next morning, after a cold bath and breakfast, as fresh as if he had had a long night's sleep. His physical endurance was extraordinary, beyond anything I have ever known. His commanding qualities were those of judgment, earnestness, and moral force, lightened by a keen sense of humor.

Still the "man's man" he had been before becoming sheriff, he continued to enjoy fishing and hunting and spending leisure time with men of similar interests in hotel lounges and saloons such as Louis Goetz's, Gillick's, and "the Shades," where customers helped themselves to beer from kegs because there was no bar. On Sunday nights he was likely to be found dining on sausage and sauerkraut at the more refined Schenkelberger's restaurant. He also prided himself on being a charter member of "the seven bachelors." Other members were Wilson "Shan" Bissell, attorney John Milburn, and the man who had defeated him in the contest for district attorney, Lyman Bass. Kindred spirits fond of amusement, though not of the parlor or theater variety, they favored hotel lounges, card games played in the swirl of cigar smoke in the back rooms of saloons, fishing, duck hunting, and clambakes at a spot on the Niagara River known as the Beaver Island Club.

A close friend was his former partner, Oscar Folsom. A man of genial high spirits and impressive intelligence, Oscar had a passion for fast horses and owned a trotter named White Cloud which he delighted in matching with spirited competitors, frequently on the streets of Buffalo. An ardent Democrat, he had read election returns indicating that Ulysses S. Grant had defeated Horace Greeley for president in 1872 and greatly amused Grover by grumbling, "The country's gone to hell."

In 1874 Oscar was the father of a pretty eight-year-old girl named Frances. While the child was the apple of her father's eye, this did not prevent him from once almost leaving her behind. The occasion was a challenge to a buggy race. Assigning Frances to the care of the wife of the proprietor of the Sandpit Hotel, Oscar eagerly took up the challenge, won the contest handily, and celebrated the victory at Cassidy's bar. Only after he had proceeded almost all the way home did he turn to Grover and exclaim, "Frances! Gosh, where did I leave that girl?"

One day, in the tradition of men who have discovered happiness in married life, Oscar asked Grover when Grover might be expected to find a wife. Grover looked smilingly at Frances and replied, teasingly, "I'm only waiting for my wife to grow up."

When one of Grover's sisters asked whether he had ever thought of marrying, he replied, "A good many times; and the more I think of it the more I think I'll not do it."

This expressed disinclination toward marriage did not, however, constitute a complete lack of interest in women. He was not a misogynist. Indeed, around the time he completed his term as sheriff he found himself drawn to an attractive widow by the name of Maria Crofts Halpin. A year younger than Grover, she had come to Buffalo from Jersey City, New Jersey, in 1871. Employed as head of the cloak department of Flint & Kent dry goods store, she had two children and attended the fashionable St. John's Episcopal Church. Graceful, quite amusing, well educated, and fluent in French, she resided close to Grover's apartment and won not only his amorous attentions, but those of a few unattached gentlemen who were Grover's acquaintances. She also caught the roving eye of more than one of his wedded friends.

Consequently, when Maria gave birth to a son on September 14, 1874, speculation and tremors of trepidation as to the paternity of the child ran rampant through Grover's circle of friends and associates. But this crisis passed for all but one of them when Maria declared that Grover was the father and that she had named the infant Oscar Folsom Cleveland. With no way of ascertaining the truth of the allegation, and because other possible fathers were married—but with no intention of admitting parentage by agreeing to marry Maria—Grover reluctantly gave his consent to provide for the boy financially.

Unfortunately, that was not the end of the matter. Soon after the birth Grover learned that Maria had begun drinking heavily and was neglecting the boy. Seeking confirmation of these reports, he sought the assistance of Judge Roswell L. Burrows. When his investigation proved the story true, the jurist, without consulting

Grover, arranged for Maria to be temporarily admitted to an asylum for the mentally deranged operated by the Sisters of Charity. While Maria was confined, the judge took steps to see that the boy was committed to an orphan asylum in Buffalo, the $5-a-week fee to be paid by Grover through Judge Burrows. Grover also agreed to fund Maria in a business in Niagara Falls.

This arrangement proved satisfactory for all concerned until Maria reneged on the deal by retaining a lawyer to regain custody of the boy. Why she took this step remains a mystery but has been attributed by Cleveland biographers to a mother's loneliness and to Maria's realization that in entering into the agreement she had surrendered any hold she might have had on Grover. Some historians contend that Maria's consistent purpose throughout this unpleasant episode had been to coerce Grover into marrying her.

Much more likely is an equally unhappy deduction that Maria was, indeed, mentally unbalanced. This scenario gained credence on April 28, 1876, when Maria took the bizarre step of kidnaping the boy. Once again Judge Burrows intervened by obtaining a court order to permanently revoke Maria's claim by recommitting the boy to the orphanage. Adoption of the child by one of western New York's best families relieved Grover of any obligation he felt to continue supporting him.

When the boy's mother later remarried after admitting to her lawyer that Grover had never promised to marry her, lending further credence to the theory that she had accused him of being the child's father to force him into wedlock, Grover supposed that the embarrassing affair was at last behind him.

Later, at a crucial moment in his political career, he would discover that he was wrong.

Since leaving the office of sheriff, Grover had endured two personal crises. First had come the deaths of his brothers in 1872; then, Maria Halpin. As though these calamities were not enough, while the latter affair was going on he suffered the loss of one of his dearest friends. On July 23, 1875, while Grover was looking forward to seeing his friend Oscar Folsom that evening, Oscar was thrown from a carriage and instantly killed.

Three days later, those events were uppermost in Grover's mind as he stood before the Erie County Bar Association to offer a memorial tribute to Oscar. "In the course of a life not entirely devoid of startling events," he said, "I can truly say I never was so shocked and overwhelmed as when I heard, on Friday night, of the death of Oscar Folsom."

As he concluded the eulogy for "a kind and generous heart" he searched the faces of those listening to him. Looking at Oscar's daughter, Frances, he said, "Let our tenderest sympathy extend to a fatherless child."

Despite being a lawyer, Oscar Folsom had died without having prepared a last will and testament. When the court appointed Grover administrator of Oscar's estate, he assumed a duty beyond his legal ones to see to the welfare of Mrs. Folsom and Frances.

Allan Nevins eloquently wrote in his biography of Grover Cleveland that as the 1870s drew to a close, Grover "seemed to have found his permanent place in the life of Buffalo." He was a substantial and highly esteemed lawyer; a true friend; a good Democrat; a boon companion on a fishing or hunting trip; fun to spend an evening with at cards, at dinner, or in a saloon; and evidently a contented confirmed bachelor.

Of his work as a lawyer, Shan Bissell said that his every act "was characterized by the highest sense of honor and by the most delicate appreciation of and compliance with all the rules of professional ethics." One of the judges, Edward W. Hatch, recalled, "He was a good jury lawyer, and frequently became eloquent before juries. He practiced no subterfuge. This was impossible for him. His great strength was his candor, his thorough integrity."

Others saw him as slow, unimaginative, and narrow. One contemporary described his thinking process this way: "First, there came a somewhat wistful look of perplexity, as if bewildered, almost distressed; second, there was a mental circling around the idea in a receptive attitude of mind; and then, third, a sudden grasping of the idea, never to let go."

According to a friend, his approach to writing was equally tortured and brooding.

A list of adjectives applied to his manner of work invariably included "steady," "toiling," "tireless," and "determined." Hardly anyone proposed "overly ambitious politically."

These assessments were all correct.

At some point in the 1870s, for a reason known only to him—perhaps because he thought it more dignified—he also decided to ask his friends, other lawyers, clients, judges, and everyone else to apply another word to him. He wished to be called by his middle name.

2

✦

Mayor Veto

On official registration rolls of the Democratic Party, the proprietor of the restaurant at the corner of Eagle and Pearl streets was listed as Henry W. Dranger. To his patrons, though, he was Billy, and for as long as he'd owned the place it had been a favored resort of the upper echelons of the party leaders. Accordingly, convened there on a Saturday evening in October 1881 were members of a committee which had been appointed by Erie County Democratic Chairman Peter C. Doyle. Their mission was to find someone who would be willing to carry the party's standard in the forthcoming mayoral election in a city which was overwhelmingly Republican. Thus far, the members—Warren F. Miller, John B. Sackett, and William J. Runcie—had been turned down by everyone they had dared to approach. Having toiled for several days and with the nominating convention scheduled for Tuesday, they had about sixty hours remaining in which to come up with a man willing to run, and knew full well that the brutal reality was, as one political wag had noted, "Running for mayor on the Democratic ticket was not classified among the favorite sports in Buffalo."

But as they glumly picked at Billy Dranger's food around 7:30 that evening, the door to the restaurant opened and Grover Cleveland walked through it. Recognizing a golden opportunity, they grasped it. Whether the object of their attention would view their proposition as enthusiastically as they offered it remained to be determined. Invited to join them at their table, Grover accepted, plopped heavily into a chair, and asked, "What brings you fellows together on a Saturday night?"

That Grover didn't know illustrates how far out of touch he'd become concerning party politics. But exactly how desperate the men at the table were quickly became evident as they recited names of those who had brushed aside their invitations to become the party's mayoral candidate. Which of the committeemen asked Grover if he might be interested in running is not known. His logic in inquiring is. Grover had been elected sheriff in a Republican county and left the office with an exemplary record, to say nothing of his service as assistant district attorney. It was true that, as sheriff, he'd angered a great many politicians, but that was nearly ten years ago. He was respected as a fine lawyer and, despite his recent inactivity in the party, he was still a Democrat in good standing. He was the only Democrat who could attract a significant number of independent Republicans, a vital element if a Democrat were to win. And he was honest.

All this was flattering, Grover replied, but if he were to consider accepting the nomination he would insist on a nonnegotiable condition. "The rest of the ticket," he declared, "has to be made up to suit me."

His meaning was not lost on the savvy politicians around the table. Without saying it in so many words, Cleveland was ruling out a run for reelection by the incumbent comptroller, an old political hack of dubious character named John C. Sheehan. A warhorse of the Democratic Party and boss of the predominately Irish waterfront, he had been elected comptroller on the Democratic ballot despite a Republican landslide in the previous election. To challenge Sheehan was such a daring move that it was speculated that Grover had done so in the expectation—even the hope—that his demand would be rejected out of hand. If that was his reasoning and intent, he failed. Confident that Grover Cleveland could win the mayoralty, the party leaders persuaded the nominating convention to dump Sheehan.

On October 25, 1881, delegates unanimously nominated Grover Cleveland and for the first time he addressed a political convention. Beginning by admitting he had hoped their choice might have fallen upon someone "worthier," he declared, "I believe much can be done to relieve our citizens from our present load of taxation, and that a more rigid scrutiny of all public expenditures will result in a great saving to the community."

He continued: "There is, or there should be, no reason why the affairs of our city should not be managed with the same care and the same economy as private interests. And when we consider that public officials are the trustees of the people, and hold their places and exercise their powers for the benefit of the people, there should be no higher inducement to a faithful and honest discharge of a public duty."

In his formal letter of acceptance he digested his speech into the phrase "Public officials are the trustees of the people."

Next came the campaign, known then as "the canvass." Candidates went from place to place where they could find voters in the largest numbers and explain why they believed they deserved to be elected. While these face-to-face encounters afforded some candidates a chance to introduce themselves to the electorate, Grover had no problem with what political managers and campaign advisers and pollsters of a century later would call "name recognition." The majority of Buffalo's voting-age citizens knew him well, either as their former assistant district attorney and sheriff or as a prominent lawyer. Denizens of the city's saloons and restaurants knew him even better. The city's upper class (almost entirely Republican) was keenly aware that in 1877 he had founded the City Club and served as a member of its board of directors.

By all accounts, Grover plunged into the canvassing enthusiastically. One eyewitness to the candidate's style recorded him standing on a table in Charles Diebold's beer garden exhorting the patrons of the First Ward to rally under the banner of municipal reform. Addressing a rally in the more sedate environment of Schwabl's Hall, he declared, "It is a good thing for the people now and then to rise up and let the officeholders know that they are responsible to the masses." Another group heard, "We believe in the principle of economy of the people's money, and that when a man in office lays out a dollar in extravagance, he acts immorally to the people."

These appeals won the editorial endorsement of the Buffalo *Express*. The always-friendly *Courier* extolled his honesty, inflexibility, and contempt for meanness. Even the rock-ribbed Republican newspaper *Commercial Advertiser* conceded that the worst thing to say about him was that he tended to be too haughty in attitude and carried "his head so high, as a rule, that he cannot see ordinary persons."

Evidently the ordinary people of Buffalo did not view him that way. They turned out at the polls to hand him 3,592 more votes than his Republican opponent, Milton C. Beebe. His toll was double that of the Democratic candidate for comptroller and more than ten times the vote for the nominee for city treasurer. Making this an even more impressive personal triumph was the fact that the Republican candidates for state offices carried Buffalo decisively, meaning the city's voters had split their tickets in order to send Grover Cleveland to City Hall by the largest majority ever given to a mayor.

Not yet forty-five, he stood before the Common Council of sixteen Republicans and eleven Democrats on January 1, 1882, and made it clear that the theme of his campaign had not been easy, empty election-year rhetoric.

"We hold the money of the people in our hands to be used for their purposes," he said. "It seems to me that a successful and faithful administration of the government of our city may be accomplished, by bearing in mind that we are the trustees and agents of our fellow-citizens, holding their funds in sacred trust, to be expended for their benefit; that we should at all times be prepared to render an honest account to them touching on the manner of its expenditure, and that the affairs of the city should be conducted, as far as possible, upon the same principles as a good business man manages his private concerns."

Why was it, he wondered, that the city auditor only checked the accuracy of the sums of columns in financial documents, rather than actually *audit* the billings handed in by firms doing business with the city? And why did the auditor not *examine* the legitimacy of the claims filed against the city?

On another subject which proved particularly irksome to the hardworking people of the city, he said, "I am utterly unable to discover any valid reason why the city offices should be closed and the employees released from their duties at the early hour in the day which seems now to be regarded as the limit of a day's work. I am sure no man would think an active private business was well attended to if he and all his employees ceased work at four o'clock in the afternoon. The salaries paid by the city to its officers and their employees entitle it to a fair day's work. Besides, these offices are for the transactions of public business; and the convenience of all our citizens should be consulted in respect to the time during which they should remain open."

Should the Council require an example of how a diligent public servant ought to carry out his duties, they had only to look to the new mayor. Although he continued his partnership in his law firm (as the law allowed), he devoted long hours to mayoral responsibilities. No one would ever question whether the citizens of Buffalo were getting full value for the $2,500 salary they allowed their chief magistrate.

Any cynical doubts nurtured by members of the Council concerning Grover Cleveland's sincerity and determination in regarding himself as guardian against raids upon the treasury were quickly dispelled when the Council routinely sent him a resolution accepting, by a 15 to 11 vote, a bid of slightly under half a million dollars for a five-year street-cleaning contract by the firm of George Talbot. After looking into the circumstances and noting that five other companies had bid much lower, Grover became convinced that Talbot's inflated figure included graft payments. He vetoed the measure and penned the Council a blunt explanatory message. It began, "This is a time for plain speech."

He was withholding approval of the resolution, he explained, "because I regard it as the culmination of a most bare-faced, impudent, and shameless scheme to betray the interests of the people, and to worse than squander the public money."

Reported the *Courier* gleefully, "Rarely have we heard such a universal round of public applause as that which everywhere yesterday greeted Mayor Cleveland's message."

Flustered and red-faced, the Council voted again, with the result that the veto was upheld 23 to 2 and the street-cleaning contract awarded to the low bidder. But in sustaining the veto, the Council had done more than attempt to get out of a politically embarrassing situation and move on. They crowned Grover Cleveland with a halo of political courage and enshrined his street-cleaning veto as the beginning of the most astonishing and rapid ascent from political obscurity to the pinnacle of governmental power in the annals of the United States. American historians and Cleveland biographers agree that if the Buffalo Common Council had overridden the veto of the street-cleaning contract, Grover Cleveland could not, that very year, have become governor of New York, and only two years after that, have been elected the twenty-second President of the United States.

Yet these same chroniclers also agree that should such an outcome have been suggested to Grover as he basked in the praise of his triumph on behalf of the people's public purse, he would have bellowed a laugh and signaled the barkeep to draw him another lager. To the surprise of none of his cronies, Mayor Grover Cleveland proved to be the same happy-go-lucky fellow. He continued to live in a room above his law offices in the Tweed Block and take meals (often by himself) in one of his favorite restaurants or at the City Club. If public office beyond being mayor were of any interest to him, his intimates assumed, the position most likely to hold out appeal to him might be a judgeship. Marriage didn't appear to be in the cards.

While his oldest friends could still call him Big Steve, he discovered that those who lauded his defiance of the Council had given him a new nickname: "our veto mayor."

He used his veto pen to improve public health. It closed contaminated water wells, approved construction of a sewer system, and empowered the Board of Health to ban feeding cows the waste of distilleries. He rejected Common Council approval of a measure to pay three German-language newspapers $800 to publish synopses of its proceedings. He gave thumbs-down to gifts of city money to the Firemen's Benevolent Association and the Fourth of July fund of the G.A.R. (Grand Army of the Republic). He also vetoed payments to officers of the city street department for providing livery services using city horses and wagons. When the Council created the job of morgue keeper, the mayor voided the action and cited as his reason the failure of the legislation to specify the duties of the job. A resolution providing for new sidewalk construction contained no specifications regarding materials and was denounced as the "worst kind of jobbery and swindling."

On July 3, 1882, six months into the job and confident of public support, he spoke with brimming optimism at a ceremony marking the semicentennial of his adopted city. "It seems to me," he said, "that of all men the resident of Buffalo should be the proudest to name his home."

Without question Grover Cleveland had cause to express a rosy view of Buffalo. He had arrived penniless in 1855 and now he was an able and respected lawyer, financially comfortable, well liked in Buffalo's drawing rooms as well as in its saloons, a resounding success as mayor, and only forty-five years old. He spoke of the "Queen City" at the age of fifty being in the "heyday" of its life. "The face is fair, the step is light," he said, "and the burden of life is carried with a song; the future, stretching far ahead, is full of bright anticipations, and the past, with whatever of struggle and disappointment there may have been, seems short, and is half forgotten."

The personal future into which Grover Cleveland stepped to the accompaniment of applause on that sultry summer evening would indeed prove to be full of bright anticipations, but instead of stretching far ahead, it would be swift in unfolding. Over the next 181 days he would find himself courted by bosses of the New York State Democratic Party, nominated for governor, elected by the largest plurality in the state's history, and sworn into office.

He would also lose his mother.

During those last days of waiting as she lay dying in Holland Patent, a friend wrote, "Never once did he leave the home town." When Ann Cleveland died on July 19 she was surrounded by seven surviving children and buried next to their father. Returning to Buffalo, Grover lamented "the desolation of a life without a mother's prayers."

Back in the "Queen City," the mourning mayor discovered that he had become the man of the future, at least in the minds of friends and admirers who envisioned him going on to even greater achievements in politics, beginning with the governorship. Such a proposal a year earlier would have been unthinkable. The widely held belief, reinforced by a decade of political indifference on Grover's part, was that he had no interest in seeking public office.

But his agreeing to run for mayor; his emphatic victory, which bridged party lines and social strata; and his triumphs as the veto mayor had triggered reconsideration of the assumption that Grover had chosen to enjoy the pleasures of private life and leave the reforming of government to others. As mayor, he'd shown that he was not only a willing and able politician, but a darn good one in whom the fires of reform burned brightly.

Among Buffaloans welcoming the reemergence of Grover Cleveland onto the political stage was the editor of the *Courier*, Charles W. McCune, who also happened to be a member of the Democratic State Committee. Regarding whom the party might choose as its candidate for governor in the forthcoming election, he told a meeting of the committee in early summer that he knew of no one better than Grover Cleveland. But the mayor of Buffalo had also attracted the attention of a spirited orator and influential, though quietly behind-the-scenes, leader of the New York State Democratic Party. His name was Edgar K. Apgar and his reading of the newspaper accounts of "the veto mayor" had left him mightily impressed—so much so that he remarked to a friend, "This man Cleveland would make a good candidate for governor."

Whether other party leaders would agree with this assessment remained to be seen. One of those whose approval was essential was Daniel Manning. Head of the party's upstate organization centered in Albany, he was recognized as the leading opponent of the downstate organization rooted in New York City and known as Tammany Hall. If Cleveland were to win the approval of Manning, there would have to be a meeting of the two men. But first Apgar needed to know whether Grover Cleveland had an interest in running for governor. To find out, he wrote him a letter. Dated August 23, it appealed to Cleveland's record as an honest reformer.

Apgar wrote, "The Democratic party has so often, in recent years, abandoned its principles and made dishonest alliances for the sake of temporary success, which even in most cases it has failed to secure, that it has, naturally, lost the confidence of the people. It has fallen, in so many instances, into bad hands, that thousands of Republicans, tired of their own party and longing for a change, have been fearful to trust our promises of reform."

The letter proposed a Cleveland-Manning meeting. Grover's immediate impulse was to be wary of becoming involved in a struggle between upstaters and downstaters. He believed that if anything were to come of his candidacy, it depended on remaining aloof geographically and ideologically from the centers of the two wings of the party. He sought "an entire freedom from the influence of all and every kind of factional disturbance" and believed that in not becoming enmeshed in such factionalism, should he become the gubernatorial nominee, he "could be the instrument of bringing about the united action of the party at the polls."

After weighing this strategy for six days, he sent Apgar a letter in which he flattered Mr. Manning as a man "who has it in his power to assist my cause so much." But to meet with him, he went on, might be "misconstrued and misinterpreted," and it might be "falsely alleged, that an understanding had been arrived at between us, and pledges made which make me his man."

Such a conference, he believed, might serve to undermine his strength as a candidate free of entangling alliances. He preferred to be his *own* man, in fact and unquestionably.

A meeting with Manning did occur, but not until almost a month later, when the entire Democratic Party was in place at the nominating convention in Syracuse. Grover had gone to the parley at the insistence of his backers, who felt it was to his advantage to make himself known to delegates, many of whom still had no idea who he was and why an unknown figure from Buffalo ought to be their standard-bearer in November.

Recalling the experience years later, Grover found some amusement in learning that "the principle thing that was wanted was a chance to look me over, with the result that, in spite of the difficulty of submitting to such an unusual test, I came rather to enjoy it."

Coatless in sweltering mid-September heat, he remained in his hotel, "being introduced to delegates from every part of the state, talking freely with Mr. Manning and the various gentlemen attached to my fortunes."

Politicians were not the only individuals taking the measure of the man from Buffalo. He was carefully scrutinized by newspaper reporters. The gentleman who represented *The New York Times* saw—and wrote of—a man "a little above the medium height, with a portly and well-proportioned figure." The head, "set squarely upon a pair of broad shoulders and surmounted by a thin layer of dark hair tinged with gray," was "well shaped." His features were "regular and full of intelligent expression, his eyes dark and penetrating." He was beardless, "but a heavy dark mustache completely covers his mouth, and underneath is a square, firm chin." In his movements he appeared "deliberate, dignified, and graceful."

To be sure that delegates would recognize the candidate, a group of Buffalo men had gone to Syracuse a few days early to plaster the environs of the convention with Cleveland lithographs and to talk up their candidate with anyone who would listen. When one of the delegates asked, "Who is your second choice?" the astonished Cleveland man replied, "Grover Cleveland."

"Yes, but after you know he can't win, after you get through voting for him, who next?"

Pasting up another portrait, the Buffalo man replied, "Grover Cleveland."

While Democrats converged on Syracuse, the Republicans were assembled for their party conclave in Saratoga to decide whether to endorse Governor Alonzo B. Cornell for a second term. The issue was in grave doubt because Cornell had vetoed legislation favorable to the interests of party boss Roscoe Conkling and President Chester A. Arthur. He had also thwarted the interests of financier Jay Gould. These men had thrown their considerable weight behind Charles J. Folger, Arthur's secretary of the treasury. Reform-minded Republicans were so infuriated that many of them spoke openly about sitting out the election.

Keenly aware of the prospect of fragmented Republicans, the Democrats in Syracuse had before them a golden opportunity—if they could demonstrate to voters through their selection of a candidate that the future of political reform lay with them. Arriving for their convention, they had three choices: Civil War general Henry W. Slocum of Brooklyn, financier Roswell P. Flower of Watertown, and the "veto mayor" of Buffalo.

Called upon to second Cleveland's nomination, Edgar Apgar justified his reputation for oratory. He warned of the dangers of party factionalism exhibited by Republicans in Saratoga and argued that a Democratic victory could be achieved only by an independent figure with a record as a reformer who could attract disenchanted Republicans.

The majority of delegates on the first ballot did not agree. The convention gave Cleveland only 66 votes. On the second ballot he picked up five more. On the third go-round a shift of some upstate delegates moved him within reach of nomination. Rather than suffer a humiliating defeat on a fourth ballot, Tammany boss John Kelly ordered his delegates to Cleveland, as did Manning, allowing Grover to claim that he had won the nomination unencumbered by debts to any party bosses.

When the convention nominated David B. Hill, the thirty-nine-year-old, unmarried mayor of Elmira, as Grover's running mate (for lieutenant governor), Grover told him in a congratulatory letter, "Now let us go to work to show the people of the State what two bachelor mayors can do."

3

Grover the Good

The night Grover Cleveland returned to Buffalo as Democratic candidate for governor, he stood on the balcony of the Buffalo Democratic Club and gave a speech. He began sentimentally as he thought back to 1855, "when I came among you, friendless, unknown, and poor." He then expressed sadness at leaving "good friends of Buffalo to enter upon another sphere of activity." He meant the campaign. When he finished his remarks he joined an enthusiastic crowd at Billy Dranger's bar, and the next day he resumed his duties as mayor.

Official acceptance of the gubernatorial nomination took the form of a letter to the state party chairman, Thomas C. E. Ecclesine. It was a blunt declaration of war on those who would pervert public affairs to private ends. He vowed that if he was elected, "interference of officials in any degree, and whether State or Federal, for the purpose of thwarting or controlling the popular wish" would not be tolerated. "Public officers," he said, "are the servants and agents of the people to execute laws which the people have made, and within the limits of a constitution which they have established."

The nitty-gritty of the six-week campaign would be left to others, such as his old friend Shan Bissell, following a plan laid out by Daniel Manning. It was a strategy based on hopeless division in the Republican Party and an appeal to disgruntled political reformers to cast their votes for the man who dared to insist that public office is a public trust.

"Had Grover Cleveland been a politician, with the record of a spoilsman behind," wrote his biographer Robert McElroy, "his promises would mean little. They might have deceived a few of the simple, disgusted a few of the honest, caused mirth to a few other spoilsmen, and thus fulfilled their intended mission; for Americans had long since learned that, as the devil can quote Scripture, so the most dangerous type of demagogue can sing of ideals in false notes not easily distinguishable from true. But Mr. Cleveland had already put into practice the ideals which he announced, and Republicans bent on reform rallied to his support with an enthusiasm equal to that of his Democratic followers."

This revolt of political dissidents from both parties into a movement for reform would later be given a name by a colorful newspaperman, Charles A. Dana, editor of the influential *New York Sun*. He called them Mugwumps. An Algonquin word taken out of Eliot's Indian Bible of 1872, "mugwump" meant "chief." Dana made it plural and used it to refer derisively to political amateurs and idealists, including Henry Ward Beecher, Carl Schurz, William Everett, Charles Eliot Norton, and Leverett Saltonstall. An incipient, disorganized group of disenchanted Republicans, they would constitute a major force in the gubernatorial election of 1882 and again in the presidential election of 1884. What appealed to them in Cleveland in both instances was his honesty and avowed commitment to their kind of government reform; also, as a corporation lawyer, he had shown himself to be not just conservative, trustworthy, competent, honest, and courageous, but a friend of business.

For evidence of his reforming zeal they needed only refer to Grover Cleveland's letter of October 28 to the New York Civil Service Reform Association. The organization had written to him seeking his views on the subject. He had replied, "I believe that the interests of the people demand a reform in the national and State administrative service. [They] should speedily become an accomplished fact, and that the public should receive honest and faithful service at the hands of well-fitted and competent servants."

Keenly aware of the disaffection of influential members of the party, the Republican candidate, Folger, sought to reign in the doubters by fomenting fear. He asked the wayward, "Do the business interests of the country dread a return of the Democratic Party to power? Will the election of Cleveland increase this dread? These are questions for hesitating Republicans to ponder."

Henry Ward Beecher responded by declaring that in the Republican convention's choice of Folger over Governor Cornell, "Avarice and Revenge kissed each other."

This Republican dissension bolstered Democratic expectations, and none more than those of their candidate. After casting his vote on November 7, 1882, Grover Cleveland returned to his office in City Hall to write to his brother, William. Indicative of how the election was expected to end in the view of the editors of *Frank Leslie's Newspaper* was the presence in the mayor's office of an artist assigned to make a sketch of the candidate.

Noting the presence of the artist, Grover admitted in his letter to feeling confident of the outcome of the balloting. "I have been for some time in the atmosphere of certain success," he said. "But the thought that has troubled me is, can I well perform my duties, and in such a manner as to do some good to the people of the State? I know there is room for it, and I know that I am honest and sincere in my desire to do well; but the question is whether I *know enough* to accomplish what I desire."

After a brief digression to admit "much anxious thought" about the social life awaiting him as governor in Albany, and pledging to "spend very little time in the purely ornamental part of the office," he told William, "first of all others," that the policy he intended to adopt was to regard his election as "a business engagement between the people of the State and myself, in which the obligation of my side is to perform the duties assigned me with an eye single to the interest of my employers. I shall have no idea of re-election, or any higher political preferment in my head, but be very thankful and happy I can well serve one term as the people's Governor."

He concluded the letter with thoughts of his late mother. "Do you know that if mother were alive, I should feel much safer? I have always thought that her prayers had much to do with my success."

Not long after he completed the letter, a Mutual Union telegraph wire began chattering out the first returns. By midnight it was clear he'd won. The final tally would be a landslide plurality of 192,854 (Cleveland: 535,318; Folger: 342,646)—the largest victory in New York history.

To mark the occasion, his friends presented him with a roomy chair with back and arms handsomely carved with the horns of a steer.

Before he assumed the governorship, there would be one more veto as mayor of Buffalo. It was a rejection of authorization of payment of $1,000 for reimbursement of legal fees incurred by a city employee accused of neglect of duty. The man was guilty but had been given only an official censure. Said the mayor, "I am very much disinclined to aid in establishing a precedent that the city shall pay the expenses of the defense of any official accused of neglect of duty."

A few hours after the veto message arrived at City Hall on November 20, 1882, the Council received another Cleveland communication:

> I hereby resign the office of mayor of the city of Buffalo and respectfully ask that such resignation be accepted by your honorable body.

Four months short of his forty-sixth birthday, Grover Cleveland was not a well-traveled man, even in the state he was preparing to govern. Except for the time he had spent in New York City at the Institution for the Blind, he had lived the years since age nineteen entirely in or around his adopted city of Buffalo. There had been one notable excursion to the state capital in January to plead with Governor Cornell for the commutation of a death sentence imposed on a Buffalo grain elevator worker convicted of first-degree murder in the stabbing death of his foreman. He argued that the killing was not premeditated and that the trial jury had not been properly instructed. They had not been told they were allowed to consider the fact that the defendant's state of inebriation at the time of the killing could be a mitigating factor in deciding between murder and manslaughter.

Nine months later, the man whose argument had persuaded Cornell to grant the commutation was preparing to succeed him as governor, with sobering recognition of his lack of experience in

dealing with a legislature considerably larger in number and consisting of two chambers filled with individuals who could be
expected to be infinitely more independent-minded than members
of the unicameral Buffalo Common Council. Nor were the issues
before the New York State Assembly and Senate likely to be as relatively easily handled as the purity of water in wells, the condition
of sidewalks, and the rightness of the people picking up the legal
bills for a public official accused of neglecting his duty. Pending on
the legislative calendar in Albany were such items as civil service
reform, tax policy, banking and insurance regulations, revamping
the state militia, and affairs affecting the city of New York, from
demands for home rule to revamping the harbormasters system and
a popular proposal to roll back the city's transit fare to a nickel.

Compounding the complexity of these issues was the state of politics within the legislature itself. The two chambers were not simply divided between Democrats and Republicans, with the
Democrats in control of both houses; they were suffused with
intraparty rivalries which pitted, for example, the forces loyal to
the Republican Party boss, U.S. Senator Thomas Platt, and a small
group of reformers led by the firebrand Minority Leader of the
Assembly, Theodore Roosevelt. On the Democratic side of the
aisles of both Assembly and Senate were factions following the lead
of contesting downstate and upstate bosses. Added to this splin-
tered scenario was a determined cadre of lobbyists working for the
interests of corporations and business tycoons who sent them to
the capital with seemingly limitless funds with which to buy alle-
giance.

For advice and assistance in preparing to wade into these
uncharted waters, the governor-elect appealed to Daniel Manning
to dispatch someone who knew his way around Albany. Just such

Democratic State Committee member <u>Daniel Manning</u> served as chief political adviser to Governor Cleveland and went on to be <u>secretary of the treasury in his first presidency.</u>

an individual sprang immediately to Manning's mind. Energetic, boyish in looks and in his enthusiasm, Civil War veteran, journalist for the *Albany Argus*, secretary of the Democratic State Committee, and clerk of the Assembly, he was Daniel S. Lamont. Grover immediately liked him.

Among the most pressing matters for the two men was preparation for a meeting of the Manhattan Club scheduled for December 5. Gathered to hear Grover would be the leading Democrats of the country—eight hundred of them—from the party's titular leader, General Winfield Hancock, to outgoing and incoming mayors of the city, the bosses of the party's factions, and members of the legislature. Few members of the audience convened in the stately parlors of the club at 96 Fifth Avenue had ever laid eyes on Grover Cleveland. If they were anxious, so was he. "This scene and these surroundings are new and strange to me," he said, "and, notwith-

As Cleveland's private secretary during his governorship and presidency, Daniel Lamont eventually became secretary of war.

standing all that is calculated to reassure and comfort me in the kindness of your welcome, when I am reminded of the circumstances which give rise to this reunion, a sense of grave responsibility weighs upon me and tempers every other sentiment. We stand tonight in the full glare of a grand and brilliant manifestation of popular will, and in the light of it how vain and small appear the tricks of politicians and the movements of party machinery."

If that hint that Governor Grover Cleveland would not be bossed were not sufficient, he went on to remind the assembled Democrats that "my majority was so large as to indicate that many, not members of the party to which I am proud to belong, supported me."

Back in Buffalo, while Lamont was at work on his behalf in Albany, he worked on his next scheduled speech—his inaugural address, to be delivered on New Year's Day. Writing to Lamont on the day after Christmas, he said he expected to arrive in Albany the following Saturday—New Year's Eve. He did as promised, traveling only with his friend Shan Bissell (he had asked friends not to form delegations to attend the swearing-in), and found as they walked from the train station to the Executive Mansion (already vacated by Governor Cornell) that nobody recognized him.

The next noon, a curious audience braved the cold and clear weather with a brilliant sun glinting on the snowy grounds of the capitol not only to see him in the flesh and mark what their new governor had to say, but to hear his voice for the first time. They found it ringing and clear, and many marveled that he spoke without a script or notes. After the expected obsequies to the man he was succeeding, he put into words what everyone in his audience surely had to be thinking. He said, "You have assembled today to witness the retirement of an officer, tried and trusted, from the highest place in the State, and the assumption of its duties by one yet to be tried."

This was certainly true. Few of those listening to him knew much about him. All had been surprised that a man of such slight experience in politics had been nominated and elected by more votes than any governor in New York's history, a reality underscored by

State Street, Albany, New York. When Cleveland was sworn in as governor on January 1, 1883, the New York State House (in the distance) was still under construction.

a feeling of anticipation and not a little measure of anxiety concerning what he intended to do in office. The usual barometers for gauging such men were useless. He had not come to power as the result of the accustomed political management, nor as the result of a long service in one or the other branch of the legislature. He'd been the mayor of Buffalo, and that for less than a year. He had a reputation for honesty and ability and had done his duty without fear or favor, which imbued him with an aura of independence— and he was a successful lawyer—but could he measure up to such illustrious predecessors in the governorship of New York as William H. Seward and Samuel J. Tilden?

In an age of long speeches, his inaugural address was so brief as to provide few clues to the future. It ran seven paragraphs and less than five hundred words without clarion calls to greatness. No galvanizing words. No indelible phrases. Only a call for "vigilance on the part of the citizen" and a summons to be "contributors to the progress and prosperity which will await us." A plea for "the forbearance of a just people" and his hope for "the guidance of a kind Providence" to "aid an honest design."

With so little offered in the inaugural address, those looking for guideposts to exactly what Governor Grover Cleveland intended to do in office turned to the next event on his agenda, his message to the legislature. Delivered in writing the following day, it had been the object of intense work by him and Dan Lamont. Many years later, Grover would tell biographer George F. Parker that he had never undertaken a harder task than preparation of his first message as governor. In this, his first experience in state politics, he felt he could deal only in generalizations "because it was impossible that any man, coming unprepared to such a place, should have the sure grasp of State affairs which would enable him to import into his message any considerable measure of original suggestion."

He chose to sound notes which had served him well as mayor. He appealed to the legislature to keep "a jealous watch of the public funds" and to refuse to "sanction their appropriation except for public needs." To this end he demanded abolition of "all unnecessary offices . . . and all employment of doubtful benefit." And he called for "absolute fairness and justice" when exacting "from the citizen a part of his earnings and income for the support of the government."

★   ★   ★

Among the members of the legislature studying the new governor's first message with a great deal of interest was the leader of the Assembly's Republican minority. Beginning his second term in Albany, Theodore Roosevelt was the youngest member of the legislature (age twenty-five) and widely considered a rising Republican star not only by New York political observers but by those as far from Albany as Iowa, where one admirer had hailed him as "the rising hope and chosen leader of a new generation." Savvy political pundit William C. Hudson of the *Albany Argus* predicted that " 'Teddy' would be heard from in the upper regions of politics."

Yet Roosevelt found himself the leader of only forty-two Republicans in the lower body of the legislature dominated by exactly twice as many Democrats. This commanding posture in the legislative branch was reinforced by a majority in the Senate of 18 to 14. While this seemed to be a slender edge, the reality was that there often existed an alliance between Tammany Democrats and machine Republicans, the result of which was that neither Governor Cleveland nor the Assembly minority leader could rely on strict party-line discipline.

That brutal fact of life quickly manifested itself on the question of whether the transit fare in the City of New York was to be reduced as a matter of law from ten cents to five. As discussed earlier, the issue proved to be a test of political courage for both Cleveland and Roosevelt in defying the consensus of their respective parties. But the governor's veto of the measure was just one of several which hit the legislature like an Albany blizzard. In rapid fire during the period between January 26 and March 1, he vetoed eight measures. One of these rejected a bill to reorganize the Buffalo fire department, an effect of which was to scuttle a grander Tammany scheme to revise the charter of the city of New York. He also refused to allow the county of Montgomery to borrow money; amendment of the charter of Elmira to change its liability for injuries as a result of unsafe and dangerous streets; permission for the library association of Fredonia not to pay local taxes; and the county of Chautauqua to appropriate money for a soldiers' monument. Sentimental attachment to the village of Fayetteville did not dissuade him from vetoing a measure to permit borrowing to buy a steam fire engine, and for the village of Mechanicsville to do the same.

In disposing of these measures the new governor exhibited a work habit which had been noted by his admirers (and detractors) when he practiced law, as assistant district attorney and sheriff, and during his term as Buffalo's mayor. Whatever action he took was the consequence of long hours spent studying the issue, reading and parsing every word and phrase, careful weighing of pros and cons, and presentation of a laboriously worked out explanation of his rationale.

To assist him in gubernatorial chores that were many times those he'd been called upon to handle as mayor, and to pilot him through the shoals of Albany politics, he elevated Dan Lamont from unofficial adviser to the post of private secretary. He confided to a friend that he had never seen Lamont's like. He saw in Lamont a political man with "no friends to gratify or reward and no enemies to punish." These were useful attributes for Lamont in the role the governor assigned him as a bridge between the Executive Office and the leaders of all factions of the Democratic Party. Maintaining comity with them was vital in the matter of gubernatorial appointments. These had almost always been considered compensation for

In the spacious "governor's room" of the New York State House in 1883, Republican Assemblyman Theodore Roosevelt formed an alliance with Democratic Governor Cleveland.

the party faithful. Rather than handing out patronage in the accustomed manner, the governor had pledged to fill hundreds of posts entirely on the basis of merit. Accordingly, the newly created jobs of railroad board commissioners went to nonpoliticians with the technical and engineering knowledge required. Instead of a former assemblyman for the post of superintendent of public works, he picked an engineer with no party affiliation. Competency over politics was also the rule in naming a superintendent of insurance.

On the subjects of these appointments and the flurry of vetoes, the editor of the Republican *Albany Evening Journal* declared in print, "Grover Cleveland has shown himself what we took him on trust to be last fall—bigger and better than his party."

How big the governor was physically was seen by any citizen who cared to take the time to pay a call on him. His office door was open to all, and so many people walked through it seeking an audience with the governor that Lieutenant Governor Hill joked, "Governor, you might as well put your desk on the grass in front of the capitol."

Most who took advantage of the governor's availability came seeking jobs and justifying their requests by service to the party, only to be greeted by steely blue eyes and the words "I don't know that I understand you."

While striving to be true to his pledge to see to it that those who undertook public service treated it as a public trust, he also stuck to the pledge he had made in his election-night letter to his brother, William, to "spend very little in the purely ornamental part of the office." The man who'd shunned dances, parties, and other socializing in Buffalo would not suddenly fling himself into such frivolities in the state capital. Although there were some receptions and dinners which could not be avoided, he felt no need to add to them.

70

He had come to Albany to work. This he did by getting out of bed at seven, having breakfast (often in the company of Dan Lamont and a stack of correspondence to be answered), walking about a mile to the capitol building, and arriving at the office before nine. Lunch was half an hour. The office work usually ended at five, followed by dinner at home, generally alone. The evenings more often than not found him back at the office until after midnight.

This diligence to duty did not go unnoticed by a reporter for the *Albany Evening Journal*. He wrote on March 21, 1883, "There was not a night last week when he departed from the new Capitol before one A.M. Such work is killing work."

Nor was the Lord's Day exempt, although he frequently allowed himself a few hours on a Sunday afternoon to get in a few games of cards with friends. Mindful of the likelihood of being criticized for this, he joked, "My father used to say that it was wicked to go fishing on Sunday, but he never said anything about draw poker."

In a letter to the Reverend Charles Wood, minister of the Fourth Presbyterian Church in Albany and formerly a pastor in Buffalo, he apologized for not having taken time to greet Wood when he had called to offer congratulations on Grover's birthday. The governor explained this lapse in courtesy to being so busy that he was "not always akin to the best sensibilities."

Visitors to the executive mansion who had called on previous governors in the modest yellow-brown, turreted house provided and furnished by the people of New York as their governor's residence found it unchanged by the current occupant, with two exceptions. Most obvious was the conversion of an upper hallway into an office used for working on Sundays. The other modification was the installation of a billiard table. Expenses for running the house were paid out of his annual salary of $10,000.

71

As his surroundings had changed (even if his work and social habits had not), so had his circle of friends. Although his associates in Buffalo had been from the ranks of politicians and lawyers, the Albany men of those persuasions who gathered around him did not do so in the back rooms of saloons. Nor were they concerned with affairs which, from the perspective of the state capital, seemed to be quaintly provincial. These men were interested in matters considerably loftier than the condition of wells, sewers, and sidewalks. Their subjects were the soundness of the currency, taxes and tariffs, the state of commerce and business on a national scale, and the place and destiny of the United States as it struggled to put the divisions of the Civil War behind it while expanding over a continent and emerging as a power to be reckoned with on a world stage. Associating with new friends such as Daniel Manning and other prominent Democrats with a national and world view, as well as a handful of journalists and editors, could only broaden Grover Cleveland's horizons. Their very presence drove home to the new governor the fact that there was a world of difference between serving as mayor of Buffalo and being leader of the most powerful state in the Union.

The majesty of the State of New York was symbolized by construction of a new capitol building. Designed in French Renaissance style by Thomas Fuller and commandingly situated at the top of State Street hill, with a small park in front, it had been started in 1869 and was still being built. Its exterior walls were of light-colored granite supporting red-tiled roofs. Set on three acres and laid out in the form of a quadrangle, it consisted of a central tower designed to rise 300 feet and contain a central court that was 137 feet long and 92 feet wide. Ground-floor space was devoted to offices and committee rooms, with the southeast corner designated the Governor's Room or Executive Chamber. Its decor consisted of mahogany wainscoting and a ceiling of red Spanish leather.

The second floor, reached by way of elegant marble staircases, housed the chambers of the Senate and Assembly. The latter, designed in a style which *Baedeker's United States* termed "a fine example of a civic Gothic interior" stretching 140 feet long and 40 feet wide, was spanned by the largest groined arch in the world. Supported by four red granite columns, the wooden ceiling was praised for its excellent acoustics, although the quality of the speeches which it reflected was frequently questioned, along with the sincerity of a good many of the orators who took to the floor beneath it.

One assemblyman whose manner of speaking left much to be desired and who never fell into the category of dubious sincerity, but who fascinated the man occupying the office below the legislative chambers, was the unexpected ally in the Five-cent Fare fight and on the Civil Service Reform measure, Theodore Roosevelt. Among the colorful assertions offered by the Manhattan Republican which would have amused Governor Cleveland was a denunciation of a newspaper, the *World*, owned by financier Jay Gould, as a "stock-jobbing sheet of limited circulation and versatile mendacity, owned by the arch-thief of Wall Street." So, too, Grover Cleveland welcomed Theodore Roosevelt's characterization of enemies of civil service reform as a "vast band of hired mercenaries." Assemblymen and newspaper reporters might ridicule Roosevelt's speaking style, but no one could dismiss his effectiveness in propounding causes close to the heart of Governor Cleveland.

Roosevelt in 1883.

That Roosevelt was a Republican did not matter. He was an ally, and as a man of principle, Grover Cleveland stood ready, if needed, to return the favor.

Just such an opportunity arose when Roosevelt was appointed to a three-man Assembly committee to look into whether legislation was needed affecting the working conditions in the thriving cigar business in New York City's tenement district. The bill had been introduced at the request of a cigar-makers' union. Its announced reason for seeking a law was an altruistic one: elimination of appalling working conditions. An unstated motive was to ensure that cigars would be made in genuine factories employing union members.

Because one member of the investigating committee was on the union's side of the issue and the second admitted to Roosevelt that he was beholden to "certain interests which were all-powerful" and opposed to the proposed law, Roosevelt considered himself an unbiased free agent and set out to inspect the working conditions himself. He saw that many of the workers in at-home factories were immigrants and that most of the work was being done by children. In these squalid places which poor, oppressed families called home, he discovered tobacco stowed where mothers, fathers, and children worked day and night in shockingly unhealthy conditions.

Outraged, he returned to Albany determined to champion the bill in the legislature and then in the Executive Chamber. Aware that the measure had the backing of Governor Cleveland, he recognized that the Big One had never posed as a special friend of labor. Presented with a bill to prohibit drivers and conductors on street railways from working for more than twelve hours a day, he'd vetoed it on the basis that the issue was none of the state's business and that such a law constituted an assault on the powers of localities.

This record notwithstanding, and convinced that the Big One simply was not cognizant of the facts underlying the Cigar Bill, Roosevelt felt that if he were given a chance to personally report his finds, the governor—a Christian gentleman and proven humanitarian—would embrace the outrage and switch his position. Cloaking himself in the mantle of spokesman, in Roosevelt's words in his autobiography, "for the battered, undersized foreigners," he asked for an appointment in the Executive Chamber to lay out a case for a Cleveland signature when the bill reached his desk, an eventuality of which Roosevelt was confident if he could return upstairs to spread the news among legislators that the Big One would not stand in the way of its enactment. Welcomed into the governor's office, the young Republican, a nonsmoker because of asthma, faced the cigar-smoker chief executive and launched a vivid description of all he'd seen. He described families eating, living, and sleeping in the same cramped room where they worked. Huge stacks of tobacco stood alongside the foul bedding, and in a corner where there were scraps of food. He said such conditions rendered it impossible for families of tenement-house workers to live so that their children might grow up fitted for the exacting duties of American citizenship.

Moved by Roosevelt's impassioned plea and goaded by his own conscience, and perhaps not wishing to lose a possible ally in the future over a bill which by all accounts stood little chance of passage, the Big One allowed that if Roosevelt could get the bill passed, he would sign it. Had it been any other legislator who'd left the Executive Chamber that day, no "sporting man" would have bet on his chances. In the hearts and minds of opponents of the Cigar Bill, the measure was, as Roosevelt recorded in his memoirs, "contrary to the principles of the *laissez faire* kind." Businessmen who spoke to him about it shook their heads and insisted it would "prevent a man doing as he wished and as he had a right to do with what was his own."

Though this argument was vigorously presented in debate, it proved to be insufficient to overcome the passion of Roosevelt and his "men." Always a man of his word, Grover Cleveland signed the bill into law. But to the dismay of both the Big One and the firebrand Republican whom few in Albany now ridiculed as "the Dude," the same *laissez faire* argument was carried into the courts by one of the very cigar makers Roosevelt had championed. The Court of Appeals ruled the law unconstitutional. Still seething about the reversal decades later as he undertook his autobiography, Roosevelt wrote, "The judges who rendered the decision were

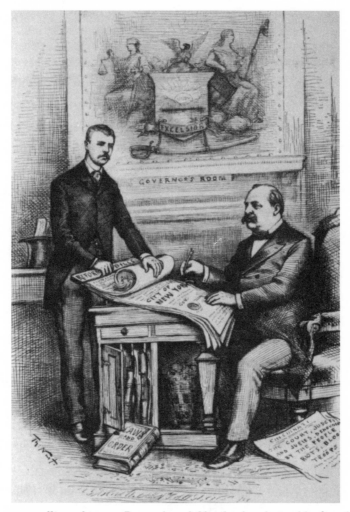

The strange alliance between Roosevelt and Cleveland as depicted by famed car-toonist <u>*Thomas Nast*</u>.

well-meaning men. They knew nothing whatever of the tenement-house conditions; they knew nothing whatever of the needs, or of the life and labor, of three-fourths of their fellow citizens in great cities. They knew legalism, but not life."

Cleveland biographer George F. Parker summed up Governor Cleveland's labor policy this way: "He came into office at a time when the conflict between labor and capital was perhaps sharper than at any previous period." For several years the conflicting interests of capital and an emerging concern for the status of labor had been coming into focus, particularly in New York City. In addition to maintaining its supremacy as the country's most important commercial city, it was the largest center for manufacturing industries and had the greatest concentration of workers. The burning question was, how to balance these interests?

Cleveland's policy was to deal with this tension between capital and labor so as to avoid unnecessary clashing and to ensure the enactment of laws which were both just and conservative. In his letter accepting the nomination for governor, he'd written, "The laboring classes constitute the main part of our population. They should be protected in their efforts to assert their rights when endangered by aggregated capital, and all statues on this subject should recognize the care of the State for honest toil, and be framed with a view of improving the condition of the workingman."

A time was coming, and would not be long in arriving, when President Grover Cleveland's views on capital and labor would be put to a far more severe test than that presented in the form of the working hours of streetcar men and immigrant families trapped in sweatshops of cigar makers.

★ ★ ★

As the 1883 legislative session wore on, friends and other observers of Grover Cleveland were worried. The consensus was that he was working too hard. On March 23 the Albany *Evening Journal* ran a story to that effect: "The visitors who go into the executive chamber are met affably by the large-headed man, and he listens patiently to what they have to say. Still there is only a slight glimmer of ideas in response. The words are few and they are listlessly said. The eyes of the large man look glassy, his skin hangs on his cheeks in thick, unhealthy-looking folds, the coat buttoned about his large chest and abdomen looks ready to burst with the confined fat. Plainly he is a man who is not taking enough exercise; he remains within doors constantly, eats and works, eats and works, and works and eats."

The weight of work and its demands on him made its way into a letter sent to Shan Bissell a month later. "I will tell you the deadest secret in the world," he wrote on April 22, 1883, "that for the last few days I have felt the effects of long hours, steady work, and worse than all, incessant pesters about offices. I honestly think I can't stand it more than two weeks longer. My head a good deal of the time don't [sic] feel right, and when a man begins to talk about office I begin to get irritable and my head begins to ache. Lamont acts and looks as if he needed a rest too. I shall enter upon this next week with apprehension that I may make a mistake before it closes."

Office seekers were not the only individuals demanding attention from the governor. A number of individuals petitioned him for far more compelling reasons than getting public jobs. These men turned to him for their very freedom. Inmates of state prisons, they begged him for executive clemency, commutations of sentences, and outright pardons. Between his taking of the oath of office on January 1 and July 15 he granted twenty-one commutations and pardons. Told that these were fewer than those ordered in a similar period by Governor Cornell, he was repelled by the notion that he was in some kind of competition with his predecessors.

When he was accused by some newspapers of being too lenient, he retorted sarcastically, "I shall pardon when I see fit. I shall be governor until the end of my term, notwithstanding all the would-be governors there are in the state. I am going to do just as I have a mind to about this pardoning business, whether the newspapers like it or not. I am going to be governor one term, and then if these editors want to be, and the people let them, they can be [governor]."

He continued, "One of these days I'll grant a pardon just because, in my judgment, it ought to be granted, and I shall say that is my reason, and shall not give any other. Justice, mercy, and humanity are the things alone to be considered in the application for a pardon. And if I find a poor fellow has been unjustly imprisoned, or there is any good reason why he should be pardoned, I'll pardon, and will not regard the record at all. That's all there is about that business. There are a whole lot of people who want to be governor. All of these people will have to wait till I have got done, and the people have turned me out."

Outbursts like this, combined with his haggard and weary appearance, indicated to friends and allies that the governor was close to the breaking point physically, mentally, and emotionally. As the date for adjournment of the legislature neared, they did their best to persuade him to plan a vacation. He agreed, but departing lawmakers left behind a large stack of bills which demanded attention. Studying them in his painstaking and plodding manner would consume another month. Many of the measures he was being asked to approve left him so downhearted that he wrote a friend, "I sometimes feel that the fight for the good against the bad is a discouraging contest with the odds on the wrong side; this is when it seems to me that the people and the press are not going to give me aid and encouragement. But I straightaway grow ashamed of my unbelief, when I win a word of encouragement from men whom I *know* are right. I look for better things. I am where I *must* and *have* and *shall* feel the strain and wrenching of the change. I hope I shall hold fast. I believe I shall. It is exceedingly unfortunate that those in public places battle with the jobbery and treachery fronting them, must constantly feel that malice, uncharitableness, and misrepresentation are treacherously fighting them in the rear."

His answer to anyone who sent him proposed legislation he considered not in the public interest was a veto couched in language which called attention to shoddy thinking and sloppy draftsmanship, and frequently to the fine print and clauses that he deemed to be attempts to mask a raid on the treasury. After signing his name to the final veto, he rose from his desk and gave in to the pleadings of aides and allies to take a rest by heading for Buffalo.

Old friends joyfully welcomed him back to old haunts and old habits of late nights of food, drink, and loud singing of old songs. But what Grover longed for most was to do battle with the fish in the streams and lakes of the Adirondacks. On June 24 he sent a note to Dan Lamont back in Albany in which he gleefully reported having "very respectable" sunburn on neck and face. A note two days later stated, "I have much to do yet in the way of fishing, etc., and a great many fish are waiting for me." But he confessed in a letter to Lamont, "I am in disgrace, with myself at least, just at present. I had a beautiful shot at a deer Saturday and missed him. We are preparing to start again for my last chance."

Eighteen years after this outing, he published *Fishing and Shooting Sketches*. In the book he extolled the virtues of both pastimes and called sport and outdoor life a "mission" in which he sought relief from "the wearing labors and perplexities of official duty." Yet his obligations as governor could not be escaped, no matter how deeply he penetrated Adirondack forests or how remote the stream or lake. He wrote to Lamont, "You will see by the enclosed that I am doing business here and don't propose to entirely neglect executive duties." Among the items dealt with during the respite were (ironically) appointments to the Fish and Game Commission and a batch of pleas from convicts for pardons. He referred grumpily to papers sent by Lamont for signing as "grist." In another message to his private secretary, he closed with, "Don't fail to let me know by telegraph if I am needed."

Two rumors going around about his vacation angered him. The first was an anonymous accusation that he and his companion anglers had committed the unforgivable fisherman's sin of stealing someone else's bait. "I think this is pretty mean treatment to begin with and suspect that this is a pretty tough country," he wrote to Lamont. "At this rate, I am liable to be accused of rape before I get back."

A second report, carried in some newspapers, was that he vacationed in the seaside plush homes of millionaire August Belmont and other wealthy New Yorkers in Newport, Rhode Island. He had been invited to visit them in palatial houses they called "cottages" but had declined. "But that fact did not prevent certain of the newspapers of New York from stating it as if it were really so," he complained. "How is it that these things get in newspapers out of nothing?" The baseless report still nettled him in 1901. In *Fishing and Shooting Sketches* he complained of "mendacious" newspapers having called his fishing excursions "dishonest devices to cover scandalous revelry."

He learned that no matter where he might go to spend time away from his duties, someone was ready to find fault. He wrote that when he was not being chastised for "residing in a non-sporting but delightfully cultured and refined community" he was castigated for being willing to "associate in the field with any loafer who is the owner of a dog and gun."

At last, from the rustic confines of a fishing and hunting lodge called Camp Corlies, he wrote to Lamont on September 3 that he planned to "start for civilization tomorrow morning" and be back in Albany in two days.

Pending in the capital on his return was an issue of harmony within the factions of the Democratic Party regarding choosing a slate of candidates for the state legislature and the office of secretary of state in the November elections. Hoping for nominees who would be on his side in "the cause of good government," he expected fierce opposition to his efforts. In a letter to Shan Bissell, he predicted, "The lines will be sharply drawn, though there will probably be a great effort to conceal them. All the spoilsmen, little and big, all the disappointed seekers after personal interest, all those hoping to gain personal ends, and all those who desire a return to the old, corrupt, and repudiated order of things in party management, will, under one specious guise or another, be ranged on one side." On the other front would be "true and earnest men."

The form of the fight was not long in taking shape. Back in Albany, a rested and sunburned governor learned that Tammany boss John Kelly was prepared to strike at the heart of everything Grover Cleveland stood for. A report reached the Executive Chamber that Kelly was determined to force the party's nominating convention to renominate to the State Senate the man who had led the fight for the Five-cent Fare Bill and opposed every one of Governor Cleveland's attempts at reform. His name was Thomas Grady, and in the Big One's opinion he was the very embodiment of the detested old, corrupt, and repudiated order of things. But what could Grover do about it?

After two days of mulling his options and contemplating the possible consequences for his political future, on October 20 he settled into his enormous chair, laid a sheet of stationery on the big desk, picked up a pen, dipped it in ink, and wrote a letter to Kelly. When he handed it to Dan Lamont, the trusted and politically astute veteran of countless political skirmishes and outright carnage was shocked to read:

> *It is not without hesitation that I write this. I have determined to do so, however, because I see no reason why I should not be entirely frank with you. I am anxious that Mr. Grady should not be returned to the next Senate. I do not wish to conceal the fact that my personal comfort and satisfaction are involved in the matter. But I know that good legislation, based upon a pure desire to promote the interests of the people, and to the improvement of legislative methods, are also deeply involved. I forebear to write in detail of the other considerations having relation to the welfare of the party and the approval to be secured by a change for the better in the character of representatives. These things will occur to you without suggestion from me.*

Lamont knew a gauntlet had been thrown down. He exclaimed, "You can't send this." Taking back the letter, Grover replied, "Well, I'm going to send it."

Kelly received it, tucked it into a pocket, said nothing about it to anyone, and coolly proceeded, to Grover's regret though not surprise, to engineer Grady's renomination. But on the eve of the election the contents of the letter (but not the name of its author) appeared in the *New York World*. Accompanying the text was a statement from Kelly laying blame for disaffection in the party on "the Executive." Grover acknowledged authorship but said nothing more. Pleased and motivated by the Democrats' disarray, Repub-

Tammany Hall leader John Kelly.

licans smelled blood in the water and tossed aside their own factional disputes to see their man elected secretary of state and win control of both houses of the legislature. In the Senate the division would be nineteen Republicans and thirteen Democrats. The Assembly would see Republicans in a slightly closer split with Democrats of seventy-three to fifty-five.

Thomas Grady would not be one of them. Despite Kelly's power and influence, Grady's Sixth District leaders rebelled, refusing to back his nomination. An effort to have him nominated by another district failed because its leaders had already picked a candidate. With no means of being nominated, Grady withdrew his candidacy, shrouding the act in the guise of "retirement."

Four days after the balloting debacle, he bitterly attacked Cleveland in a fiery speech to Tammany Hall loyalists and blamed the defeat on "attempted interference of the Executive with the action of the people in choosing their representatives."

The object of the attack continued to hold his tongue until a reporter for the *New York Herald* showed up in Albany seeking an interview. The outcome made its way into the paper's pages on November 23 in narrative form:

Mr. Cleveland sat in his large revolving chair, alone. He looked vigorous and buoyant.

"This letter of yours to Kelly," said the correspondent, "has caused a great deal of talk."

The heavy chair of the Governor moved a little nearer as he replied:

"Indeed? Well, I suppose so. Why?"

"That is for you to say," the reporter responded.

"I hold," said the Governor, "that it was the proper thing, under the circumstances, to send that letter."

"You think Grady was not a proper representative to send back to the Senate?" queried the visitor.

"I do, most assuredly," Mr. Cleveland answered. "His action in the Senate has been against the interests of the people and of good government, and his ready tongue gave him power to be of great aid to bad men. I believed that the Democratic party could not afford to endorse such a course, and that his rejection would be a great benefit to the party and to the people."

"But about the letter, Governor?" asked the reporter.

The big armchair again moved closer, and the Governor said: "I sat down with the knowledge of any person and wrote to Kelly—this man who had been assuring me of his anxiety to give me aid in my work."

Grover then recounted the events which ensued, bitterly criticizing the publication of the letter which had been written "for his eyes only." Asked if he regretted having sent it to Kelly, Grover said he did not, adding, "If this be treason I can't see how I can escape its consequences."

Cleveland biographers and other historians agree that in a bold stroke Grover Cleveland had done more than slap John Kelly in the face. He forever severed a bond with Tammany and, by implication, all political machines. Allan Nevins wrote, "This letter marked the beginning of Cleveland's marvelous career as a national leader." Widening circles in New York had noted Cleveland's courage. Now the entire nation saw it. Rexford G. Tugwell's biography said, "That Cleveland was hated by the whole Tammany crowd was his best credential for future success."

Of course, these judgments were for the years ahead. At the time, Grover Cleveland had no way of knowing that his letter would have any effect other than to throw doubt on his political survival. Neither could he know whether daring defiance of Kelly and Tammany would have the result he sought in the removal of Grady as a stumbling block in the way of reform in the State Senate. And he possessed no crystal ball to show him that a hazardous gamble with his future would have, as Tugwell charmingly noted, "the odd result of collaboration between Cleveland and Theodore Roosevelt."

When TR, as he preferred to be called, read the election results he was "dee-lighted" to find himself in the majority with a governor who pledged in his second annual message to the legislature, "The most practical and thorough civil service reform has gained a place in the policy of the State."

Between the election and the message to the lawmakers, the governor had time to assess his first year in office and found ample reasons to be pleased with himself. On New Year's Eve he wrote to Shan Bissell, "I congratulate myself upon the close of my first year of gubernatorial life—and a close, I'll say to you and myself, which brings no disgrace or regret."

Pleased with himself and invigorated by the successes of his first year as chief executive of the state, Governor Cleveland sent the new Republican-controlled legislature his second message with more than a little self-congratulatory crowing and patting himself on the back. He offered a litany of accomplishments, from introduction of "business principles" in continuing construction of the new capitol, a law imposing better administration of the immigration bureau, protection of the public against abuses by insurance companies, establishment of a court of claims to handle demands of citizens against the state, and a law protecting rights of voters in primary elections, to prohibition of sale of forest lands at the source of streams, "thereby checking threatened disaster to the commerce of our waterways," and, most important of all, "practical and thorough civil service reform" as the policy of the state.

Looking ahead, he expressed agreement with critics of the legislature who said lawmakers took too much time off by recessing frequently for inadequate reasons. He expressed a need for regulation of corporations to curb immense salaries to officers, transactions which profited the directors of companies while stockholders lost money, and large sums of money spent under various disguises in efforts to influence legislation. "The honestly conducted and strong corporations would have nothing to fear," he said, but those "badly managed and weak ought to be exposed."

Other calls for action involved establishing a statewide system of bank examiners, abuses in the running of charitable organizations, and changes in the management of state prisons.

His purpose in all these matters, he explained to a friend, was to deal with "the practical things relating to State affairs and in which my people are interested."

"The fact is I am growing to be a kind of crank on all that pertains to the commonwealth and the citizens of New York," he continued. "I haven't the material, I think, to do more for the people, the party, nor myself than I can do in that role."

Having laid out his goals for the new legislative session, the cranky governor soon found his resolve tested by his ally in the Five-cent Fare fight. In the reshuffling of power from Democrats to Republicans, Theodore Roosevelt had been given the chairmanship of the Assembly's Committee on Cities with oversight of the affairs of the biggest of them all—the Democratic Party bastion of New York City. He immediately launched investigations into all aspects of the city's administration. The result was a trio of bills giving the mayor of New York power to appoint heads of all city departments, including the most corrupt of all, the police: stripping city alderman of the power to confirm mayoral appointments to city offices: and substituting salaries for the fee system by which county officers were paid, thus eliminating a source of governmental blackmail.

Each of these measures was an arrow aimed at the heart of political bossism in both the Democratic and Republican parties. However, knowing of Grover Cleveland's commitment to the rooting out of government corruption, opponents of the Roosevelt bills crafted their appeals to the governor to veto them by arguing that they threatened the balance of power in the state and put too much local authority in the hands of one man. Grumblings were heard to the effect that the bills, if passed, would turn the mayor of New York into a czar.

Roosevelt replied from the floor of the Assembly, "A czar that will have to be re-elected every second year is not much of an autocrat." He added that he would rather have "a responsible autocrat than an irresponsible oligarchy" of contemptible aldermen "protected by their own obscurity." Under his proposed reorganization of New York City government, he continued, a mayor stands in view of the press and "in the full glare of public opinion; every act he performs is criticized, and every important move that he makes is remembered."

One man in Albany not requiring a definition of the office of mayor occupied an oversize chair on the floor below the Assembly chamber. When the Roosevelt reforms reached his desk he brushed aside the contrary pleadings of his party and signed them.

"The Democratic game of bluff and bulldozing did not succeed with Governor Cleveland," said the editor of the *Albany Evening*

Journal, Harold Frederick, on March 18, 1884. Those who'd predicted otherwise, he went on, were "astray in their estimation of the man."

The magazine *Harper's Weekly* published a cartoon of Cleveland and TR standing with arms linked as Tammany's symbol, a tiger, was declawed, toothless, and slinking away with its tail dragging.

Roosevelt's comity was not constant, however. Cleveland's "reckless heroism," as TR described the signing of the New York City bills, was found wanting on the question of a measure known as the Tenure of Office Act. It authorized the next New York City mayor to appoint a new register of deeds and commissioner of public works. The target of the legislation was the current occupant of the latter post, Hubert O. Thompson. A longtime, loyal member of Daniel Manning's organization, he had figured importantly in nominating Cleveland for governor. When the bill to kick Thompson out of his job landed on Cleveland's desk, Roosevelt rushed to see the Big One.

"You must not veto those bills," he demanded of the governor. "You cannot. You shall not. I won't have it."

Grover slammed a fist on his desk. "Mr. Roosevelt, I am going to veto those bills!"

He did so not because he was paying a political debt, as critics charged. He rejected it, like so many other bills placed before him as mayor of Buffalo and governor, because he considered it poorly drafted. This was an objection in which the author of the measure eventually concurred, calling his own bill "a very shabby piece of legislation, quite unfit to find a place in the statute book." Roosevelt was not assuaged and said so in harsh language in a widely published speech. Grover discounted it as typical but momentary Roosevelt passion.

With the 1884 legislative session moving inexorably to an ending in May, later than usual but in time for New York politicians to join their brethren across the country in preparing for the summer's two presidential nominating conventions, Cleveland and Roosevelt found themselves in agreement on spending almost a million and a half dollars to create a state park at Niagara Falls. Neither Roosevelt, a self-taught naturalist and committed environmentalist, nor Cleveland, the devoted outdoorsman from Buffalo, found amusement in Grover's predecessor, Governor Cornell, who had vetoed a similar bill with the question, "Why should we spend the people's money when just as much water will run over the Falls without a park as with it?"

The present question was whether the newly constituted legislature agreed with Cornell. Grover's strategy was to present the matter differently; in effect, to trick the lawmakers. This act of political gamesmanship—some would say political artistry—was described by Grover in a speech at Adirondack Park on January 24, 1891:

> If we had gone to the legislature for a bill asking so much money to buy so much land around the falls, we certainly would have failed. We might have gone there and pleaded that we only wanted $1,500,000 until we were black in the face, and we would have been answered every time that the $1,500,000 we asked for was only an entering wedge. Our opponents would have pointed to the Capitol building at Albany and shaken their heads.
>
> What did we do? We got the legislature to pass a law authorizing an appraisal of lands we wanted to preserve. As good luck would have it, the appraisal amounted to just about the amount we said the lands would cost. We continued to win supporters for our project. We then asked the State to buy the lands, and to her credit, she did so.

Again left with a pile of legislation to be read, studied, weighed, and signed or not, the governor declined an invitation to dinner for May 13. He sent a note of regret to Mrs. John V. I. Pruyn in which he said he had such an "economy of time I am afraid the night will not be long enough to do all I have at hand. Need I say any more—except to assure you that 'It's fun to be governor'?"

4

★

Ma, Ma, Where's My Pa?

Republicans swarming into the sultry city of Chicago to open their 1884 presidential nominating convention carried with them the weighty baggage of political scandal in the nation's capital. Eight years earlier, one United States senator from Massachusetts had risen to lament, "I have heard in the highest places the shameless doctrine avowed, by men grown old in public office, that the true way by which power should be gained in the Republic is to bribe the people with the offices created for their service, and the true end for which it should be used when gained is the promotion of selfish ambition and the gratification of personal revenge. I have heard that suspicion haunts the footsteps of the trusted companions of the President."

Since the end of the Civil War the federal government had been in the control of such men. A Republican legislative oligarchy vehemently opposed to attempts at genuine reconciliation between

Grover Cleveland in 1884.

North and South had humiliated President Andrew Johnson with an impeachment which had failed by one vote in the Senate. During the administration of Ulysses S. Grant they smoothed the way for favored groups to win land grants, favorable tariffs, various governmental subsidies, and generous pensions. Bribery and venality were rampant. "This selfish materialism of the worst wing of the Republican party," as Allan Nevins correctly described these power brokers, continued to hold sway in the administration of James Garfield. But after he was assassinated in 1881, his successor, Chester A. Arthur, surprised everyone by backing efforts to end patronage through civil service reform. As a result, the question nagging Republicans as they convened in Chicago in June 1884 was whether to nominate Arthur to be president in his own right, or offer the nomination to the Speaker of the House of Representatives, James G. Blaine.

Among a growing movement of political reformers who were repelled by government corruption and abuses of power, few men in the Republican Party (perhaps none) embodied all that was wrong more than Blaine. He'd been intimately involved in and had profited from the granting of valuable rights to the Little Rock and Fort Smith Railroad. An otherwise able and intelligent man who loved nothing more than politics, he found nothing amiss in using power and position for personal profit. As Republicans headed for their convention, he represented a viable alternative to the suddenly unpredictable "Chet" Arthur.

On Monday, June 2, Theodore Roosevelt assessed the Chicago gathering and confided to his diary, "All the corrupt element in the Republican Party seems to be concentrated here working in behalf of Blaine."

Opposed to the nomination of Arthur and appalled at the prospect of Blaine, reform-minded delegates and others in the Mugwump movement marshaled themselves against the two prospects. Their efforts and those of backers of Arthur and a third candidate, George F. Edmunds, failed. When the Republicans nominated Blaine, one newspaper reporter called it "Black Friday" for the reformers.

An outraged leader of the movement, Carl Schurz, railed at those who had nominated Blaine, "Do you not see that the best Republican principles have already been defeated by that nomination? Do you not see that those principles, which were the great soul of the

Republican party, command you maintain good government at any cost, be it even the timely sacrifice of party ascendency?"

Theodore Roosevelt was so dismayed that he growled to a reporter from the *New York World,* "I am going cattle-ranching in Dakota for the remainder of the summer and a part of the fall. What I shall do after that I cannot tell you."

The *World* asked if Roosevelt would support Blaine from out west.

TR replied, "It is a subject I do not care to talk about." But late that night he told a man from the *Evening Post* that he was prepared to throw "hearty support" to any decent *Democrat.*

★   ★   ★

As the party of Abraham Lincoln was burdened by governmental scandal, the political heirs of Thomas Jefferson and Andrew Jackson approached their convention in the first week of July 1884 collared with the albatross of the Civil War, for which popular judgment held that they had been responsible. In consequence there had not been a Democrat elected to the White House since James Buchanan in 1856, when a newcomer to Buffalo named Stephen G. Cleveland had been two years short of the voting age. Amazingly, in early June of 1884, *Governor* Grover Cleveland found himself boosted as the Democratic candidate for president of the United States by friends, political allies, increasingly vocal disaffected Republicans, and a spreading array of admiring newspaper reporters.

One of the latter group wrote in the Boston *Advertiser*:

Cleveland is stout, has a well-fed look, is indeed a good liver, has the
air of a man who has made up his mind just how he ought to behave

in any position where he may find himself. He is getting bald; he is getting gray—though his white hair does not show conspicuously, as his complexion is sandy. He dresses well, carries himself well, talks well upon any subject with which he is familiar, and upon subjects with which he is not familiar he does not venture to talk at all. He has the happy faculty of being able to refuse a request without giving offense. It has been my fortune to see him several times during the past winter upon business in connection with some of the State Institutions. He has impressed me always as one heartily desirous of getting to the bottom of any matter he may have in mind, and acting wisely on it.

Might the object of this honest and at the same time affectionate journalist's portrait be the sort of Democrat worthy of an endorsement by Theodore Roosevelt and others like him in the ranks of the party of Lincoln? Was Governor Cleveland available?

William C. Hudson, the Albany newspaperman who also served as an adviser to Grover, found himself among a group of Cleveland associates in the Executive Chamber when one of the men predicted that the forthcoming Democratic National Convention would recognize the wisdom of giving the presidential nomination to the governor of New York.

Grover replied, "Go away, boys, and let me do my work. You're always trying to get me into a scrape."

Three days before New York State Democrats were to meet in Syracuse to choose their delegation to the national convention in Chicago in mid-July, another Cleveland associate, Frank W. Mack, visited the Executive Chamber and found the governor's greeting to be "that of a man who welcomed other comradeship than his own thoughts."

Cleveland said, "Well, you come from the outside world?"

"Yes, Governor, and things seem to be coming your way."

Grover gave Mack a look that was half quizzical, half apprehensive. Mack saw in the blue eyes "no glint of pleased ambition." When Grover sighed heavily, Mack would recall, "it was more than half a groan."

The governor turned a tired face toward a window.

"You seem not highly gleeful as to the outlook, Mr. Governor," said Mack, amazed at the "spectacle of a man saddened by the prospect of a presidential nomination."

"Yes. Yes, I believe things are coming this way," Grover said, "and I feel certain now that I cannot escape it."

Mack blurted, "Escape the nomination?"

"Yes, the nomination—escape the nomination, I say. Tell me this. Can you understand me? Might anybody understand me when I say that, if I were to indulge my personal impulse at the moment, I would go away into some forest, hide in some fastness where no man could reach and where this awful burden might never reach me?"

Nearly forty years after this candid conversation with Mack when destiny appeared to be closing in on the governor of New York, the earliest of Grover Cleveland's twentieth-century biographers, Robert McElroy, wrote, "Few men reach the heights of power unless, in some important respects at least, they are gifted above their fellows. Grover Cleveland had the homely gift of unflinching courage, the rare gift of long patience, and the divine gift of unimpeachable honesty. For such a man the times were calling."

But making the case that a governor who was a year and a half into his first term could be taken seriously as a candidate for president was left to others. To do so, the Cleveland minions would have to tangle again with the forces within the party who just two years earlier had sought to keep the mayor of Buffalo from occupying the governor's chair. The fresh contest would pit Daniel Manning against Tammany's John Kelly. Hoping to be one step ahead of Kelly, Manning sent a lieutenant, William C. Hudson, to Chicago to set up a Cleveland headquarters in the Palmer House hotel in advance of the gathering of the convention delegates. But upon Hudson's arrival he discovered Kelly's advance man and Cleveland's old nemesis, ex–state senator Thomas F. Grady, already ensconced in the opulent hotel and working on behalf of Kelly's efforts to deny Cleveland the nomination.

In fact, Manning himself would have preferred someone else. But he had turned to Grover when the venerable but old and ailing former New York governor, Samuel J. Tilden, removed himself from consideration for what he called "a task which I have not the physical strength to carry through."

This announcement cleared the way for the young lions of the party to assert themselves for the first time since the Civil War. Regarding the Cleveland candidacy, Kelly set his heart and mind on defeating it, no matter the cost. The Tammany boss soon found eager allies in many quarters. The editor of the Louisville, Kentucky, *Courier-Journal* declared Cleveland unknown and inexperienced in national affairs. Charles Dana of the *New York Sun* continued its opposition to Cleveland by depicting him as a man with "plodding mind, limited knowledge and narrow capacities." Backers of Blaine also managed to inject themselves in the anti-Cleveland campaign by sowing fear and apprehension among Irish delegates from New York City, describing him as an irreconcilable enemy and a bigoted Presbyterian. Because a rule of the national party required that New York's delegation vote as a unit (72 votes), Tammany hoped to prevent Cleveland from winning the nomination by denying him votes from the city, and thereby the votes of the entire New York slate.

Scrambling to persuade the city delegates to back Cleveland, Manning found himself without two votes on the morning of the day of the first ballot. Those who would cast these votes were nowhere to be found. When at last they were located and brought to a meeting of the city caucus, each voted Manning's way. To bring them into line, Manning's lieutenant, Hudson, had promised one a state office and the other an enticement which Hudson did not reveal. The two votes swung the majority to Cleveland, and the unit rule gave him all the New York delegation's votes. Said Hudson, "By what small chances do we live in history."

Nominating speeches were given on Wednesday, July 9. A glowing presentation of the virtues of Grover Cleveland was offered and

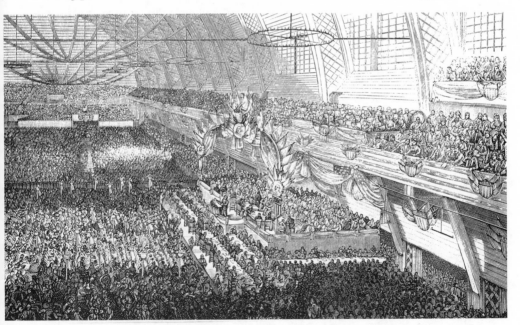

The Democratic Party presidential convention, 1884.

then immediately challenged from the convention floor by Grady. Leaping to his feet, he shouted, "Cleveland cannot carry New York State."

Another Tammany stalwart declared, "We have been told that the mantle of Tilden has fallen upon Cleveland. The mantle of a giant upon the shoulders of a dwarf!"

Words which settled the matter of Grover Cleveland's worthiness sprang from the lips of General Edward S. Bragg of Wisconsin. Speaking for the young men of his delegation and explaining why they backed Cleveland for the nomination, he said, "They love him because of the enemies he has made."

Undaunted, Grady moved on the floor that the convention absolve the New York State delegation from the unit-rule obligation. The attempt was rejected. With the New York votes in the Cleveland column, Manning now had to garner two-thirds of the convention (547 of 820 delegates) for Grover to win the nomination. This proved impossible on the first ballot. He had 392 votes. His nearest opponent, U.S. Senator Thomas F. Bayard of Delaware, had 170. The others were divided between several states' favorite sons, including Allen G. Thurman of Ohio (88), Samuel J. Randall of Pennsylvania (78), and six others, including a single vote for Thomas A. Hendricks of Indiana and one sentimental ballot for Tilden.

Having failed again to thwart the Cleveland forces, Kelly and Grady decided to turn to a political trick—packing the public galleries with hired agents to attempt to stampede delegates on the floor below away from Cleveland to someone else. But to whom?

After a discussion of names, Kelly, Grady, Benjamin F. Butler, and other Cleveland foes settled on Thomas Hendricks, and they ordered their men to raise the cry "Hendricks for President" at the moment he appeared at the morning session. Unfortunately for Kelly, Manning somehow got wind of what was planned and sent messengers scurrying to collar delegates and advise them of the plot. When Hendricks arrived at the convention the next morning, he was greeted noisily by the galleries but with cheers on the floor from only a knot of Tammany stalwarts. The attempt to stampede delegates had failed.

During the call of the roll of states on the second ballot the movement was clearly toward Cleveland, but the tally left him 72 votes short of the two-thirds needed. In expectation of a third ballot giving him the nomination, delegations clamored for recognition by the chair in the hope that by switching their votes they might go home knowing they had put Cleveland over. At one in the afternoon it was done. Grover Cleveland had 683 votes, 136 more than required. 3 AP

At the Democratic Party presidential convention, John Kelly hoped to prevent Cleveland's nomination by using Thomas Hendricks (pictured here).

The delegates then nominated Thomas Hendricks for vice president and after a rendition of the hymn "Praise God from Whom All Blessings Flow," the convention adjourned.

Presently, in Albany, the quiet summer afternoon was shattered by the boom of a cannon. A west wind wafted the sound into the capitol's Executive Chamber. Then came a second and third report. Exultantly jumping up from his chair, Adjutant General John G. Farnsworth exclaimed, "Governor, they are firing a salute to your nomination."

Grover looked at Dan Lamont quizzically.

He nodded his head. "That's what it means."

"Do you think so?"

Confirmation came from Chicago via a phone call.

Grover's face brightened. "By Jove," he said, "that is something, isn't it?"

That evening, July 18, after watching a fireworks display and reviewing a parade of five thousand celebrants, the Democratic presidential nominee spoke. "Let us, then, enter upon the campaign now fairly opened, each one appreciating well the part he had to perform, ready, with solid front, to do battle for better government, confidently, courageously, always honorably, and with a firm reliance upon the intelligence and patriotism of the American people."

★   ★   ★

Having assisted in winning the nomination for Cleveland, William Hudson wasted no time in returning to Albany, not in his capacity as newspaperman, but to do all he could to ensure a win for Cleveland in November. The task assigned him by Lamont was the writing of a campaign document asserting the achievements of the candidate's political career. Being a newspaperman, he appreciated that such a document, if it were to be read by anyone, needed a catchy summarizing phrase at the top, of the sort found in newspaper headlines. With that in mind he began by gathering Grover's papers and addresses going back to the campaign for the mayoralty of Buffalo. Among them he found the speech accepting that nomination, along with the text of his first message to the Buffalo Council. In the former he had said, "Public officials are the trustees of the people, and hold their places and exercise their powers for the benefit of the people." In the latter he declared, "We are trustees and agents of our fellow citizens, holding their funds in a sacred trust."

Continuing his reading of papers and speeches, Hudson discovered similar language in the speech accepting the nomination for governor: "Public officers are the servants and agents of the people, to execute laws which the people have made and within the limits of a constitution which they have established."

These repeated assertions certainly expressed the heart of Grover Cleveland's political philosophy. Hudson's objective was to state this recurring theme effectively but in the boiled-down form which his successors in the field of political propagandizing in the distant era of the automobile and TV screen would provide through bumper stickers and sound bites.

Recalling the challenge he faced in July 1884, Hudson wrote that he sought a "dogmatic form of what [Cleveland] had expressed with greater elucidation."

The document heading Hudson came up with was "Public Office Is a Public Trust."

"I took it to the Governor for his inspection," the journalist-politician wrote. "His eye went to the top line and, pointing to it, he asked, 'Where the deuce did I say that?' "

"You've said it a dozen times publicly, but not in those few words."

"That's too bad," Grover said. "That's what I believe. That's what I've said a little better because more fully."

"But this has the merit of brevity, and that is what is required here. The question is, Will you stand for this form?"

"Oh, yes. That's what I believe. I'll stand for it and make it my own."

Eleven days after the high-minded intentions expressed in a July 10 speech, both the candidate and Hudson's catchy slogan were severely tested. The blow fell in Grover's adopted city on July 21. Buffalo's perennial anti-Cleveland newspaper, the *Telegraph*, blared a sensational headline:

A TERRIBLE TALE
A DARK CHAPTER IN A PUBLIC
MAN'S HISTORY

———

THE PITIFUL STORY OF MARIA
HALPIN AND GOVERNOR
CLEVELAND'S SON

———

A PROMINENT CITIZEN STATES THE RESULT
OF HIS INVESTIGATION OF CHARGES
AGAINST THE GOVERNOR—
INTERVIEWS TOUCHING
THE CASE

When it was revealed during the 1884 presidential campaign that Cleveland had fathered a son out of wedlock, his gleeful opponents chanted, "Ma, Ma, where's my Pa?" The theme was picked up by Puck *magazine's political cartoonist Frank Beard.*

The accompanying story began, "A child was born out of wedlock. Now ten years of age, this sturdy lad is named Oscar Folsom Cleveland. He and his mother have been supported in part by our ex-mayor, who now aspires to the White House. Astute readers may put the facts together and draw their own conclusions." The "prominent citizen" who wrote these words was the Reverend George H. Ball, D.D., a Republican loyalist and pastor of Buffalo's Hudson Street Baptist Church. In terms both vivid and moralistic in tone and condemnation, the preacher-turned-investigative-reporter depicted Grover's bachelor digs in Buffalo as "a harem" from which he trolled for victims "in the city and surrounding villages."

As for the hapless Halpin, Ball and the *Telegraph* portrayed a woman cruelly used by a man who'd deceitfully promised to marry her, abandoned her along with their child, and then had the poor woman committed to an insane asylum.

Newspapers from coast to coast picked up the story. The equally persistent critic of Cleveland, Charles A. Dana, wrote in the *New York Sun,* "We do not believe that the American people will knowingly elect to the Presidency a coarse debauchee who would bring his harlots with him to Washington and hire lodgings for them convenient to the White House."

In a state of alarm, if not panic, Cleveland's friend Charles W. Goodyear wrote him to ask what the party should say. Grover replied by telegram on July 23: WHATEVER YOU DO, TELL THE TRUTH.

The truth, as a highly respected cleric, Rev. Kinsley Twining, attested, was that when Mr. Cleveland "was younger than he is now, he was guilty of an illicit connection; but the charge, as brought against him, lacks the elements of truth in these substantial points; there is no seduction, no adultery, no breach of promise, no obligation of marriage."

Yes, continued Twining, there had been at that time "a culpable irregularity of life, living as he was, a bachelor," but the deplorable episode had been followed by conduct which was "singularly honorable, showing no attempt to evade responsibility, and doing all he could to meet the duties involved, of which marriage was certainly not one."

Defense of Cleveland was waged in more than words. Within days of the newspaper article a small army of investigators descended on Buffalo. Described by Allan Nevins in his Cleveland biography as "hounds of truth on the heels of the worst fabrications," they quickly demolished most of Rev. George Ball's story and eventually forced him to write a letter to the *Courier,* ever faithful to Cleveland, in which Ball admitted that he had falsified several claims. Finally, a report published by sixteen well-known Buffalo Republicans concluded:

> Our examination of the general charges which have been made against Governor Cleveland's private character shows that they are wholly untrue. In every instance in which the reports and insinuations have been tangible enough to furnish us a clue to guide us in our investigations they have been positively proved to be false. The attack upon Governor Cleveland's character is thoroughly discredited when we consider the sources from which it comes.

None of the investigators, pro-Grover and not, nor Rev. George Ball, spoke with Maria Halpin, whose whereabouts proved to be untraceable. Yet none of their evidence prevented Cleveland's enemies from subsidizing national distribution of a song, ostensibly written by "H. R. Monroe" and issued by the National Music Company of Chicago.

Titled "Ma! Ma! Where's My Pa?" it left no doubt as to its target:

Little Tom Tid was a frolicsome kid,
A cute little cuss, I declare,
With eyes full of fun,
And a nose that begun
Way up in the roots of his hair.
Jolly and fat was this frolicsome brat,

As he played thro' the livelong day,

But one eve, to his cost,

His papa got lost,

And he and his ma say a lay, Oh,

CHORUS

Ma! Ma! Where is my Pa?

Up in the White House, darling,

Making the laws, working the cause,

Up in the White House, dear.

Ma! Ma! Where is Papa?

Up in the White House, darling:

Making the laws, working the cause,

Up in the White House, dear.

While the song was being promoted by Republicans, another story was circulated by, of all people, the friendly editor of the *Buffalo Courier*, Charles McCune, claiming that the reason Grover had never denied fathering the child was that he was protecting the identity of the real parent, Oscar Folsom.

When word of McCune's story reached Grover, he wrote a letter to Daniel Lockwood angrily denying that he had shielded Folsom. Speaking of McCune, he asked, "Now is this man crazy or does he wish to ruin somebody? Is he fool enough to suppose for a moment that if such was the truth . . . that I would permit my dead friend's memory to suffer for my sake? And Mrs. Folsom and her daughter at my house at this very time! I am afraid that I shall have occasion to pray to be delivered from my friends. How often I wish that I was free and that some good friend of mine was running instead of myself."

As though dealing with the Halpin matter were not enough to worry about, the candidate found himself under fire for not having served in the army during the Civil War. Because a large segment of the electorate consisted of veterans of the war, this posed a serious problem. Grover's response came in an answer to a letter on the matter from the vice-commandant of a New York City veterans' post. Branding the draft-dodging allegation "this new development of political mendacity," Grover explained the circumstances which had led him to hire a substitute. The issue was defused. In September he was able to write to Shan Bissell, "I hope now that the scandal business is about wound up that you have a little freedom from the annoyance and trouble which it necessarily brought in its train. I think the matter was arranged in the best possible way, and that the policy of not cringing was not only necessary but the only possible way."

Thus began a campaign that would be condemned by contemporary observers as the vilest ever waged (overlooking previous contests in which mudslinging and outright lies about opponents had been at least as bad, if not worse). But in the summer of 1884 the smears were not the property of Democrats. From the moment the Republicans nominated Blaine, the Mugwumps carried on a tirade of attacks on Blaine that were violent in their tone and personally offensive. Carl Schurz set the standard, referring to Blaine's "unclean record." The general theme was dishonesty, giving rise to a Democratic chant to counter the Republicans' "Ma, Ma, Where's My Pa?" Almost everywhere Blaine went he found himself confronted by the singsong taunt:

> Blaine, Blaine, James G. Blaine,
> The continental liar from the State of Maine.

Unable to control what Mugwumps and other passionate partisans did, and uncomfortable and embarrassed by their tactics, Grover Cleveland declined to participate in character attacks on Blaine. When presented with papers which purported to be extremely damaging to Blaine, he grabbed them, tore them up, flung the shreds into the fire, and decreed, "The other side can have a monopoly of all the dirt in this campaign."

The following passage from Robert McElroy's two-volume biography of Cleveland may seem extravagant in its praise, but it is nonetheless a true portrayal of his character in the heat of the campaign:

> Unskilled in sophistry and new to the darker ways of national politics, Grover Cleveland faced his accusers, his slanderers, and his judges, the sovereign people, conscious of the general rectitude of his life, and courageously determined to bear the burdens of his sins in so far as guilt was his.

While the Halpin, Civil War draft, and other assaults on Cleveland's character faded as issues, Republicans floated other balloons which could not be so easily deflated. They stirred fears. Democratic rule would be dangerous to the welfare of the Union. The policy of low tariffs favored by Democrats would wreak ruin on business. Manufacturing industries would be left prostrate. Currency would be debased, public credit ruined. Civil and political rights would be in jeopardy. The Supreme Court would be reorganized. Constitutional amendments were earmarked for repeal. Reconstruction was to be reversed. Veterans' pensions were to be slashed and then eliminated. Forces favoring prohibition of alcoholic drink, led by radicals such as Frances E. Willard, strident head of the Women's Christian Temperance Union, would succeed in imposing prohibition.⌉

Historian and Cleveland biographer Horace Samuel Merrill wrote in *Bourbon Leader: Grover Cleveland and the Democratic Party*, "The depiction of Blaine as an unrestrained public plunderer and Cleveland as town drunk and debaucher was just a part of the material used to fill the vacuum of a campaign devoid of issues. Hence, lingering Civil War prejudices, pension-conscious war veterans, the Catholic issue, anti-British sentiment, nativism and prohibition received much attention. As the outlandish, issue-starved campaign approached its end, it was apparent to both sides that the outcome was very much in doubt."

Hanging in the balance were Connecticut, Indiana, New Jersey, and New York. Although Grover honored a tradition in presidential campaigning in which candidates did not carry their messages directly to voters and remained at home, leaving the barnstorming and stump-speaking to surrogates, he agreed to make public appearances in October. The first was on October 2 for a colorful torchlight parade and rally in Buffalo. He found his welcome "much beyond anticipations and in point of fact the largest they have ever seen." Late in the month he delivered speeches in Newark, New Jersey, and Bridgeport, Connecticut, on the themes of civil service reform, tax reduction, and labor.

Abandoning the no-campaigning tradition, James G. Blaine, feeling confident and cocky, had taken to the hustings in a strenuous speech-making tour in the Middle West. The windup of this precedent-shattering and whirlwind excursion came in Philadelphia. Fatigued and weary, Blaine settled into his headquarters at the Fifth Avenue Hotel on Wednesday, October 29, only to be greeted by a delegation of clergymen, all ardent reformers who had refused to enlist in the ranks of Mugwumps rushing to embrace "Grover the Good."

Among these loyalist Republican clerics was Dr. Samuel Burchard, a preacher with a reputation for coming up with a well-turned phrase intended to not only save the souls of sinners, but drive home the points of the reverend's sermons in Murray Hill Presbyterian Church. Despite Blaine's weariness and evident inattention, Burchard, fired by the Blaine campaign's theme of the ruination facing the nation if the White House went to a reform-minded Democrat who was unsympathetic to high tariffs and prohibitionists, proudly declared, "We are Republicans, and don't propose to leave our party and identify ourselves with the party whose antecedents have been Rum, Romanism, and Rebellion."

The Reverend Samuel Burchard.

Listening to Burchard's rhetoric were newspaper reporters who evidently found nothing remarkable to report to their readers. When the meeting with the clerics ended, Blaine proceeded to the next event on his crowded calendar. It was called a "prosperity dinner" and those attending it were millionaires. They gathered at Delmonico's restaurant where, as the *New York World* would report, "champagne frothed and brandy sparkled in glasses that glittered like jewels."

One man who had been present and more attentive than Blaine and others at the Fifth Avenue Hotel during Dr. Burchard's remarks, but who did not trail the Republican presidential candidate to the Delmonico festivities, was a stenographer who had been engaged by Democratic campaign manager Arthur Pue Gorman. When the stenographer read the reverend's words to Gorman, the campaign manager's eyes flashed. He exclaimed, "Write that out!"

Within hours, "Rum, Romanism, and Rebellion" was on placards and handbills on their way to the principal cities up and down the East Coast and wherever there was a heavy concentration of Irish Catholic voters. Hundreds of the hastily printed signs and leaflets were in evidence as Blaine passed through New Haven, Connecticut, the next day. But being confronted with them was not nearly as infuriating and embarrassing to Blaine as that day's edition of the *New York World*. Half its front page was taken up by a cartoon by Walt McDougall showing the "prosperity dinner" and labeling it "The Royal Feast of Belshazzar Blaine and the Money Kings."

In Albany, far from such frivolities, Grover Cleveland sat in his big chair to compose a letter to his dear friend Harold Frederick, even more removed from New York in London. It is a remarkably candid self-portrait of a man at a personal and historic moment:

I sometimes feel that I do not fully appreciate the solemn responsibilities of my position, and, again, that I do not fret enough and am not anxious enough. At times the whole question is presented to my mind in such a way that in the midst of wonderment I say to myself, "There is a God!"

Imagine a man standing in my place, with positively no ambitions for a higher position than I now hold, and in constant apprehension that he may be called to assume burdens and duties the greatest and highest that a human being can take upon himself. I can not look upon the prospect of success in this campaign with any joy, but only with a very serious kind of awe. Is this right?

Another man with doubts regarding the prospect of Grover Cleveland becoming president of the United States was just back from the Wild West. Brushing aside earlier expressions on the unacceptability of James G. Blaine, and recent legislative alliances with the Democratic governor of New York notwithstanding, Theodore Roosevelt told a group of reporters, "I think he is not a man who should be put in that office, and there is no lack of reasons for it. His public career, in the first place, and then private reasons as well." What these were, he chose not to specify. Nor did he offer an explanation for the change which had occurred in his attitude toward Blaine in the interval between June and October which he had spent as a cowboy in Dakota. Some students of Theodore Roosevelt have speculated that he was simply assuring himself of good standing in the view of the candidate who was widely expected to win the White House, thereby positioning himself for an appointive position in a Blaine administration. Others credit his turnabout as his duty to his party.

Roosevelt biographer Nathan Miller's analysis in *Theodore Roosevelt: A Life* concluded that TR had decided to be a political professional. Had he bolted to Cleveland, Miller wrote, he would have been devoid of influence within the Republican Party.

Roosevelt himself saw his position in October 1884 as a no-win situation. He explained to his mentor, Senator Henry Cabot Lodge, that "chance placed me where I was sure to lose whatever I did." Disconsolate over the recent deaths of his wife and mother on the same day, left without support of the Mugwumps, and seeing no future for himself in politics, he soldiered through the waning days of the campaign, making speeches on behalf of the party. He then declared his belief that he would "ever be likely to come back into political life," remanded the care of his infant daughter to a sister, sold his Manhattan house, and went back to Dakota.

★　★　★

With election day drawing closer, Grover remained in Albany in the welcome company of Oscar Folsom's widow and their pretty daughter, Frances, officially his ward. Awaiting the vote, he was assured of the support of two of New York's mightiest newspapers. The influential *Herald* had informed its readers, "We are told that Mr. Blaine has been delinquent in office but blameless in private life, while Mr. Cleveland has been the model of official integrity, but culpable in his personal relations. We should therefore elect Mr. Cleveland to the public office which he is so well qualified to fill, and remand Mr. Blaine to the private station which he is admirably fitted to adorn." Joseph Pulitzer's *New York World* gave four reasons for endorsing Cleveland: "1. He is an honest man; 2. He is an honest man; 3. He is an honest man; 4. He is an honest man."

The dawn of election day brought dismal rain squalls across upstate New York as Grover traveled from Albany to vote in Buffalo. At the same time in Cambridge, Massachusetts, a twenty-one-year-old junior at Harvard, William Randolph Hearst, cast the first ballot of his life, marking it for the Democratic candidate, then dipped into his very considerable inheritance to plan a huge celebration for the victory he joyously anticipated personally leading. That evening, as early tallies were reported running in favor of Cleveland in the traditionally Republican districts of Murray Hill and Brooklyn Heights in New York City, there was reason to believe that young Hearst's expectations would be met. But an exception to this thinking was voiced by Blaine's managers, who knew that the count which truly mattered would come not from Mugwump strongholds, but in Irish Catholic wards controlled with an iron fist by the Tammany machine. These savvy pols counseled, "Wait till you hear from the slums."

Back in Albany, Grover awaited the returns in a second-floor sitting room of the Executive Mansion, accompanied by Dan Lamont and his assistant secretary, Colonel William Gorham Rice. Assessing the first returns, Rice found a slight Cleveland edge which, if it held, would provide a breathtakingly narrow winning margin—about 2,000 votes. Lamont agreed. With votes trickling in without change and the hour nearing midnight, the candidate rose from his chair and informed his associates he was going to bed.

Remaining awake and growing increasingly alarmed, Lamont and Rice conferred with Edgar Apgar and discussed the likelihood that the outcome of such a close election in Blaine's favor might be the result of Tammany-dictated fraud in the counting process. Hoping to abort that possibility, they fired off a telegram in the name of Daniel Manning to Democratic leaders in every county, ordering them to round up their "vigilant and courageous friends" to see that "every vote cast is honestly counted." This message was followed in the morning by telegrams requesting them to obtain certified copies of official tallies in all county clerk offices across the state and send them by courier to Albany.

When Grover awoke on Wednesday, November 5, the election still hung in the balance, with the Associated Press reporting Blaine ahead and gaining. In Boston, still hoping to stage an extravaganza to hail a Cleveland victory, "Willie" Hearst held his breath. An angry throng of New Yorkers, suspecting that Jay Gould had ordered his telegraph company, Western Union, to put out falsified returns, streamed down Broadway to the firm's offices and chanted, "We'll hang Jay Gould from a sour apple tree." A similar group serenaded Gould with the same grim threat outside Gould's Fifth Avenue mansion.

Central to concerns of Democrats was the fact that it was not the popular vote nationally which determined the winner in presidential elections. That lay with the Electoral College. While the unquestionable result of voting in Connecticut, in New Jersey, across the South, and in Thomas Hendricks's Indiana spelled a Cleveland victory, in other states of the Midwest the old-soldier vote turned out for Blaine. This put the focus on New York. Lacking its electoral vote, Grover could not prevail.

As Wednesday passed with messengers delivering the official tallies from county seats across the state to the Executive Chamber, Lamont studied them and satisfied himself, as he wrote later, that "Mr. Cleveland's majority in the state was more accurately known than anywhere else." The margin was razor-thin, under 2,000 votes, as Lamont and Rice had predicted. Persuaded of the accuracy of the count and Lamont's assessment of the outcome,

Grover sent a telegram to a concerned supporter in Troy, New York, dated November 6: "I believe I have been elected president and nothing but grossest fraud can keep me out of it and that we will not permit."

But, as Lamont noted in a memoir of those tense days, "it was not until about 10 o'clock in the morning of Friday, November 7, when the manager of the Western Union Telegraph company in Albany, Mr. F. W. Sabold, delivered into Mr. Cleveland's own hands a message received over a special wire, that the situation was relieved of doubt." The wire was from Jay Gould:

GOVERNOR CLEVELAND—I HEARTILY CONGRATULATE YOU ON YOUR ELECTION. ALL CONCEDE THAT YOUR ADMINISTRATION AS GOVERNOR HAS BEEN WISE AND CONSERVATIVE, AND IN THE LARGER FIELD AS PRESIDENT I FEEL THAT YOU WILL DO STILL BETTER, AND THAT THE VAST BUSINESS INTERESTS OF THE COUNTRY WILL BE ENTIRELY SAFE IN YOUR HANDS.

Lamont noted for the record, "Coming from the most conspicuous of his [Cleveland's] opponent's supporters—from one who was the head and center of the group of interests which had continued to claim that opponent's election—it satisfied Mr. Cleveland that the contest was over and the victory won."

The official margin of victory in New York was 1,047.

Yet diehards, such as the *New York Tribune*, refused to concede. As did James G. Blaine. Not until the towel was thrown in on Saturday by the Associated Press would Blaine admit he'd lost New York and therefore the White House. Said Grover to friends, "I am glad of it. I am glad they yield peaceably. If they had not, I should have felt it my duty to take my seat anyhow."

He had carried twenty states with a total of 219 electoral votes to Blaine's eighteen states with 182. The plurality over Blaine in the national popular-vote total of more than nine million had been under 24,000.

The night Willie Hearst threw his party in Cambridge the music was provided by a brass band from Boston. Fireworks illuminated the sky. A deft cartoonist for the Harvard *Lampoon*, Fred Briggs, unfurled a Hearst-commissioned banner painted with the portraits of Cleveland and his running mate. A parade ended at Holyoke and Mt. Auburn streets with a flag-raising. An observer noted "such a red-blazing, ear-splitting, rip-roaring, all-night racket as to scandalize old Cambridge." Among those irked by the din were students and Harvard dons, jolted from their sleep at dawn on Sunday by dozens of roosters (then the symbol of the Democrats) set loose in venerable Harvard Yard.

Demonstrations also erupted in the streets of Buffalo, Albany, and cities across the nation, particularly in the states of the South. In Atlanta a session of the legislature was brought to a halt by five thousand exultant Georgians delivering "a message from the American people." Cannons thundered and hymns were sung across the former Confederacy to salute the ending of a quarter century of punishing retribution for the Civil War under Republican presidents.

Some Cleveland celebrants, recalling the mocking ditty "Ma, Ma, Where's My Pa?," ran around chanting one of their own:

> Hurrah for Maria.
> Hurrah for the kid.
> We voted for Grover
> And we're damn glad we did.

On November 13, with the last ballot examined and verified and victory his beyond the shadow of a doubt, the president-elect wrote to his old friend and ally Shan Bissell, and provided an illuminating and instructive self-portrait:

> *As I look over the field I see some people lying dead whose demise will not harm the country, some whose wounds will perhaps serve to teach them that honesty and decency are worth preserving, and some whose valor, fidelity, and staunch devotion are rewarded with victory and who have grappled themselves to me with "hooks of steel." In this last array stand my true Buffalo friends. You don't, I'm sure, want me to be invidious, but you must trust me to appreciate all that you have done. I am busy all day long receiving congratulations of friends in person, while through the mail and telegraph they are counted by the thousand. It's quite amusing to see how profuse the professions of some who stood aloof when most needed. I intend to cultivate the Christian virtue of charity toward all men except the dirty class that defiled themselves with filthy scandal and Ballism. I don't believe God will ever forgive them and I am determined not to do so.*
>
> *I look upon the four years next to come as a dreadful self-inflicted penance for the good of my country. I can see no pleasure in it and no satisfaction, only a hope that I may be of service to my people.*

Two weeks later, concerning "a fine Newfoundland dog" which had been sent to him as a gift by an admirer, William J. Leader, he responded, "I hope you will not deem it affectation on my part when I write you that I am very averse to the receipt of gifts—especially in the relation of strangers which you and I sustain to each other. . . . The acceptance of presents of value which could involve an obligation, I should deem in my present position entirely inadmissable."

The dog was returned the next day by express at Grover's expense.

5

✦

Gone to the
White House

Except for Grover Cleveland himself and Chester A. Arthur, the Republican he would replace on March 4, 1885, no American would be affected more directly by the arrival at the White House of the twenty-second president of the United States than the chief disbursement officer of the President's House. For one thing, Colonel William H. Crook had never served a Democrat. He'd come to work for Abraham Lincoln and risen to his current post from that of doorman. He'd been on duty the evening of the surrender of Robert E. Lee's Army of Northern Virginia, April 12, 1865, when the president asked a Union Army band to strike up "Dixie," and two nights later had wished President and Mrs. Lincoln a pleasant time as they departed for a lively comedy at Fords's Theatre. He was on hand when the assassinated president's body was carried into the East Room to repose until a state funeral at the Capitol. He liked to boast that he had been the one who rushed

On March 4, 1885, President Arthur accompanied Cleveland from the White House to the Capitol for the inauguration.

down Pennsylvania Avenue to the White House from the U.S. Senate to inform the impeached President Andrew Johnson that he had been acquitted by one vote at the trial. He could spin fond tales of President Ulysses S. Grant and spoke of Grant's wife affectionately as a "quaint old lady." He had served the administration of President Rutherford B. Hayes and endured a second assassination, that of James A. Garfield. For almost four years he served the president who waited to greet Grover Cleveland on March 4, 1885, prior to the ceremony at the Capitol for the oath of office by which the power and majesty of the executive branch of the federal government passed into fresh hands. In the parlance of historians a hundred years hence, Crook possessed "the institutional memory" of the White House. One of those chroniclers, William Seale, wrote of Crook in his two-volume *The President's House*, published by the White House Historical Association in 1986, "A line of succession through six Republican Presidents led back to the Republicans' first triumph in 1860 and the mighty visage of the Civil War. The Grand Army of the Republic still marched young in memory, although in reality with the beards and paunches of middle age."

What Crook knew of his future boss was that Mr. Cleveland had been a sheriff for two years; in private law practice for seven; the mayor of Buffalo, New York, for two years; governor of New York for the same number; and elected president. He'd considered all these offices "a business engagement" between the people and himself. What Crook knew of Cleveland's personal life was gossip and a scandal in the newspapers: he was a bachelor, soon to turn forty-eight years of age, very fat, and had fathered a child out of wedlock. Former President Hayes had said that Cleveland was "a brute with women," but that Cleveland's "greatest deficiency" was not having served in the Civil War.

In the twenty-two years since Grover Cleveland paid $150 for a substitute to represent him in the war, the "one nation" which Lincoln strove to preserve had become a place dramatically different from anything the Great Emancipator could have anticipated. The United States of America over which the twenty-second occupant of the White House would preside found itself in the throes of changes driven by industrialization, explosive growth of the importance of cities, and expansion into the West of which Theodore

Roosevelt had become recently enamored. All these factors, noted Richard E. Welch Jr. in *The Presidencies of Grover Cleveland*, fostered confidence in American society on Inauguration Day 1885. This optimism evidenced itself in a general prosperity for American industry, if not for individuals—the workers—who were the linking strands of the social fabric. Yet the feeling abroad among the working class of the nation as the president-elect came to Washington to take office was one of confidence in the future, not restless discontent.

Allan Nevins described a changing nature of America in which winds had whistled and waves had swept high, but the fountains of the great deep had not been broken up. There was no crisis demanding dramatic action. "Men expected Cleveland to display not an excursive boldness," he wrote, "but simply a greater honesty and earnestness than his predecessors, and he understood this perfectly."

The consensus of Cleveland biographers is that the president-elect was appalled to see how unprepared he was for the magnitude of the duties he had obligated himself to assume. He was also aghast at how little time he had to ready himself for the presidency, while at the same time writing his third message to the legislature as governor and preparing to hand over the reins of that office to Lieutenant Governor Hill. He planned to do so on January 6, 1885, leaving two days less than two months to devote himself entirely to forming a presidential administration.

Immediately besieged by individuals looking for jobs in the government, he wrote to Shan Bissell on Christmas Day, "The plot thickens. I am sick at heart and perplexed in brain during most of my working hours. I almost think that the professions of most of my pretended friends are but the means they employ to accomplish

President Cleveland at the beginning of his first term.

personal and selfish ends. It's so hard to discover the springs of action and it seems so distressing to feel that in the question as to who shall be trusted, I should be so much at sea. I wonder if I must for the third time face the difficulties of a new official almost *alone*?"

Not quite. Dan Lamont was at hand. Informed that he was expected to transfer his duties from Albany to Washington, D.C., he demurred until the president-elect said, "Well, Dan, if you won't go, I won't." Lamont's title would be presidential secretary. In that role he would leave a model for a century of men who followed him. He would stand at the head of an administrative team whose appointments Theodore Roosevelt characterized as "the Apotheosis of the Unknown." This was not entirely deserved. Several of the men Cleveland appointed knew their way around Washington very well indeed.

Also ready to assist in the transition from governor to president were his sisters Rose (unmarried) and Mary (Mrs. Hoyt). They were there to help set up temporary housing after he moved from Albany's Executive Mansion and would be present to assist their brother in settling into the White House.

There were also people offering advice, especially a Democratic Party leadership which knew as well as Grover Cleveland that they had no claims on him because of political debts. Not since James Buchanan had a Democrat been called upon to appoint federal officials ranging from postmasters to revenue collectors. Of a government payroll of about 126,000, all but 16,000 got their jobs by appointment by the president. This well-established political payoff mechanism was commonly known and denounced by reformers as the spoils system. Worried that their choice for president might find himself succumbing to it, leaders of the Mugwumps arranged for him to receive a letter from the National Civil Service Reform League seeking assurances that the president-elect remained committed to the cause. They asked for a pledge that he would observe the new civil service law of 1883. They needn't have fretted. He replied that no "consideration shall cause a relaxation on my part of an earnest effort to enforce this law."

He then went further, vowing not to remove on partisan grounds anyone in the government service who was doing his job. "Efficient employees" would keep their posts for their full terms; "inefficient employees, offensive partisans, and unscrupulous manipulators" would be removed. He also noted that faithful party work would be rewarded by office, but that the appointee would first have to be deemed fit for the post.

Assessing the Cleveland appointments from the vantage point of 1923 in his two-volume biography, *Grover Cleveland, The Man and the Statesman*, Robert McElroy wrote, "It has been said that a President is known by the appointments he makes. And this is partly true. A small President is likely to choose small men to surround him, unwilling to invite the cooperation of great minds, lest his own be dwarfed by comparison. As an appointing agent Mr. Cleveland was not inerrant, but his mistakes came from no such petty jealousies. The average of his appointments is high compared with any executive of his time, nor did he in his choice of men make secret concessions to standards which he was unwilling to profess openly."

Guided by that precept, he began filling the most important posts in his administration—his Cabinet—as soon as the election results were confirmed. His intention in announcing selections quickly was to allow ample time for the choices to be judged by public and party before they were sent to the Senate for confirmation.

The consensus of historians is that the choices were not only well distributed geographically, but laudable in their quality. Each was a man of integrity, moral strength, and intelligence with conservative views and a sense of responsibility. They were self-assured with records of success in politics, business, or law. Allan Nevins wrote that in ability the Cleveland Cabinet "had not been surpassed since Lincoln's day." Historian Horace Samuel Merrill, in *Bourbon Leader: Grover Cleveland and the Democratic Party*, depicted it as "the fusion of interests that were to control the Democratic party and were greatly to influence the nation during the 'Cleveland era.' "

Cabinets in presidential "eras" of the twentieth century would be known as "the brain trust" of Franklin D. Roosevelt, Dwight D. Eisenhower's "board of directors," and "the best and the brightest" of John F. Kennedy. But it was the chief executive who would dominate his time in office, and be the one judged by history. So it would be with Grover Cleveland.

It was he, after all, not his Cabinet, presenting himself at the White House on March 4, 1885, to be greeted by Colonel Crook

Grover (fourth from left) *and members of his first Cabinet* (left to right): *William F. Vilas, postmaster general; Thomas B. Bayard, secretary of state; William C. Whitney, secretary of the navy; William C. Endicott, secretary of war; Daniel Manning, secretary of the treasury; Augustus H. Garland, attorney general; Lucius Quintus Cincinnatus Lamar, secretary of the interior.*

in the same manner with which the majordomo of the President's House had welcomed Lincoln, Johnson, Grant, Hayes, Garfield, and Arthur.

★   ★   ★

Although the president-elect had been invited by President Arthur to stay in the White House the night before his inauguration, Grover chose to ensconce himself in the Arlington Hotel on Vermont Avenue. He'd bidden farewell to Albany on March 2 and traveled down to Washington, D.C., by train. In keeping with his policy of not accepting gifts, he had turned down an offer from the railroad of a special train at no cost. The longest train ride he'd ever taken terminated in a city he had never visited.

As the seat of the federal government, Washington, D.C., had grown accustomed to the every-four-year pageantry of presidential oath-taking. But everyone standing along Pennsylvania Avenue for the festivities to begin on the fine clear morning of March 4, 1885, did so in the full appreciation that power had not been exchanged between opposite parties since James Buchanan and Abraham Lincoln had done so in 1861. That point was uppermost in the mind of Cleveland biographer and friend George F. Parker. In *Recollections of Grover Cleveland*, he gave this account of the day:

> Few inaugural ceremonies have been marked with more of pageantry or have had in them a greater rejoicing on the part of the successful party, and, at the same time, more of genuine grief on the part of the defeated, than that which ushered Grover Cleveland into the Presidency. The day was in every way perfect, the first in the long list which grew to have the distinctive name of "Cleveland

weather." An elaborate program had been planned, and the men assigned to the work of handling the crowds were expert in the management of great occasions. The military features—participated in by the army, the marines, the navy, and the artillery—were increased by detachments from the militia of the several states, especially from Pennsylvania.

The day's schedule began with the arrival of the president-elect at the White House for an official greeting by President Arthur, followed by a carriage ride from the Executive Mansion to the Capitol. When the two men entered the Senate to await the signal to proceed to the east front of the Capitol Building, all eyes turned to a physically enormous figure in a long, double-breasted, black Prince Albert coat and gray striped pants, a man about whom hardly any of those gathered knew much. Among them was Republican Robert M. La Follette, freshman member of the House of Representatives from Wisconsin. He recalled, "The contrast with Arthur, who was a fine, handsome figure, was very striking. Cleveland's coarse face, his heavy inert body, his great shapeless hands, confirmed in my mind the attacks made upon him during the campaign."

The Washington correspondent of the *Cleveland Leader*, understandably present to see a descendant of the city's namesake become president of the United States, proved less judgmental than La Follette, but just as brutally candid in his report's description. "What a Big Man President Cleveland is! He must weigh nearly three hundred pounds, and a line drawn through the center of his stomach to the small of his back would measure at least two feet. He is six feet tall, has a great width of shoulder, and his flesh, unlike that of most fat men, is solid, not flabby."

The right of the "great, shapeless hands" clutched the Bible on which he would place the left to repeat the oath of office as administered by the chief justice of the United States, Morrison R. Waite. The Bible bore an inscription on the flyleaf: "My son, Stephen Grover Cleveland, from his loving Mother." After the oath the clerk of the Supreme Court would write below it, "It was used to administer the oath of office to Grover Cleveland, President of the United States, on the fourth of March, 1885." Throughout Grover's eight years as president, the Bible would be kept in the upper left-hand drawer of a massive desk which had been a gift to the White House from Queen Victoria.

Oath taken, the twenty-second president of the United States stepped to the podium to deliver his inaugural address, and to secure a place in the history of such speeches by making it without a manuscript. As astonished as every one of the onlookers, but perhaps not aware of the deserved reputation of "Big Steve" Cleveland as a winning cardplayer, Senator John J. Ingalls muttered, "God, what a magnificent gambler."

Not really. "Preparing every public utterance with the greatest of care, not only as to word, phrase, and sentiment, but as to punctuation," noted George F. Parker, "he had the rare gift, with only the slightest effort, of so memorizing his own writings that he could deliver an address of an hour in length without loss or change of a word." Nonetheless, the audience arrayed on the east plaza of the Capitol that day stirred with amazement at the composure and self-confidence—"the spectacle," as Parker put it—of a man who had been elected president of the United States in less than three years after he'd been an obscure lawyer in a small city, and yet was able to stand below the Capitol dome and speak to them of his goals without a note before him, flawlessly.

The feat of memorization is all the more remarkable because the printed text of the address in a book of Cleveland speeches runs more than five pages. To those who knew the speaker and his record in public office, its keynote was familiar: "The people demand reform in the administration of the government, and the application of business principles to public affairs."

In that enterprise, he said, he would give the nation economy, isolation from foreign entanglements, an executive branch "guided by a just and unrestrained construction of the Constitution, a careful observance of the distinction between the powers of the federal government and those reserved to the State or to the people," and assurance that "the common interest is subserved and the general welfare advanced."

He called for "a spirit of amity and mutual concession" and abandonment of "all sectional prejudice and distrust" in the country and between the White House and a Congress with a majority of embittered and dubious Republicans in the Senate.

On the subject of those who once had been slaves but were now free, he said, "The fact that they are citizens entitles them to all the rights due to that relation, and charges them with all duties, obligations, and responsibilities."

Such matters as pressing national controversies over taxation, business interests verus those of labor, tariffs, currency and the gold standard versus silver, and other questions of the hour were passed over in generalities. His aim was to allay a prevailing fear that the advent of a Democrat in the presidency for the first time in twenty-four years was a potentially dangerous event.

The speech ended with acknowledgment of "the power and goodness of Almighty God, who presides over the destiny of nations, and who has at all times been revealed in our country's history." The audience which applauded and then made its way from Capitol Hill did so of three minds. Some departed in the hope that the new president would prove a strong one, in contrast to his immediate predecessors. Others left feeling relieved that the Republicans still held power in the Congress. Most went away willing to wait and see what would transpire, and content for the moment to observe and enjoy inaugural festivities which the nation's capital held in store for the first bachelor to reside in the White House in a quarter century.

★   ★   ★

Not officially named "the White House" until President Theodore Roosevelt assumed the Executive Mansion in 1901, the home of the president of the United States would by the end of the twentieth century become symbolic of everything which would change about the presidency since the evening of Inauguration Day when Grover Cleveland first listened to a rousing salute by the U.S. Marine Corps band. In 1885 if there had been the term "superpower," it would have been applied to Great Britain. In a world where freedom was scarce and dreams of it scarcer, no one had coined for the president of the United States the phrase "leader of the free world." Fireside chats of Franklin D. Roosevelt via the radio were fifty years in the future and an address by a president on television from "the Oval Office" was, like that chamber itself, unimaginable. Indeed, eight years after the twenty-second president of the United States moved into the mansion at 1600 Pennsylvania Avenue, the first edition of the traveler's guide *Baedeker's United States 1893* saw "Executive Mansion of the President of the United States" as so unimpressive that it was afforded one paragraph.

A sentence in that text, read more than a hundred years later, profoundly illustrates the changes which have occurred in the intervening century. The guidebook noted, "The East Room is open to the public from 10 to 2. Two or three times a week the President receives all comers here at 1 P.M., shaking hands with each as they pass him in single file."

There was no White House "visitors' center" with metal detectors to screen those who came. No tickets. No eagle-eyed Secret Service agents in uniforms and plain clothes scanned the line of callers for the potential assassin. Nor was there an electronic security system, a tall iron fence turning a presidential residence and offices into a "compound," or sentries at gates, assorted color-coded passes to be displayed on clothing, antiaircraft and missile defenses on the roof, sharpshooters, and barriers closing Pennsylvania Avenue and other surrounding streets to traffic. A citizen was free, if he or she desired, to walk right up the lane or across the front lawn and up to the front door unchallenged. The white mansion stood alone, unextended by east and west wings to accommodate staffs of the president and the first lady. No swimming pool. No room set aside for reporters. No photo ops. Not even a press secretary.

The entire staff at Grover Cleveland's command in 1885 was no more than a handful, led by the indispensable Dan Lamont. A personal servant, William Sinclair, had been brought down from Albany. For a short time there was a butler named Arthur, but he was let go because Grover considered the job unnecessary. A coachman was available for carriage rides out of the city, although the president frequently decided to leave the carriage in order to walk. There were no bodyguards. On many occasions foot excursions were made alone across the unfenced south lawn (where band concerts were held in the summer) for strolls around the recently completed Washington Monument.

There was also a French chef, prompting Grover to gripe in a letter to Bissell, "I must go to dinner. I wish it was to eat a pickled herring, Swiss cheese, and a chop instead of the French stuff I shall find."

Finally, fed up with the continental cuisine, he begged his successor in Albany's Executive Mansion to let him bring his former cook, Eliza, down to the nation's capital. When she arrived the French chef was dismissed.

Thanks to a demand by President Arthur in 1881, the mansion had been refurbished. He'd taken one look at the deplorable condition of the house and the things in it and declared that unless decades of worn furniture and an accumulation of outright junk were removed, he would not live there. As a result, Grover settled into the two-story combination residence and offices with no need to modify any of the public spaces on the ground floor or living quarters and working areas in the eastern end on the second, which he entered no later than nine o'clock each morning.

The first order of business was meeting with Lamont for about an hour on pending matters and taking care of correspondence, both official and from the public. One of the earliest letters from a woman pleaded, "Mr. President Cleveland, I would love to have something from the White House. Please send me scraps of your cravats and your cabinet to make a block in my crazy quilt."

Another letter suggested, "If you could see your way clear and the right material in a colored man for your Cabinet, you would thereby clinch the lip-service of the Democrats as scouted by the Republicans, and attach the race to the party which would be to the advantage of both."

After finishing with Lamont (at least for the morning), he was ready to see visitors on business. Afternoon conferences with the Cabinet were convened Tuesdays and Thursdays in the adjoining Cabinet Room. At 1:30 Monday, Wednesday, and Friday afternoons he went downstairs to the East Room to shake hands with people who chose to drop in at the White House to speak with the president on subjects of importance to them, to see him up close, or to take advantage of a custom dating back to the 1841 inauguration of President William Henry Harrison of shaking a president's hand.

After a session which lasted for three hours Abraham Lincoln had sat at a desk to sign the Emancipation Proclamation and found his right arm "almost paralyzed." Having a difficult time holding on to the pen, he told those gathered around him to witness the historic event. "Three hours of hand-shaking is not calculated to improve a man's chirography." Two years later, he took the hands of more than six thousand persons in one evening.

Pressing the flesh of citizens was not new to Grover Cleveland, however. At a Chicago rally during the campaign, he'd matched Lincoln's record. It wouldn't be long before he surpassed it.

6

This Man Cleveland

Soon after the inauguration, Washington correspondent Carp Carpenter reported to readers of his newspaper in Ohio, "This man Cleveland is a hard worker. He rises at half past seven each morning. As soon as he is dressed, he reads the daily newspapers, and at eight he is ready for his breakfast. This is not a large meal. After breakfast, with no exercise, the President goes directly to his office."

Because Congress imposed financial strictures on the size of the White House office staff, limiting Grover to a total which never rose above fifteen, many of the routine matters involved in running an office fell to him and Lamont. There was no stenographer and clerical assistance was limited. If the single White House telephone rang and a steward was not at hand to pick it up, the president answered it himself. He was also known to respond to knocks on the front door. But in the early days of his term the greatest consumer of time was dealing with the seemingly limitless appointive federal jobs to be filled in a government bloated by decades of political patronage. A survey taken soon after the Cleveland inauguration found that of 958 minor jobs in the bureau of printing and engraving, 539 were superfluous. Similar waste existed throughout the government.

With so much spoils to be garnered, thousands of Democrats eagerly sought them in the expectation that their party's first president in a quarter of a century would routinely and happily dole out the jobs. Within two weeks of taking office, the new president found himself inundated with pleas for employment ranging from ridiculously inept to downright toadying. One letter began, "My Lord," and went on, "I, the undersigned, come most humbly and most respectfully to the feet of Your Most Gracious Majesty's throne, to offer this humble petition of mine to Your Most gracious Presidential Majesty . . . Receive me, My Lord, as your soul-son."

Another asked "Your Excellency for an assignment after your private secretary or a position as Master of Ceremonies, Steward, or Door Keeper." The writer's qualifications were then delineated. "I am a single man and was never married—prematurely Snow headed and Bearded, I wish to live in Washington and make myself agreeable with everybody that I come in contact with, and will serve you with a perfect heart without vanity, egotism or anything else, with truth, integrity and probity. All I write is strictly true."

A plea arrived from "an orphan, without kindred—literary by nature." Another, addressed to "Der and respectable sir," stated, "Thrusting in hope I will be so free to ask your Honor for a situation. I have receive a good eddication."

From somewhere on the Western Frontier came, "It is verry dull out here. There is nothing to enliven things except the possibility of being impaled by a live Indian and I dont want to be impaled. I aint got any money to pay Rail Road fare and I want to get out of this. I thought if you could give me an office, I then could get a pass I voted the Republican ticket last fall but if you think there will be any chance of your being elected another term I will vote for you that is if I get an office."

While wading through the deluge of applications on paper, Cleveland also fended off job hunters who accosted him during the East Room handshaking rituals. Even as he heard pleas by party leaders there were cries of apprehension from Mugwumps that he might suddenly give in to partisan pressures.

He shot off a letter to a politician who had knowingly endorsed a worthless and corrupt office seeker:

Executive Mansion
Washington, D.C., August 1, 1885

Dear Sir:
  I have read your letter with amazement and indignation. There is one—but one—mitigation to the perfidy which your letter discloses, and that is found in the fact that you confess your share in it. I don't know whether you are a Democrat or not, but if you are, the crime which you confess is the more unpardonable.
  The idea that this administration, pledged to give the people better officers and engaged in a hand-to-hand fight with the bad elements of both parties, should be betrayed by those who ought to be worthy of implicit trust, is atrocious, and such treason to the people and to the party ought to be punished by imprisonment.
  I can only say that, while this is not the first time I have been deceived and misled by lying and treacherous representations, you

*are the first one that has owned his grievous fault. If any comfort is
to be extracted from this assurance you are welcome to it.*

Grover Cleveland

Again in frustration he looked up from a fresh stack of imploring letters, thought for a moment about his own job, and exclaimed to a friend, "My God, what is there in this office that any man should want to get into it?"

When a leading Democrat appeared at the White House on a mission to land someone a job, the president growled, "Well, do you want me to hire another horse thief for you?"

To his physician, Dr. W. W. Keene, he complained, "Those office-seekers. They haunt me in my dreams!"

Three months before taking office he had written to the National Civil Service Reform League, "If I were addressing none but party friends, I should deem it entirely proper to remind them that, though the coming administration is to be Democratic, a due regard for the people's interest does not permit faithful party work to be always rewarded by appointment to office."

Among the supplications reaching his desk on behalf of strict party-line appointments was one from Wisconsin's congressman General Edward S. Bragg, who at the presidential nominating convention had declared, "They [the men in his delegation] love him because of the enemies he has made." Bragg demanded that every Republican postmaster in his district be removed for a Democrat.

Such tactics obviously were not welcomed by Republicans, who made up their minds to preclude them by means of invoking a statute known as the Tenure of Office Act. The measure took away from the president the power to make removals and replacement appointments except with the permission of the Senate. It had been passed in 1869 over the veto of President Andrew Johnson. And despite questions of constitutionality and objections by President Grant that the law was "inconsistent with a faithful and efficient administration of the government," it remained on the books. It now afforded Senate Republicans an opportunity to counteract the effects of the November election and render Grover Cleveland's presidency, in the words of one historian, "an office much like that of the Doge of Venice, one of ceremonial dignity without real power."

The stage was thereby set for a confrontation between the executive branch and the Senate. But ironically, it was not a removal of a Republican in the manner General Bragg demanded which triggered the fight. The test which was to arise would have to do with whether the Senate had authority to force the president to surrender White House documents, or if those documents were, in the legal sense, "privileged." Could a president of the United States defy the expressed will of Congress (in this case the Senate) by claiming "*executive* privilege"?

The issue was the unexpected result of Senate Republicans questioning the legality of the appointment of a district attorney for the Southern District of Alabama who had been named to the post in place of a man who was suspended, but whose term of office did not expire until some months later. A provision of the Tenure of Office Act required the president to seek approval of the Senate for persons appointed to vacant offices, even if the appointment was temporary.

Accordingly, the Senate Judiciary Committee commanded the attorney general, Augustus Garland, to transmit "all papers and information in the possession of the Department of Justice regarding "the suspension and proposed removal from office" of the former federal attorney in Alabama, along with all documents and papers in relation to the conduct of the Alabama office since January 1, 1885.

President Cleveland believed, as he later explained, that he "could not avoid the conviction that a compliance with such requests would . . . be a failure to protect and defend the Constitution, as well as a wrong to the great office I held in trust for the people, and which I was bound to transmit unimpaired to my successors; nor could I be unmindful of a tendency in some quarters to encroach upon executive functions, or of the eagerness with which executive concession would be seized upon as establishing precedent."

Dismayed by what he considered "animus" on the part of Republicans in the Senate, he directed Garland to inform the Senate committee that the documents would be withheld because "it is not considered that the public interest will be promoted by a compliance."

The Judiciary Committee reported this to the full Senate, framing the controversy in terms of rights of the legislative branch of the government. "The important question, then," it said, "is whether it is within the constitutional competence of either House of Congress to have access to the official papers and documents in the various public offices of the United States, created by laws enacted by themselves."

The Republican majority on the committee recommended adoption by the Senate of a resolution expressing "condemnation of the refusal of the Attorney General, under whatever influence, to send to the Senate" the documents desired. After reading the resolution, the president of the United States was left with no doubt that the phrase "under whatever influence" was meant as a gibe at himself. If the charges in the resolution were true, he reasoned, they were grounds for "the impeachment of the Attorney General—if not the President under whose 'influence' he concededly refused to submit the papers demanded by the Senate."

He believed that the Republican motive was to discredit civil service reform pledges he had made to the people. His response was blunt. "I am not responsible to the Senate," he said, "and I am unwilling to submit my actions and official conduct to them for judgment."

Senate debate on the proposed resolution of condemnation lasted more than two weeks and ended with its passage by a vote of 32 to 25. But by the date of the voting, the man who had been suspended had been reappointed to the post and the man who had temporarily replaced him had gone on to other pursuits.

"The earnest contention that beat about their names ceased," Cleveland noted, "and no shout of triumph disturbed the supervening quiet."

During the tempest the attorney general had been condemned, but the issue of a president invoking executive privilege in refusing to comply with a demand by Congress for documents and other materials related to the chief executive's actions had been resolved, in Grover's view, with a victory for the executive branch. In a book of essays, *Presidential Problems,* published in 1904, he said proudly that the presidency, freed from the Senate's claim of tutelage, became again the independent agent of the people, representing a coordinate branch of their Government, charged with responsibilities which, under his oath, he ought not to avoid or divide with others, and invested with powers, not to be surrendered, but to be used, under the guidance of patriotic intention and an unclouded conscience.⸸

The claimed sanctity of executive privilege in dealings with the legislative branch would remain untested for nearly a century, until the refusal of President Richard M. Nixon to surrender to a Senate investigating committee secret White House tape recordings during the Watergate scandal of the 1970s. His claim of privilege was rejected by the Supreme Court. A quarter century later, the Court again struck down executive privilege when President Clinton fought subpoenas issued by Independent Counsel Kenneth Starr in his 1990s investigations of a failed real estate venture and other matters known as Whitewater and Zippergate.

★   ★   ★

While battle lines were being drawn around executive privilege, the president who claimed the right continued his struggle with job seekers. On June 25, 1885, he wrote to Bissell, "For three months I have stood here and battled with those of my party who deem party success but a means of personal success. They have been refused and disappointed, [but] my administration is strong and popular, because those thus refused and disappointed cannot say that I have refused them in order to make place for personal friends [and for] payment of personal political debts."

Pride in accomplishment aside, the letter turned melancholic as Grover confessed that he often thought how solemn a thing it is to live and feel the pressure of the duties which life—the mere existence in a social state—imposes; but I have never appreciated the thought of its full solemnity until now. It seems to me that I am as much consecrated to service, as the religionist who secludes himself from all that is joyous in life and devotes himself to a sacred mission.⟡

He then pleaded with his old friend from Buffalo to "not think that I am always blue and always unhappy."

Indeed he wasn't. He frequently escaped, at least momentarily, through the companionship of Dan Lamont and his wife and their two small daughters, with whom he relished the simple joy of watching goldfish in a fountain on the south lawn. On some days the Lamonts would join him for breakfast, lunch, and dinner. However, when he invited them to move into the White House, Lamont declined, saying he wished to spare the children the inevitable glare of publicity.

The press never failed to note who called on the president. The reporters had exhibited fascination with a friend of his sister Rose on a visit from Albany. Her name in the guest book was "Miss Van Vechten." Good-looking, with an aristocratic air, she was once engaged to General Philip Sheridan and was widely believed to be interested in the possibility of marrying a president. But press interest in her faded with the arrival in April of Mrs. Oscar Folsom and her daughter for a two-week visit.

A student at Wells College, Frances Folsom was to graduate in June and seemed, to a reporter for the *New York World*, to have "made many friends" during her brief time in the nation's capital.

Everyone who met her came away charmed by the beautiful twenty-year-old for whom, they all knew, the president had stood almost in loco parentis since the death of Oscar. The gesture was regarded as so endearing that it gave the lie to the sort of ugly gossip bandied about by Congressman La Follete and others that the occupant of the White House was a brute regarding women.

By all accounts of persons who witnessed the attention paid to

Mrs. Folsom during the two weeks she spent visiting the president in April, it was natural to assume that there might be more to his interest in the widow of his former law partner than either friendship or a sense of obligation to her and her charming daughter imposed upon him as administrator of Oscar Folsom's estate. It was widely believed in Buffalo society that he had gone well beyond the discharge of such legal responsibilities to the widow and the child who called him "Uncle Cleve."

Washington wags and Buffalo residents wondered if it might not be very long before the admittedly lonely president abandoned bachelorhood, gave the nation a first lady, and the very winning young girl whom Grover called "Frank" started addressing him as "Stepfather."

If there were to be such an eventuality, it would have to wait until Mrs. Folsom and Frank returned from an extended excursion in Europe.

Meanwhile, journalists and capital society would have to make do with the woman who, since Inauguration Day, had filled the demanding role of official White House hostess. Reporters already had made an assessment of Rose Cleveland and judged her "charming" in that capacity. The first such occasion had been on March 21 for members of Congress and the diplomatic corps, who had been invited to meet the Cabinet. Among the guests had been James G. Blaine and his son Walker, both of whom discreetly departed early. Like her brother, Rose was large of frame (some thought her mannish), direct in manner (some said "brusque"), and all in all an impressive personality. She was generally addressed as Miss Rose, although to her brother she was "Libbie." Allan Nevins (writing in 1932) considered Rose one of the most cultivated women ever to reign over the White House.

149

Cleveland's youngest sister, Rose, served as official White House hostess until Cleveland shed his bachelorhood.

A graduate of Houghton Seminary, she taught there and in Lafayette, Indiana, and had published a book, *George Eliot's Poetry and Other Studies*. The book went through twelve editions in one year and reportedly earned Rose more than $25,000 in royalties. An excellent conversationalist, she was portrayed by White House historian William Seale as an ardent feminist who saw her position "as an excellent platform from which to buttonhole politicians who might be of service" in the cause of women's rights. Although her personality appeared at first to be somewhat off-putting, she could be warm and even humorous. These traits, combined with her intellect, eventually made her a well-liked and respected Washington figure. It was rumored that her way of dealing with the tedium of standing in a reception line and smiling as she greeted the guests was to mentally conjugate Greek verbs.

Although not "the first lady," she was unquestionably in charge of every nonpolitical aspect of the unique household at 1600 Pennsylvania Avenue. As a member of the Women's Christian Temperance Union, she frowned on the use of alcohol, but her views could not persuade the former carouser of Buffalo saloons to adopt the "dry" policy of Mrs. Rutherford B. Hayes, who had banned serving wine in the White House.

When Grover was not hosting a formal social occasion, shaking hands with strangers in the East Room, or working in his upstairs office, he sought relief from the burdens of office by spending time alone in the White House conservatory admiring the flowers. He could have gone for a ride on a yacht frequently used by President Arthur, the *Dispatch*, but he regarded it as unseemly, just as he'd deemed unseemly the gift of a dog and an offer of a free special train.

On the first of each month, all business of government came to a halt during however much time it took the president of the United States to write personal checks for personal and household expenses.

The glamour of living in the White House was so unimpressive to him that while he was penning a letter late one night to Shan Bissell, he noted, "It is nearly one o'clock. Colonel Lamont is gone and William [his valet] too. If I did not keep one of the waiters here, I should be absolutely alone in the upper part of the house. That's splendor for you, sleeping alone in the White House."

A *Baltimore Sun* story pictured the president's life as "very much like that of any active business man having large and important interests committed to him. There is a difference, however, in the fact that Mr. Cleveland does an amount of work much in excess of that performed by the average first-class business man. The President's whole indoor life is under one roof. He transacts all the affairs of this great nation which come under his jurisdiction separated only by a few feet from the apartments where he eats, sleeps, and is supposed to enjoy his rest."

Spending long days and evenings at his desk, still plagued by incessant demands for jobs, harassed by Democratic leaders who criticized him for many of the appointments (and for keeping Republicans employed), and frequently feeling lonely, he labored through the spring and into the summer while Congress adjourned and members rushed home to escape the brutal heat of June, July, and August. Again as in Albany, Lamont and others urged him to take some time off. Again he demurred, insisting he had too much work to do.

In late July, after a long war with cancer, Ulysses S. Grant died, necessitating the president's attendance at the funeral in New York City. In honor of the commander of the Army of the Potomac in the Civil War and eighteenth president of the United States, Grover first proclaimed a state of national mourning. The document said in part, "The great heart of the nation that followed him when living with love and pride, bows now in sorrow above him dead, tenderly mindful of his virtues, his great patriotic services, and of the loss occasioned by his death."

Reviewing the mournful procession as it wended through thronged Manhattan streets, Grover could not fail to notice that taking part in the grand but solemn spectacle was Theodore Roosevelt, resplendent in the uniform of a captain in the New York National Guard. After all due honors were rendered to the hero who had accepted Robert E. Lee's surrender at Appomattox in

1865 and subsequently presided, evidently unwittingly, over an administration rife with greedy men and governmental corruption of unprecedented magnitude (but who'd died almost penniless himself), Grover seized the opportunity of being so close to his beloved Adirondacks to allow himself a two-week vacation. He was feeling tired. And he looked it. But the unanticipated news of a vacation in the mountains raised eyebrows among a suspicious press, especially editors of the *New York World*. Wondering if this abrupt change in presidential scheduling might be an attempt to mask an illness, the paper dispatched a reporter to track him down.

The reporter found Grover Cleveland in the company of a physician, S. B. Ward, of Albany, and a few other friends. Their guides were Gard Maloney, who was a boatman familiar with the lakes; Charley Brown, a skilled hunter; Wesley Wood, a cook; and a rugged woodsman by the name of Dave Cronk. Surprised by the arrival of a reporter as they sat around a campfire for breakfast, Grover declared to Wood, "Place one more plate."

The meal was broiled venison, baked potatoes, hot biscuits, and tea with condensed milk, served on a table built of a rough board and stakes for legs. Large logs were used as chairs. From his place the reporter had an excellent opportunity to observe the object of his hunt. In his story for the *World*, he noted that the president seemed to have "gained considerable flesh since he entered the mountains, and his manner betokened some fatigue and lassitude."

This appearance, he was advised by Dr. Ward, was attributable to "the arduous journey through the forest" which had "exhausted him so much that for two days after reaching camp he had been unable to move freely about."

"Small wonder," the reporter wrote, "speaking from my own experience!"

Another reporter, sent by the *Chicago Tribune* to locate the nation's chief executive, was on hand to provide an account of fishing for pickerel using live frogs as bait. Fixing a hook into the skin of the back of a fine small one, Grover cast it into the water, squatted on the muddy ground, lit a cigar, and waited for a pickerel to bite.

"It was not long before there was a rush in the water," wrote the *Tribune* reporter in a story dated August 21, 1885, "and a little later the doctor landed a fine pickerel. The President looked enviously at the dappled sides of the fish and watched his own line with increased interest, but it did not stir."

Peering across the water toward a log on which a frog sat sunning himself, Grover said, morosely, "I don't see how it is, doc, that you catch so many fish while I don't get even a nibble." He looked at his line, then at the doctor, and back to the frog. "Jehoshaphat!"

"What is it?" shouted Ward. "What's the matter?"

Shaking his great head, Grover grumbled, "I'll be hanged if that isn't my frog on that log. He's swum across and climbed up on it, hook and all, and here I've been sitting and waiting on him all the afternoon—waiting for pickerel to bite! Great Scott!"

The reporter's account continued. "The sympathizing doctor crossed the creek and prepared to toss the frog and hook back into the water, but the President said he guessed he wouldn't fish any more that day. The frog was released with all care, and tossed into a puddle."

On the return to camp, Grover blamed himself. "I've been daydreaming," he muttered. "I ought to have attended to business."

A few days later, back in the White House and back to the people's business, he lamented to Dan Lamont, "I feel that I am in the treadmill again."

The nettlesome matter on his mind that early September of 1885 was a huge number of appointments yet to be made, some 49,000 fourth-class postmasters and 5,000 more to miscellaneous posts. For every one he had to contend with an expectant Democratic official promoting a candidate. The Democrats saw no reason why he would not fill vacancies with party faithful, or make vacancies where none existed. At the same time, Republicans and their cohorts among newspaper editors who had backed Blaine found other reasons to fault him. He was denounced in print as a hypocrite on civil service reform, wolf in sheep's clothing, and camouflaged spoilsman. Never mind that he found a champion in the head of the Civil Service Reform Association, George William Curtis, who said, "No president has given such conclusive evidence both of his reform convictions and of his courage in enforcing his convictions as Grover Cleveland."

Attacks on his faithfulness to reform, coinciding with his battle with the Senate over the independence of the executive branch, were further exacerbated by the press criticism. Believing it was unfounded, he lashed out at it wherever he could. In a letter to a New Yorker who had sent him clippings of an especially scurrilous nature, he wrote, "I don't think there ever was a time when newspaper lying was so general and so mean as at present, and there never was a country under the sun where it flourished as it does in this. The falsehoods daily spread before the people in our newspapers, while they are proofs of the mental ingenuity of those engaged in newspaper work, are insults to the American love for decency and fair play of which we boast."

This was not a new presidential complaint. The first had been voiced at the very birth of the nation by George Washington and was echoed by every occupant of the White House after him to Bill Clinton. Like all presidents, Grover also learned that newspaper attention to the nation's chief executive would not be limited to his performance of official duties.

Soon after his Adirondacks vacation, while he was driving with an old friend and her daughter, the woman handed him a newspaper clipping which intimated that the president was going to marry Emma Folsom, widow of his late friend and law partner, Oscar.

"I don't see why the papers keep marrying me to old ladies," he replied. "I wonder why they don't say I am engaged to marry her daughter."

7

Burglars in the House

If the year 1885 was a time of beginnings and wrestling with the demands of spoilsmen while learning how to be a president, the year ahead for Grover Cleveland promised to be a period of tension with an impatient Democratic House of Representatives and an obstructive Republican Senate. On the agenda as he prepared his first State of the Union message for the legislators were continuing troubles over the Tenure of Office matter, civil service reform, tariff legislation, and the very foundation of the dollar.

Of significant moment in dealing with the latter would be a proposal for the repeal of the Bland–Allison Act, which compelled the government to buy and coin as much silver as could be mined. The view of the nation's bankers and financiers, shared by the president, was that the free and unlimited silver coinage and issuing of paper money (greenbacks) whose value was based on silver rather than gold undermined the gold standard and threatened the health of the economy.

In the message to be sent to Congress in December, the president would assert that the continuation of a policy of free silver coinage would result in disruption of business, reduction in the income of farmers and workers, gold hoarding by individuals, a drain of gold from the Treasury to overseas banks, and a wiping out of savings.

"When the time comes that gold has been withdrawn from circulation," he would warn, "then will be apparent the difference between the real value of the silver dollar and a dollar in gold, and the two coins will part company." He recommended "the suspension of the compulsory coinage of silver dollars."

In the midst of preparing the message for the anticipated fight over silver in Congress, Grover found himself mourning a political ally. On November 25 he learned of the death of the man whom Tammany's John Kelly and Thomas Grady had attempted to use in order to deny him the presidential nomination. Vice President Thomas Hendricks died at his home in Indianapolis. In announcing the "distressing fact," Grover lauded the "eminent and varied services of this high official and patriotic public servant" and ordered a month of national mourning.

When his message went to Congress on December 8, 1885, it began with a tribute to the late vice president. Later in the message he used the vacancy in the vice presidency to point out the need for a constitutional amendment to clear up "the condition of the law relating to the succession to the Presidency in the event of the death, disability, or removal of both the President and Vice-President." Congress accepted the wisdom of the advice on January 19 by approving the Presidential Succession Act, providing for succession of the heads of executive departments in order of the creation of their offices.

★   ★   ★

As to the call for repeal of the silver-purchase act, the silver champions in both parties in both houses heard out the president and then dug in their heels. Gold-standard adherents looked to the White House for strong and effective leadership from the man who had so forcefully fought for the independence of the executive in refusing to knuckle under in the executive-privilege battle. Just such a valiant defense of the gold standard by Grover Cleveland was anticipated by the Washington correspondent of the *New York Herald.* He confidently predicted that the administration would use pressure and patronage to win on the issue. He was wrong.

Asked by the press about the *Herald* item on January 4, 1886, Grover shocked them and the gold-standard defenders on Capitol Hill with what amounted to a shrug of the shoulders. He said, "I believe the most important benefit that I can confer upon my country by my Presidency is to insist upon the entire independence of the executive and legislative branches of the government."

The Congress was to do what it thought best, he said, without interference from him. If he didn't like the result, the Constitution empowered him to veto it. Meantime, he had no desire to influence that coequal branch of the government beyond what he had done in calling for the repeal of the silver-purchase law.

The *Herald* headlined: DEMOCRATS WITHOUT A LEADER. A congressman in the accompanying story was quoted as saying, "If only Mr. Cleveland had been content to say nothing, he had the game in his own hand."

Rather than expected vigorous leadership from the other end of Pennsylvania Avenue, all the president's men were left on their own, which spelled a stalemate on repealing the silver act that would last through both of Grover's nonconsecutive terms. It would also provide a Democratic orator, William Jennings Bryan, a chance to coin one of the most resounding and memorable phrases in American political history. On December 22, 1894, at the midpoint of Grover's second presidency, Bryan told the House of Representatives, "I shall not help crucify mankind upon a cross of gold. I shall not aid in pressing down upon the bleeding brow of labor this crown of thorns." Never a man to avoid repeating a nice turn of language, the famed orator who became the unsuccessful Democratic candidate for president in 1896 galvanized the nominating convention that year with, "You shall not press down upon the brow of labor this crown of thorns. You shall not crucify mankind upon a cross of gold."

Financial affairs of the nation were not so consuming that they outweighed the president's attention to personal finances. He sent a letter to Wilson Bissell on January 30 enclosing one check for thirty dollars to the City Club of Buffalo for annual dues, and another for fifty dollars to cover his subscription to the Music Hall. He also requested that the $4,626.96 held for him by Bissell be forwarded.

A letter of January 4 to Allen G. Thurman thanked him for an invitation to the annual reunion of the Jackson Club of Columbus, Ohio. As head of the Ohio delegation at the presidential convention in the summer of 1884, he had been regarded a contender. He'd campaigned vigorously for the Cleveland-Hendricks ticket, but had turned down appointment to the Interstate Commerce Commission, choosing to retire from active politics. In 1888 this hope would prove to have been a vain one. He would find himself nominated to be Grover Cleveland's running mate. While declining Thurman's invitation because of the press of "official duties,"

Grover heartily endorsed the purpose of the gathering, "to consult as to the manner in which the accomplishment of 'the greatest good to our people' can best be aided and assisted."

With Congress in session, bills began flowing down Pennsylvania Avenue to his desk. On February 8 he signed the Indian Emancipation Act. It authorized the abolition of the system of reservations which had been imposed on Native Americans by westward-moving white settlers with the armed support of the United States Army. The purpose was to grant American citizenship to Indians who wanted it and to parcel out reservation lands to them to farm.

★   ★   ★

Coincidentally with the signing, American soldiers under the command of General George Crook were scouring hills, ravines, and bluffs of the Arizona Territory for an Apache by the name of Geronimo. One of the wiliest and most dangerous of the "renegade" Indians, he had refused to live on a reservation. By leading warriors in off-and-on raids on white settlers in the Southwest since 1858, he had become the embodiment of Indian resistance to efforts by the government in Washington to control Indian lives, and to do so with force if necessary.

Still engaged in the contest with the Senate over executive privilege, the commander in chief of the armed forces made a formal appeal on March 1 seeking support from the country. But that struggle was eclipsed five days later when word reached him of a strike by the Knights of Labor against Southwestern railroads controlled by Jay Gould. Led by a fiery regional leader named Martin Irons, 3,700 shopmen, switchmen, and yardmen were reported to be disabling locomotives, pulling pins from couplers, and derailing trains by ripping up tracks of the Missouri Pacific, Texas & Pacific, and other lines.

If the strike continued, it would threaten the jobs of 6,000 non-railway workers and result in widespread economic distress. Yet there seemed to be nothing the president of the United States could do about it, save place his trust in the governors of the states affected to take action. They would do so on March 26, calling on railway managers to send out their trains and promising them protection from law officers.

Troubled by all aspects of the strike, from its cause in the firing of a mechanic in Fort Worth, Texas, to the violence and the lack of federal authority to intervene, and concerned about the overall issue of labor in a nation rapidly becoming industrialized, Grover decided to make history by doing what no other president had attempted. On April 22 he sent a special message to the Congress recommending legislation for the "Arbitrament of Disputes between Laboring Men and Employers."

For the first time in American history, a president asserted that the "value of labor as an element of national prosperity should be distinctly recognized, and the welfare of the laboring man" should be a concern of a federal government which dealt evenhandedly with capital and labor. "The discontent of the employed," he said, "is due in large degree to the grasping and heedless exactions of employers, and the alleged discrimination in favor of capital as an object of governmental attention."

To begin alleviating this imbalance, he proposed a "Commission of Labor" within the recently created (1884) Bureau of Labor. He asked that it be empowered to arbitrate and conciliate labor disputes. "There would also be good reason to hope," he said, "that the very existence of such an agency would invite application to it for advice and counsel, frequently resulting in the avoidance of contention and misunderstanding."

The bold and unexpectedly liberal proposal struck the fledgling labor movement as a step in the right direction and was viewed by the public and press as innovative. But on Capitol Hill, members of the House and Senate, eager to appeal to the labor vote, preferred to push legislation of their own. One of these, signed by the president, legalized the incorporation of national trade unions. Others banned importation of contract labor and cut the workday of mailmen to eight hours. A law permitting the federal government to offer arbitration and conciliation services would not be passed for two years (October 1, 1888).

*   *   *

Although the labor bill Grover wanted did not reach his desk in the spring of 1886, he had no lack of legislation sent to him for signature. On one day he received 240 special bills, among which were 198 granting claims for pensions by Civil War veterans. Eighty-one involved cases which had been rejected by the Pensions Bureau because they had been ruled baseless in fact. Another 26 were for men whose disabilities were shown to have existed before the claimants had even enlisted in the army. Twenty-one injuries could not be proved to have occurred in the line of duty. Many more had been filed for various other specious reasons. The men involved had then taken advantage of a law which allowed them to appeal the denials to congressmen and senators.

Grover considered these circumventions an outrage and said so on May 8 in a message vetoing the Andrew J. Hill special bill. As in the "It is time for blunt language" veto when he was mayor of Buffalo, he got directly to the point: "The policy of frequently reversing, by special enactment, the decisions of the bureau invested by law with the examination of pension claims . . . is exceedingly questionable. It may well be doubted if a committee of Congress has a better opportunity than such an agency to judge the merits of these claims."

Regarding Mr. Hill, he justified the veto on a technicality. He wrote, "A sufficient reason for the return of the particular bill now under consideration is found in the fact that it provides that the name of Andrew J. Hill be placed upon the pension roll, while the records of the Pensions Bureau, as well as a medical certificate made a part of the committee's report, disclose the correct name of the intended beneficiary is Alfred J. Hill."

A flurry of special pension bills was greeted by so many presidential vetoes with accompanying messages that Grover was upbraided by some newspapers for spending too much time on them. He and Dan Lamont often stayed up long past midnight disposing of them. But many other papers, including Republican ones, said the vetoes were justified because the principle underlying them was sound. The applications were without merit.

An angry Congress retaliated with a bill authored by Senator Henry W. Blair, Republican of New Hampshire. It passed the House as Bill No. 10457. Titled "An Act for the relief of dependent parents and honorably discharged soldiers and sailors who are now disabled and dependent upon their own labor for support," it offered a government stipend to *every disabled veteran with at least three months of service*. The House approved it on January 17, 1887, and the Senate ten days later.

Grover vetoed it on February 11. He pointed out that it was "the first general bill that has been sanctioned by the Congress since the close of the late Civil War permitting a pension to the soldiers and sailors who served in that war upon the ground of service and present disability alone, and in the entire absence of any injuries received by the casualties or incidents of such service." He cited the history of veterans' pensions back to the Revolutionary War and gave the cost of the annual stipends since 1861 at $808,624,811.51. The new bill would greatly balloon that figure.

"While annually paying out such a vast sum for pensions already granted," he went on, "it is now proposed by the bill under consideration to reward a service pension to soldiers of all wars in which the United States has been engaged. . . . It exacts only a military or naval service of three months, without any requirement of actual engagement with an enemy in battle, and without a subjection to any of the actual dangers of war. The pension it awards is allowed to enlisted men who have not suffered the least injury, disability, or loss, or damage of any kind, incurred in any degree referable to their military service, including those who never reached the front at all. . . ."

Demonstrating the painstaking study and reasoning which characterized his vetoes as mayor and governor, he analyzed the components of the measure and generally demolished the rationale. He pointed out instances of "no limitation or definition of the incapacitating injury or ailment," questioned the meaning of "support" and "degree," and found numerous other faults in its drafting. He then predicted what could be expected if he signed the bill into law.

"It is sad, but nevertheless true," he wrote, "that in the matter of procuring pensions there exists a widespread disregard for truth and good faith. There can be no doubt that the race after the pensions offered in this bill would not only stimulate the weakness and pretended incapacity for labor, but put further premium on dishonesty and mendacity."

Public and press opinion largely fell in behind him. *The Washington Post* called the bill one of the most reckless ever to come out of Congress. Chicago's *Tribune* pictured enactment of the measure as putting "a serpent of temptation at the ear of every veteran." Most of the din of denunciation flowed from the national organization representing the Civil War veterans and their families, the G.A.R., whose leaders had been lobbying for just such a law for years. Their reaction to the veto was a deluge of excoriation. Many members wondered aloud if it would now be suitable for President Cleveland to attend a "Grand Encampment of the Grand Army of the Republic" in St. Louis in the summer of 1887 to which he had accepted an invitation to speak partly because the occasion would take him to the West for the first time.

The possibility of his joining the G.A.R. in St. Louis and the *advisability* of doing so soon vanished. However, this was not because of the veto of the Blair pension bill. It was the result of a stumble into a gaffe involving the status of captured Confederate battle flags.

In April of 1887 Adjutant General Richard C. Drum, a Republican and a member of the G.A.R., noticed that the banners stored in an attic of the War Department since the end of the Civil War were decaying into dust. Aware that retired units of the Union Army had been allowed to claim their battle flags, Drum thought it only fitting, and in keeping with a spirit of national reconciliation, that "Rebel" flags also be given to the states of the former Confederacy. He sent his suggestion to Secretary of War William C. Endicott, who forwarded it to the White House. With little, if any, consideration of possible negative ramifications, the president gave verbal approval.

When word of this reached Pensions Bureau Commissioner Chauncey F. Black in Norwalk, Ohio, he was dubious and alarmed. He wired to Dan Lamont, "The report of alleged order returning captured flags has provoked deep feeling. If order not authentic should it not be disavowed at earliest practical moment? Mischievous men are taking extreme advantage of the situation. The public mind seems unprepared for the sentiment of such a course. I earnestly advise of the feeling as I find it."

It may be persuasively argued that no expression of disapproving public reaction of an act of the commander in chief of the armed forces of the United States which touched on public sensibilities provoked more shock than the flags decision until President Clinton established a "Don't ask, don't tell" policy regarding homosexuals in the armed services in 1993.

Governors telegraphing the Cleveland White House characterized the flags decision as "an insult to the heroic dead and an outrage on their surviving comrades." Voices raised in the Senate were "deeply saddened" and others demanded that the flags of "misguided brothers and wicked conspirators" be burned, rather than given back and allowed to become "mementoes of misapplied valor." The national commander of the G.A.R., Lucius Fairchild, who had fought at Gettysburg, exclaimed in fury, "May God palsy the hand that wrote that order. May God palsy the brain that conceived it, and may God palsy the tongue that dictated it."

General William Tecumseh Sherman, who had marched his army through the South and set fire to Atlanta, Georgia, and others cities of the Confederacy, noted that Adjutant General Drum had never been in a battle and therefore had never captured an enemy flag and could not be expected to understand what it meant to be a veteran. "He did not think of the blood and torture of battle," Sherman said, "nor can Endicott, the Secretary of War, or Mr. Cleveland."

At the White House on June 15, 1887, the commander in chief turned in full retreat. He wrote a memorandum which might have been intended as a press statement but was never released. It said, "The right of the [War] Department to make the return being questioned by the President, such right was distinctly asserted and precedents alleged, and therefore his verbal assent was given to the proposed action. The matter was dismissed from his mind until comment thereupon within the last day or two brought it again to his attention."

Upon "examining the law and considering the subject more carefully," he concluded that the flags were federal property which could not be disposed of "without Congressional action." A letter countermanding the approval went to Secretary Endicott that same day. It requested "that no further steps be taken in the matter, except to examine and inventory these flags and adopt proper measures for their preservation. Any directions as to the final disposition of them should originate with Congress."

Grover's admission of his error was dismissed by one unpersuaded governor, Joseph B. Foraker of Ohio. He saw the president sneaking away "like a whipped spaniel."

Next, the country speculated whether the president would dare attend the G.A.R. encampment. Some in the organization pleaded with him to proceed as planned. Others vowed to make him feel decidedly unwelcome. A few muttered vague threats of violence. After deliberating what to do, but longing to go ahead with a trip which would allow him to see the West for the first time in his life, Grover weighed personal desires against the dignity of his office. He wrote to the head of the G.A.R., Davis R. Francis, also the mayor of Chicago, "Rather than abandon my trip to the West and disappoint your citizens, I might, if I alone were concerned, submit to the insult to which it is quite openly asserted I would be helplessly subjected if present at the encampment; but I should bear with me there the people's highest office, the dignity of which I must protect."

In pondering the situation in which a president felt he could not subject the presidency to public dishonor, he faulted the G.A.R. for allowing itself to be "played upon by demagogues for partisan purposes" and for wandering "a long way from its original design."

★ ★ ★

No such bitterness, threats, attempts at intimidation, and calls upon the Deity to place a curse on the faculties of the chief executive of the United States surrounded an occasion planned for the great harbor of New York. He was invited to preside and make a speech at the unveiling of a colossal statue, a gift of the people of France to the people of the United States, of "Liberty Enlightening the World."

The idea for such a gift had come from an admirer of the United States, Édouard de Laboulaye, who suggested it to sculptor Frédéric Auguste Bartholdi. The notion caught on with the French people and a group of de Laboulaye's friends who shared his zest for America. But because this was to be a gift from one people to another, it was agreed that no money was to come from either government. While fund-raising proceeded, Bartholdi traveled to the

United States in 1871 to find a suitable location. He'd chosen Bedloe's Island in New York Harbor. What had been an idea and a dream was a reality requiring only official acceptance by the United States government of the gigantic statue of a woman lifting a torch holding the flame of liberty. A message "Relating to the Acceptance and Inauguration" went from Grover Cleveland to Congress on May 11, 1886. Its recitation of the history of the statue and the various authorizing resolutions and documents on the part of governments as well as private groups and citizens concluded with "The action of the French Government and the people in relation to the presentation of this statue to the United States will, I hope, meet with the hearty and responsive action upon the part of Congress, in which the Executive will be most happy to cooperate."

Along with the message, Grover transmitted to Congress a letter sent by the chairman of a private committee which had been established to raise money to pay for the pedestal on which the statue would be erected. It named Bedloe's Island as the location and proposed the date for the dedication to be September 3, the anniversary of the signing of the Treaty of Paris, which recognized the independence of the United States. Delays would push the occasion back to October.

★   ★   ★

On March 18, 1886, Grover had passed a personal milestone without ceremony, except for the receipt of a bouquet of roses from a girl named Mollie. In a letter to her he wrote, "I thought my birthday would be a pretty dull affair, and I didn't suppose that anyone would care enough about such a dreadfully old man to notice the occasion."

Three days later, the forty-nine-year-old bachelor wrote to his sister Mary Hoyt with a bit of news which would soon leave the capital and the country in a state of astonishment and excitement. He told her, "I expect to be married pretty early in June—very soon after Frank returns. I think the quicker it can be done the better and she seems to think so too."

He'd proposed to Frances about a year earlier, in a letter to her when she was visiting relatives in Scranton, Pennsylvania. She accepted and they agreed to keep the engagement secret until such time as Grover was ready to announce it. Mary and others of the family who learned of the betrothal honored his request to keep that fact to themselves. This soon would prove to be difficult as Washington, D.C., stirred with rumors and heated speculation that the president would not remain a bachelor much longer. The nominee for bride among the gossips was the widow Folsom. The more daring stated with certitude that it would be her daughter.

Many people had known of the fond relationship between Frances Folsom and the man she'd called Uncle Cleve and had been touched and charmed by it. He'd bought the little girl her first doll carriage. As the executor of Oscar's estate, he'd let her copy some of the legal papers he'd prepared in connection with the matter. He'd given her a frisky bull-terrier puppy. When she'd entered Wells College he'd properly asked Emma Folsom's permission to write to her. She and her mother had been guests at his swearing-in as governor. Although Frances had not been able to attend the presidential inauguration, she'd visited him at the White House prior to her college graduation.

In the summer of 1886, as now, and perhaps even more so, gossip of this nature was grist for the journalistic mills. *Frank Leslie's Newspaper* went so far as to publish a portrait of the young woman.

The president and Frances.

This enraged the president of Wells College so much that he rounded up all copies and burned them. When stock was immediately replenished at double the number, he gave up in disgust. At the same time, reporters dashed off to Buffalo to see what they could dig up. But in Washington, a correspondent for the *Post* set his sights closer. He sought a Cleveland crony, Colonel John B. Weber, a member of Congress. The resulting story appeared on Monday, April 19, 1886. Among its tidbits was that "the gentleman who is mentioned as the president's 'best man' " was Grover's old friend Wilson Bissell. The article continued:

Mr. Weber said to the Post reporter last night that he had never heard the matter suggested by any of those principally concerned, or by any of their friends or acquaintances, although he saw Mr. Bissell when he was at the White House on a visit a few weeks ago. He deprecates all talk and gossip about the matter. His sense of chivalry regards it as unfair to the lady to compromise her name in matrimonial gossip.

"Besides," said he, "although Mr. Cleveland is a public man, his matrimonial intentions, if he has any, ought to be considered private. The President of the United States is not a monarch or a prince and nobody but himself has any say in choosing a bride for him. That does not belong to state diplomacy. I have no reason to believe Mr. Cleveland is about to be married, but if it should happen, then I say God bless them both.

Grover read the item and immediately penned his thanks to Colonel Weber for his "due regard for women and chivalry." He continued. "This is the first glimpse I have had of American manhood since the scandalous press and thoughtless people of the country began to hunt down an absent and defenseless girl as if she were a criminal."

Frances and her mother were due back from Europe. Awaiting them in New York City was Dan Lamont. To dodge the press, he arranged for the women to be taken from their ship before it entered the harbor. A tender took them to an uptown pier. Manning found both women upset because during the crossing they'd received a cable informing them of the death of Frances's grandfather, John Folsom. Lamont's purpose in meeting them was to learn Frances's thoughts on a wedding date and the marriage ceremony. He installed the women at the Gilsey House hotel on Broadway and Twenty-ninth Street. There she selected the following Wednesday, June 2, and asked that the event be a simple affair in keeping with her state of mourning.

This accorded with Grover's wishes. In his letter to Mary Hoyt he had said, "I want my marriage to be a quiet one . . . yet I don't want to be churlish and mean or peculiar for the sake of being peculiar."

He had also given a great deal of thought to his life with Frances in the spotlight of the nation's capital. He wrote Mary, "I believe I shall buy or rent a house near where I can go and be away from the constant grind. I have thought it would be nice if Mrs. Folsom could live there and keep up the establishment. It has occurred to me that it would be nice to have the little room which William occupies fixed up for a dressing-room, etc., for Frank, or a place where she could sit and stay during the day . . . I have my heart set upon making Frank a sensible, domestic American wife, and I should be pleased not to hear her spoken of as 'The First Lady of the Land' or 'Mistress of the White House.' I want her to be happy and to possess all she can reasonably desire . . . I think she is pretty level-headed."

So much for his reputation among some detractors as a brute to women.

Where might the wedding be held? The plan had been to have it in Buffalo, but the death in the family ruled out a ceremony at the Folsom home. The Gilsey House was out of question because the president felt a wedding in a hotel would be unseemly for a man occupying the office of president. Nor was a church ceremony in store.

His father's and brother's Presbyterian clergyships notwithstanding, Grover did not belong to a congregation. Discussing his view of church membership, his biographer and friend George F. Parker wrote, "His religion was not one which took much account of profession or of mere outward form, but applied its needs and renewed itself from its own inherent sources." Grover especially disdained "sensational preaching" and what he considered nothing but politically partisan sermonizing from a pulpit. If every preacher in the country had taken occasion, upon every Sunday of the year, to preach about Mr. Cleveland, Parker recorded, it would not have changed his opinion that what the preacher said was "unchristian and the effect pernicious."

This did not mean there would not be a clergyman presiding over the wedding vows on June 2. Grover's brother, William, was invited to do so.

The strictures on the place of the ceremony left one site where a wedding had never been held. Leaving the Folsoms at the Gilsey House, Lamont hurried down to Washington to relate Frances's plans. The next afternoon Grover informed the Cabinet. That evening the news broke across the nation that there was going to be a June wedding in the White House.

As to when Frances would see Grover, the president's calendar had him coming to New York in four days to participate in Decoration Day ceremonies and review parades in Manhattan and Brooklyn. The evening before, he paid a call on his fiancée at the hotel while throngs of news-starved reporters waited hungrily on Broadway for him to leave. He stayed the night at the home of Secretary of the Navy William C. Whitney. Then it was across the East River to Brooklyn by way of a three-year-old suspension bridge which was hailed as a modern engineering marvel on the magnitude of the Seven Wonders of the Ancient World. The Brooklyn Bridge was trumpeted to the world as evidence of what American know-how could produce in the 1880s.

Wherever he went he was greeted by cheering crowds and shouts of "Long live President Cleveland and his bride." At the Manhattan parade the Twenty-second Regiment band passed by playing

Bride of the White House.

Mendelssohn's "Wedding March." He also heard brassy renditions of "Come Where My Loves Lies Dreaming" and "He's Going to Marry Yum-Yum."

The only gray cloud Grover found overhanging his plans for the wedding, other than the irritant of unrelenting press scrutiny, was worry about an alarming deterioration in the health of Daniel

Manning. In the course of the contentious debate over silver coinage, the savvy political adviser and dauntless battler against Tammany's political machine who had become Grover's secretary of the Treasury had appeared increasingly ill and verging on physical collapse. And on May 23, after attending a Cabinet meeting, he had done so. Sudden light-headedness caused him to fall on the Treasury Department building's steps. Rushed home and examined by his doctor, he was found to have suffered "a stroke of apoplexy" from a burst blood vessel at the base of his brain. Saying he was unable to carry out his duties, he offered to resign and was refused, not once but several times. When he tendered his resignation once more, three days before the wedding, Grover wrote to him, "It affects me greatly, my dear friend, to think of separating you from my official life, and from a pleasant intercourse in *every* relation of life; but I conceive it to be my duty in view of the sacrifice which your entrance into my Cabinet involved on your part, to consider the question so reluctantly met with a view entirely to your claims and needs instead of my own."

He proposed that "the matter remain as it is, and entirely confidential between us and those already informed till the first day of August." Until the question could be taken up again, Manning would stay treasury secretary, but the president insisted that Manning avail himself of "utter and complete idleness and rest during the next two months." Two days later, Grover extended the term "until the first day of October next, when, if you desire it, the question of your resignation may be resumed with, perhaps, better means of judging all the facts and probabilities which should be considered in its determination."

That Manning might not be secretary of the treasury after October first was painfully obvious. Yet he would return to the post and serve in it until February 1887, leading the fight to keep the gold standard. When Grover at last accepted his resignation, the Treasury enjoyed a surplus for the fiscal year of $94 million. The treasury secretary acceded to the president's eve-before-his-wedding order that he rest, with one notable exception. A shadow of his former 280 pounds, he was carried from a carriage into the White House's Blue Room. Decorated with tulips, white narcissis, orchids, roses, lilies, pansies, and ferns, it was aglow with light from a pair of five-foot candelabra. In the fireplace, scarlet begonias and centaureas simulated flames and ash.

A man who needed no assistance in getting into place in the entrance hall in time for the arrival of twenty-eight guests for the 6:30 P.M. ceremony was the leader of the U.S. Marine Corps band. Ramrod-straight with a neat Van Dyke beard and crisp, scarlet-and-blue gold-braided uniform, a self-confident, witty, and vigorous John Philip Sousa was, in fact, a more recognizable figure to many natives of Washington (as was he), and arguably more famous, than any recent president. In 1872 he'd led the orchestra at Kernan's Theatre Comique, a federal city variety house. He'd also played violin in the orchestra of Ford's Opera House. At the Philadelphia Centennial Exhibition of 1876 he'd been in the string section of Jacques Offenbach's orchestra, then stayed in the City of Brotherly Love to perform in the orchestra pits of the Chestnut and Arch Street theaters. He also conducted the Philadelphia Church Choir and had written the group a comic opera titled *The Smugglers*. He had been leading "The President's Own" band since 1880, taking it over when he was in his mid-twenties.

A few minutes before seven, Sousa lifted his baton to begin the wedding march for the first nuptials in White House history. Frances's pearl-white gown of heavy corded satin with a Parisian neckline was draped in delicate India silk edged with real orange blossoms. A pair of silk scarves crisscrossed the bodice. The veil was held by seed pearls and more blossoms. The train ran fifteen feet. Watching from the entrance hall, Colonel Crook thought she was as radiantly captivating as a young vision of springtime. Grover escorted her down the grand staircase.

The traditional bridal vow to "love, honor, and obey" had been revised by him, deleting "obey" and substituting "keep." After they were pronounced husband and wife and blessed by Rev. William Cleveland, church bells tolled across the capital and twenty-one guns boomed in salute from the navy yard. The newlyweds then led the guests into the East Room for a "promenade" in which the couple greeted them for half an hour before everyone moved into the State Dining Room for a candlelit dinner. The table center-piece was in the shape of a three-masted ship made of pansies and pink roses. During the meal, congratulatory messages were read from national figures and foreign heads of state, including greetings from Queen Victoria.

After the cutting of the cake and rounds of toasts, Mr. and Mrs. Cleveland left the guests to change into street clothes for their departure by way of the south portico. From there a coach took them past cheering crowds lining Pennsylvania Avenue to the train station and a private car. Their destination was a small rented cottage in a secluded part of a resort at Deer Park in the mountains of western Maryland. They arrived at four in the morning in a light rain.

So did a special express train crammed with reporters. In anticipation of their presence, the owner of the resort, John Davis, sought to keep prying eyes away from the honeymooners with a patrol made up of suitably muscular men with orders to chase away

The wedding ceremony was the first in the history of the Executive Mansion.

intruders. He quickly learned that keeping the press at bay was not that easy. A reporter from the *New York Tribune* observed that Mr. and Mrs. Cleveland had been provided a coach with four horses and dared to question Davis concerning the identity of the lender. Davis refused to reveal that the rig, the horses, and the cottage in which the couple were staying belonged to the Baltimore & Ohio Railroad Company.

Relating this story in a letter to Lamont on June 3, Grover referred to reporters as "animals and nuisances." He noted as he was writing that a group of them were "sitting on a bridge which marks one of the limits" of Davis's protective perimeter. In a later letter to the *New York Evening Post*, he railed at such tactics in typically blunt terms: "They have used the enormous power of the modern newspaper to perpetuate and disseminate a colossal impertinence, and have done it, not as professional gossips and tatters, but as the guides and instructors of the public in conduct and morals. And they have done it, not to a private citizen, but the President of the United States, thereby lifting their offence into the gaze of the whole world, and doing their utmost to make American journalism contemptible in the estimation of people of good breeding everywhere."

Looking forward to an extended August vacation with Frances in his beloved Adirondacks, he told Dr. Ward (of the frog and pickerel fishing episode), "If the newspapermen get there *I shall leave.* I will not have my vacation spoiled by being continually watched and lied about, and I won't submit my wife to that treatment."

Like each of his predecessors and every president who followed him, he found himself in a duel with an adversary that had the advantage of always being able to have the last word. Remonstrations against a prying press failed to stanch a flow of ugly stories about him and his treatment of Frances, which further infuriated him. The thrust of the items was that he was, indeed, a brute to women and that Frances was abused and unhappy. Based not on evidence but on rumor, the belief that Grover Cleveland was a wife-beater unjustly besmirched his portrait ever since. So incensed was he about treatment of Frances in newspapers which made no attempt to mask their hatred of him that he once interrupted a speech at Harvard University's Memorial Hall to blast the reporters seated at tables in front of the auditorium as "those ghouls of the press." He departed from his intended remarks and continued with such a vilifying torrent of objections to their presence that he began to weep. He proclaimed that if the American people could somehow discover the perfidy of the press, they would stamp out the "silly, mean, and cowardly lies that are every day found in the columns of certain newspapers which violate every instinct of American manliness, and in ghoulish glee desecrate every sacred relation of private life.

While these barbs were understandable against New York newspapers which had always been a vexation to him, especially Charles A. Dana's *Sun* and Joseph Pulitzer's *World*, they were misplaced regarding the attitude of the press toward Frances. The vast majority of the reporters and virtually everyone else who met the country's new First Lady fell in love with her.

Crusty old William Tecumseh Sherman thought she made things "lively" and presented a fine sample of beautiful young womanhood. Colonel Crook had never seen a woman "possessing the same kind of downright loveliness" in her voice, her marvelous eyes, or her warm smile. One Cleveland archenemy blurted a backhanded compliment. "I detest him so much," he fumed, "that I don't even think his wife is beautiful."

Of the youngest first lady, historian William Seale wrote a century later that because of her the gloomy Executive Mansion brightened with Saturday open houses for working women, sparkling dinner parties, and dances at which she wore pretty clothes and very little in the way of jewels while carrying a pink or red camellia plucked from the conservatory. But she really shone in the reception lines which her husband found tedious. Seale speculated, "She must have been bored often, yet never appeared to be and approached each new reception or tea as though it were a long-awaited joy."

Watching her at one of these events, Grover impulsively turned to his mother-in-law and told Emma Folsom proudly, "She'll do! She'll do!"

Observers of Grover Cleveland who knew him very well, and had often described him as plodding and downright glum on occasion, suddenly found him in a happier frame of mind and in brighter spirits than they'd ever experienced. But this miraculous transformation did not extend to the press, no matter how adoring the journalists might be of his wife. In hopes of deflecting the attention, he stopped what had been routine notification to reporters of times at which he was to leave the White House to attend functions in the city or to travel. He used covered carriages rather than open. And before the wedding he'd bought a house on twenty-three acres in the northern reaches of Washington (in the vicinity of the present Washington Cathedral) in which he hoped he and Frances could escape scrutiny.

Plain, square, and ugly, with a flat roof and twenty years old, it was immediately marked for extensive renovation. To achieve the transformation, architect William M. Poindexter was hired to convert the basic structure to a Queen Anne villa with porches on two levels. The shingle walls were to be green. The new roof was painted red. Frances named the place Oak View. Reporters called it after the color of the roof.

Oak View or Red Top, it was not intended as a summer or vacation getaway spot like Camp David and others frequented by twentieth-century presidents. It was meant to be a year-round retreat. A safe haven from the nosy and noisome minions of the press, it would become a full-fledged farm with a cow named Grace. In due course Frances, an animal lover, assembled a menagerie of dogs, chickens, ducks, quail, foxes, kittens, and even some white rats. A coach house and a large kitchen garden were constructed. The stable and the one at the White House accommodated five horses. Two belonged to Grover and three were provided by the government, along with a one-horse buggy, a landau, a victoria, and a brougham. To get to Red Top the president bought what he called a road wagon. He said of the house and the small farm, "I honestly think I have one of the handsomest places in the United States."

More than a hundred years after the dream hideaway became a reality, Red Top claims a unique niche in the history of Cleveland's presidency. It was the only house in the nation's capital to be used by a president as a year-round alternative to living in the White House.

Perhaps the sweetest tribute to the marriage of Grover and Frances came from one of the leading Democratic politicians in the country, though not to Grover Cleveland directly. In a letter to Daniel Lamont, Chauncey Depew said, "My only regret about it is that it will be much harder for us to win against both Mr. and Mrs. Cleveland."

He did not refer to Frances engaging directly in politics and government. She showed no interest in the activism displayed by presidents' wives who succeeded her (Edith Wilson, Eleanor Roosevelt, Lady Bird Johnson, Nancy Reagan, and Hillary Clinton). To find the most fitting comparison to Frances in the twentieth century, one must look to Jacqueline Kennedy. Like John F. Kennedy's first lady, Frances Cleveland proved to be an immediate hit as her husband's hostess at glittering socials and banquets for diplomats and visiting dignitaries. Women everywhere looked to her as a style-setter in raiment and in matters social. She also undertook a redecoration of the Executive Mansion. And she never hesitated to defend her husband if the occasion called for it.

When a Baptist minister in Worcester, Massachusetts, C. H. Pendleton, publicly claimed firsthand knowledge that the president in a drunken rage beat her and drove her out of the White House into the snow, a woman in the preacher's town wrote to Frances

Frances Folsom
Cleveland, 1887.

asking if it were true. She replied that "every statement" made by the preacher "is basely false, and I pity a man of his calling who has been made a tool to give circulation to such wicked and heartless lies. I can wish the women of our country no greater blessing than that their homes and lives may be as happy, and their husbands may be as kind, attentive, considerate and affectionate as mine."

Allan Nevins wrote of Frances, "Few young women fresh from college would have met the exacting demands of her position, which gave her hardly a free hour, without complaint. She carried her zest for life and her unselfish interest in people into the routine of dinners and calls." William Seale recorded in his 1986 history of the White House and the chief executives and their wives who resided there, "Few presidential couples have spent more time together than the Clevelands, for they were nearly inseparable."

The house they considered home, however, was Red Top. The White House was where he worked while she spent hours between her responsibilities as first lady in the small room he had set aside for her, as he'd planned. It was near his office on the second floor, facing northward to Pennsylvania Avenue and overlooking Lafayette Park. They slept together in a bed which was big enough to fit his great size and more than sufficiently strong to support his 300-plus pounds.

One night, according to a popular yarn at the time, Frances shook Grover from slumber, exclaiming, "Wake up at once! There are burglars in the house."

"No, no, my dear," said Grover sleepily. "In the Senate maybe, but not in the House."

Mrs. Cleveland in her sitting room.

8

✦

I Shall Stick to It

"The day was bleak, the sky leaden, the ground muddy, the drizzle stubborn," wrote the Cuban correspondent for an Argentine newspaper.

Indeed, a more dismal day on which to dedicate a gigantic statue on a tiny island in the middle of New York Harbor could not have been imagined. Yet on Thursday, October 28, 1886, more than a million rain-soaked people huddled along the shores of Manhattan, Brooklyn, and Staten Island, or crowded onto boats of every description, to gaze through the downpour and up into the glowering gray clouds which nearly obscured the copper head with its seven-pointed crown and right arm holding aloft a giant torch. The face was covered by the French flag. It was to be removed, according to the plan for the day, by the man who had designed and supervised the building of the 225-ton, 305-feet-and-1-inch-tall Statue of Liberty. She stood on a pedestal paid for in large part by pennies contributed by American schoolchildren, from which she would henceforth enlighten the world with a blazing beacon.

Despite the foul weather, wrote the Cuban reporter, "human joy has rarely been so bright."

Second in the attention of the spectators was another massive figure, the president of the United States, who had come up from Washington to deliver a dedicatory speech. As during his visit to the city on Decoration Day when he'd paid a brief call on his fiancée at the Gilsey House hotel, Grover had spent the previous night in the home of Navy Secretary William C. Whitney at Fifth Avenue and Fifty-seventh Street. He rode downtown with an assembly of notables from all over the United States and from France. The latter delegation was headed by the sculptor, Frédéric Bartholdi, and Count Ferdinand Marie de Lesseps, who had built the Suez Canal and failed in an attempt sponsored by France to carve an ocean-linking canal across the Isthmus of Panama. Not present for the unveiling was the man whose idea for the statue had become a reality. Édouard de Laboulaye had died in 1883.

Introduced to Bartholdi, Grover said, "You are the greatest man in America today."

From a reviewing stand at Madison Square the dignitaries watched a parade make its way down Broadway. To get to Bedloe's Island they boarded the U.S.S. *Dispatch* and sailed down the Hudson as full-rigged ships of Secretary Whitney's navy thundered a twenty-one-gun salute. Awaiting the *Dispatch* in the harbor were several French warships and a civilian armada of yachts, tugs, and excursion steamers. They formed a colorful flotilla which would not be equaled in the history of the harbor until President Ronald Reagan stood on the deck of the battleship *Iowa* to lead the celebration on the centenary of the statue's dedication. The speech Reagan made that day was much longer than Grover's remarks were in officially accepting the gift of the statue from the French to the American people.

With the removal of the tricolor by Bartholdi's loosening the rope which held it, the harbor erupted with a blaring and bellowing of horns of ships and boats to the accompaniment of booming naval guns and a brassy rendition of "My country 'tis of thee."

Barely audible through the cacophony was the day's main speaker, William Maxwell Evarts, United States Senator from New York and chairman of the Statue of Liberty committee. Trying to hear him (or at least pretending to), the drenched president sat with thick hands folded on his big belly, as one writer noted, "courteous as ever."

In addition to appreciating their portly president's reputation as a gentleman, the American people shared the view of Grover Cleveland's friends, associates in government, political allies, and even enemies that he was smart and unquestionably able, although not a man of towering intellect. He was a hard worker, diligent in carrying out his duties as he saw them which he felt the country wanted done, but mindful of balances struck by the Constitution in the separation of powers between the three branches of the federal government. Tireless in the shouldering of the demands of his office, he personified his slogan, "Public office is a public trust." Voters who had sent him to the White House, and those who had voted against him, knew they'd gotten their dollar's worth. The question was whether the value of the "buck" would continue to be based solely on gold.

After the brief visit to New York for the Statue of Liberty ceremonies, the president went back to the capital and Dan Lamont to face the task of preparing his second State of the Union message to be sent to Congress. It was due to return to its business in December following an election which was promoted by the press as offering a barometer of how the country judged the first two years of the Cleveland presidency. In addition to balloting for all members of the House of Representatives and one-third of the U.S. Senate, voters were deciding state and local contests, of which none attracted more attention than the race for mayor of New York City. Grover backed the Democrat Abram S. Hewitt, in a three-man heat involving independent Henry George and the return to politics (and from the West) of Theodore Roosevelt. The issues in the contest were local and after all the ballots were counted, Hewitt was the winner, George the runner-up, and Roosevelt a distant third. But the Democrats' win in the New York mayoralty was tempered for Grover by the congressional results. The Democratic majority in the House was cut from 184 to 160, although the Democrats narrowed the Republican majority in the Senate from eight to two.

With the verdict on his first two years in office inconclusive, Grover proceeded with the preparation of his message to Congress. As in all his writing, it was a long process. Biographer George F. Parker described it this way: "Everything was prepared with a care, a patience, and an effort. He would study for days over a question—whether it was familiar to him or not. He had a way of saying that he wanted to see it on every side so that he would not make more mistakes than he was entitled to. Then he would think it over carefully, turn it in his mind until he had fairly saturated himself, and get a point of view which must commend itself wholly to his reason, with only the smallest regard either to preconceived or popular opinion. He made few notes, except for dates and historical facts, for which his memory had no serious liking."

A speech or a message to be sent to Congress went through several drafts until the last was so cut and carved that it had only a slight resemblance to the original. Then a copy was made in his own handwriting. He would then go over it for purely verbal niceties or for insertion of new thoughts. The material was then ready for a final copying and printing.

Letters were a different matter. These were composed with an ease which showed that he knew just what he wanted to say and how to say it. They were handwritten, seldom revised, clear and concise. There were bursts of humor, but they contained few indulgences in irony, satire, or figures of speech. They did, however, frequently contain blunt expressions of opinion. These informal writings were sent with confidence that what he put into them would be known by no one except the person to whom the letters were sent.

Among the archives is Grover's "Executive Proclamation on the Death of ex-President Chester A. Arthur." Dated November 18, 1886, it announced the demise of the Republican who had yielded him the White House. He reminded the country that Arthur had been "called to the chair of Chief Magistrate of the nation by a tragedy [the assassination of President Garfield] which cast its shadow over the entire government." He said that Arthur's "assumption of the grave duties was marked by an evident and conscientious sense of his responsibilities, and an earnest desire to meet them in a patriotic and benevolent spirit."

These sentiments were not just the rhetoric expected from a living president to a dead one. The Arthur presidency (September 20,

1881, to March 4, 1885) had been well received by the American people. Said the country's most famous author, Mark Twain, "I am but one in fifty-five million, still in the opinion of this one-fifty-five-millionth of the country's population, it would be hard to better President Arthur's administration."

The second State of the Union message which Arthur's successor sent to Congress on December 6, 1886, sounded familiar Cleveland refrains. Of soldiers' pensions he insisted that every one granted be deserved, based on "actual service and injury or disease incurred in such service." He praised the results of civil service reform and asked for more. And he appealed again for the legislation he'd proposed for a system of federal arbitration in labor disputes. Recognizing the limitations of what government could do, he called on capital for "recognition of the brotherhood of our citizenship and in a spirit of American fairness, generously accord to labor its just compensation and consideration, and that contented labor is capital's best protection and faithful ally."

Labor groups, though, had little of Cleveland's patience with capital. They would recognize themselves.

Two days after the message went to Capitol Hill, some twenty-five labor groups representing about 150,000 workers met in Columbus, Ohio, and formed the American Federation of Labor (AFL). To lead it they elected a man who in 1881 had helped found the Federation of Organized Trades and Labor Unions. Born in London in 1850 and having emigrated to the United States with his family in 1863, Samuel Gompers had worked as a cigar maker in New York and joined the Cigarmakers Union in 1864. After becoming its president in 1877, he'd traveled often to Albany in the cause of cigar makers when Theodore Roosevelt was imploring Governor Cleveland to enlist in the cause of improving working conditions in that industry.

The paths of President Grover Cleveland and the president of the AFL would cross again in the not-so-distant future.

★　★　★

January 1887 brought historic action by the Congress. For the first time in history, it passed and sent to the desk of a president legislation to establish a federal regulatory commission. It set up the Interstate Commerce Commission. The purpose was to impose restraints on railroads in the matter of rates, and to constrain the power of states in an industry which was national in scope. An ardent supporter of the goals of the bill, Grover had lobbied for it (indirectly through friends) and promptly signed it. Appointments to the new commission were strong and able men with backgrounds in the issues likely to come before them. Within a year the members were able to report that the railroads had conformed to its orders and that progress had been made in creating uniformity of rates.

The early months of 1887 also brought Grover legislative successes: upholding of his veto of the Blair veterans' pension bill, which would have granted a stipend to anyone who had served at least ninety days in uniform; signing of the Hatch Act, providing subsidies for creation of state agricultural-science experiment stations; a ban on importation of Chinese opium; and the repeal of the Tenure of Office Act. February brought the often-postponed resignation of Treasury Secretary Manning (on the fourteenth, effective April 1, to be replaced by Charles Stebbins Fairchild).

On the day Manning's resignation was accepted, the presidential pen was wielded to veto a measure popularly known as the Texas Seed Bill. It authorized federal assistance in the form of an authorization for the Commissioner of Agriculture to distribute $10,000 to help farmers in Texas who had been hit hard by a drought. The money was to finance the buying of seed. Grover found no basis in the Constitution for such congressional largesse. He said he did not believe that the power and duty of the General Government ought to be expended to the relief of individual suffering which is in no manner properly related to the public service or benefit.

He included in the veto message a phrase as succinct and memorable as "Public office is a public trust." While rejecting aid to struggling Texas, he voiced a general maxim and urged that it be constantly enforced. From the moment he coined it to this day, the phrase shaped the argument of those who opposed the concept of "a welfare state."

"Though the people support the Government," Grover said, "the Government should not support the people."

★　★　★

Months of spring brought the skirmishing over the Confederate battle flags, retreat in the face of protests by Union veterans, and cancellation of Cleveland's acceptance of the G.A.R.'s invitation to attend its summer encampment in St. Louis. Another invitation which if accepted might have fanned the embers of surviving Civil War bitterness was declined in a June 24 letter to the secretary of the "Reunion of Union and ex-Confederate Soldiers." The event was scheduled for July 2, in Gettysburg, Pennsylvania, on the twenty-fourth anniversary of the three days of fighting there which had marked a decisive moment in the war. While praising the intent of the gathering to "illustrate the generous impulse of brave men and their honest desire for peace and reconciliation," Grover begged off, citing "other arrangements already made and my official duties here."

But nothing stood in his way on July 13 in marking the centennial of one his former homes. Speaking in Clinton, New York, he reminisced, "It was here, in the school at the foot of College Hill, that I began my preparation for college life and enjoyed the anticipation of a collegiate education." Nostalgia aside, he went on to talk about the office he occupied, and the pain he'd endured in obtaining it in the form of "questionable methods" and "deceit practiced to mislead the people in their choice." Asserting that a president must be "of the people," but that any president was "subject to human frailty and error," he said the generosity of the citizens should alone decree how far good intentions should excuse shortcomings. "Watch well, then, this high office, the most precious possession of American citizenship," he counseled. "Demand of it the most complete devotion on the part of him to whose custody it may be intrusted, and protect it not less vigilantly against unworthy assaults from without."

On September 17 he was in Philadelphia to observe a considerably more significant centenary. The occasion was the Constitution Centennial. He made three speeches on that day, to the banquet of the Philadelphia Hibernian Society, a dinner given by the Historical and Scientific Societies, and the chief one officially marking the hundredth anniversary of completion of the work of framing the Constitution.

Two weeks after the Philadelphia visit, he packed up for his much-anticipated trip west and the first swing by a postbellum Democratic president through states of the former Confederacy.

★　　★　　★

The journey, he declared at the outset, was to be "a social trip and every-day-kind-of-visit to the people." Like every president before him and all those to follow, he soon learned that when the president of the United States comes to town there's nothing about the occasion that is at all "everyday." In anticipation of his visit, the city of Chicago and surrounding communities declared the date of October 5 a holiday. People with the day off in four states poured into Chicago to see him and hear what he had to say to them. However, if they came expecting political oratory they were disappointed. He'd decided to leave politics behind, choosing instead to deal with topics of a noncontroversial nature. This choice prompted some criticism. One Ohio newspaper expressed its view that there were at least ten thousand men in that state who seemed as well fitted to be a president, but almost nobody was so well fitted to be a first lady as Mrs. Cleveland. When the tour reached St. Paul, Minnesota, where Frances had attended school, he expressed thanks that no one there had married "nor spoiled" her.

He added, "I had much rather have her than the Presidency."

The first stop on the odyssey had been Indianapolis (a four-hour stay), during which he lunched with the widow of Thomas Hendricks. Still hoping for a low-key trip, he informed Dan Lamont and Shan Bissell, who were traveling with him, that he considered them members of "a family party with freedom from restraint which that implies." The notion that they were all taking part in an outing of the sort enjoyed by average Americans was dispelled in Chicago. No average American had ever been expected to do what was required of Grover during a reception at the Palmer House hotel. It was there that he shattered Lincoln's record for shaking hands by clutching six thousand of them at a rate of forty-seven a minute.

The daily pace occasionally proved exhausting for Frances. During a huge procession in Chicago, her stamina gave out and she left the parade three-quarters of the way into the two-mile route. But Grover's constitution never appeared to fail. A correspondent for *Harper's Weekly* noted that after a strenuous day of touring and speaking, he routinely stayed up until three in the morning talking and smoking cigars with Lamont and Bissell, then was up and raring to go again just a few hours later. The reporter dutifully described for the magazine's readers their stout president's excursions to the shores of Lake Michigan, Wisconsin woods and farmlands, more lakes and farms in Minnesota, and the Corn Palace in Sioux City, Iowa.

In Kansas City, Missouri, on October 13, he participated in the laying of the cornerstone of a Y.M.C.A. "All will admit the supreme importance of that honesty and fixed principle which rest upon Christian motives and purposes," he said, "and all will acknowledge the sad and increasing temptations which beset our young men and lure them to destruction."

At St. Louis he admired the Mississippi River and then crossed "the Father of Waters" on the saloon deck of a steamboat to begin a swing through the southern cities of Memphis, Nashville, and Chattanooga, Tennessee. There he saw someone holding up a sign. It read, "Our Grover: he has filled the bloody chasm."

Grover accepted the sentiment as evidence of the fading of bitter memories of the Civil War and Reconstruction. Biographer George F. Parker wrote that he "saw in the South signs of a restored Union and recognized, in a more emphatic way than had been possible earlier, that sectionalism was no longer a force."

Concerning the visit to a premier city of the South which had been laid waste by William T. Sherman, there had been a frisson of worry even before the start of the journey over a report that there was a movement to invite to one of the Atlanta receptions the former president of the Confederacy, Jefferson Davis, now eighty-one years of age and regarded as a hero of the South and a traitor in the North. Learning of the possibility of Davis's showing up, Grover had warned planners of the visit to Atlanta, "If any such business as that is indulged in, the people of Atlanta will find that one of their expected guests will not listen to their talk." If there had been a movement to drag out Jeff Davis, it never got beyond the dreaming stage.

The last stops in the old Confederacy included one of its former capitals, Montgomery, Alabama, followed by brief visits to Tecumseh, South Carolina, and Asheville, North Carolina. As the train left the South and crossed the Potomac River to Washington, D.C., Grover felt his travels had contributed to erasing the scars of the Civil War and resentments stemming from the punishments imposed on the South by Reconstruction, as well as laying to rest recent unpleasantness over the battle flags.

Assessing the results of the journey west and south, Allan Nevins wrote, "This long tour through two curious sections did much to make the American public better acquainted with Cleveland; and so also did the publication, year by year, of interviews and letters which struck a personal note. The country which in 1885 had thought of him as an honest but coarse man had learned . . . that this was an inadequate view. His integrity went beyond the plain everyday honesty of the good business man or office holder. It was the integrity of a man of unbending principle and sleepless conscientiousness, founded upon a deep if simple religious conviction of which the outside world caught a glimpse."

George F. Parker expressed this belief: "The President's bearing on this extended journey, the ease and dignity with which he met his countrymen, his interest in local development, and the impressions he gathered of a restored and united country, increased his own familiarity with the needs of the country, promoted his popularity, and helped to complete the harmony of the sections so long divided, first by civil war, and, later, as the result of misgovernment and the acts of interested partisans."

★　★　★

A sure sign of the nearing of the close of 1887 was the return of Congress from its warm-weather hiatus. It had adjourned in March having done nothing to deal with a problem which was of increasingly grave concern to Grover and his advisers in terms of the continued health of the nation's economy. The federal government had too much money. At the end of the fiscal year the surplus in the Treasury was nearly $94 million. Most of that was the result of collection of high tariffs. In a final report before resigning, Treasury Secretary Daniel Manning had warned that the abundance of money must be reduced and that the way to do so would be to attack the problem at its source. He termed the current system of tariffs an "incompetent and brutal scheme of revenue." The only way to deal with the accumulation of revenue in federal coffers was to lower the rate of tariffs on imported goods. A secondary benefit of lowering the piles of money on hand which had a great appeal to Grover would be removal of a temptation to Congress to squander it.

None of this was new to Grover. He'd been calling for lower tariffs from Congress to no avail. Prior to leaving on the trip to the West and the South, he decided the time was right to stress the urgency of the issue. To do so he invited Speaker of the House of Representatives John G. Carlisle and his wife to spend four days at Oak View (Red Top). He also brought to the farm his new treasury secretary and others to discuss tariff strategy. When word of the meetings reached New York, the newspaper that had faulted Grover for not showing leadership when he had declined to lobby the Congress on behalf of gold over silver, the *New York Herald*, praised him. It said in an editorial, "The conference which he has invited marks an era in his administration. It will create a better feeling everywhere, and prepare the [Democratic] party for an attack upon some important problems during the next session of Congress. . . . What the people want is big ideas."

The meetings continued while the president traveled, and became known as the "Oak View Conferences." When he returned he studied the results of the tariff talks and began working on the State of the Union message to be sent to Congress in December. While laboring on it he found himself barraged with warnings, one of which came from the *Herald*, which had come down with a case of cold feet. The newspaper raised the prospect of the issue's backfiring and costing Grover a second term as president.

Grover grumbled to a friend, "What is the use of being elected or re-elected unless you stand for something?"

Work on the message continued, and on December 1, 1887, he wrote to Shan Bissell, "My message is done. I think it is pretty good but you will be surprised when you see it."

One of the surprises was that the message was not the smorgasbord of legislative requests he and other presidents had routinely delivered. The message of December 6, 1887, dealt only with the tariff issue. It began with typically blunt Grover Cleveland language: "You are confronted at the threshold of your legislative duties with a condition of the national finances which imperatively demands immediate and careful consideration." Among several dramatic demands in the message, the most breathtaking aspect was the course of action he proposed. He chose not to reduce the surplus with cuts in the tax rates on luxury items and reduction in internal revenue collections on items such as whiskey and tobacco. He aimed straight at protective tariffs on necessities—sugar, clothing, coffee, carpets, and other commodities of importance to the working class and farmers. He termed the levies a "vicious, inequitable, and illogical source of unnecessary taxation . . . which, without regard to the public welfare or a national exigency, must always insure the realization of immense profits instead of moderately profitable returns."

The message was both a lecture on fiscal responsibility and an indictment of a public policy fraught with dangers:

> When we consider that the theory of our institutions guarantees to every citizen the full enjoyment of all the fruits of his industry and enterprise, with only such deduction as may be his share toward the careful and economical maintenance of the Government which protects him, it is plain that the exaction of more than this is indefensible extortion and a culpable betrayal of American fairness and justice. The wrong inflicted upon those who bear the burden of national taxation, like other wrongs, multiplies a brood of evil consequences. The public treasury, which should only exist as a conduit conveying the people's tribute to its legitimate objects of expenditure, becomes a hoarding place for money needlessly with-

drawn from trade and the people's use, thus crippling our national energies, suspending our country's development, preventing investment in productive enterprise, threatening financial disturbance, and inviting schemes of public plunder. . . . It will not do to neglect this situation because its dangers are not now palpably imminent and apparent. They exist no less certainly, and await the unforseen and unexpected occasion when suddenly they will be precipitated upon us.

After a long and detailed analysis of the crisis (filling a dozen pages of fine print), he gave the Congress another example of Cleveland verbal coinage. "It is a *condition* which confronts us," he said, "not a theory."

The simple and plain duty owed to the people, he insisted in concluding the message, "is to reduce taxation to the necessary expenses of an economical operation of the Government and to restore to the business of the country the money which we hold in the Treasury through the perversion of governmental powers."

Reaction from press, public, and politicians was virtually unanimous in its praise, not for each and every aspect of the message, but for the obvious courage of the man who wrote it. The *Philadelphia Press* offered a "thousand thanks" for his "bold, manly, and unequivocal avowal" of his purposes. New York's *Commercial Advertiser* said the "concise, able and manfully candid message will have a decisive weight in the future of parties and legislation." The *Nation* called the message "the most courageous document that has been sent from the Executive Mansion since the close of the Civil War." The *Post* declared that the message "makes the revenue question the paramount and controlling one in American politics." From England came the judgment of the *London Morning Post*.

Sooner or later, it said, "this Congress will recognize the wisdom of the President's advice and resolve to reduce the Federal revenues."

A dissenting visitor in England, James G. Blaine, viewed the Cleveland tariff policy as an outright call for free trade. Also on the negative side, the *Chicago Journal*, a protectionist paper, dismissed Grover's position as "cant and humbug." The *Commercial Gazette* of New York City depicted Grover as an "ignoramus, dolt, simpleton, idiot—firebug in public finance."

But the secretary of the National Reform League, R. R. Bowker, immediately declared, "It clears the air like a thunderstorm on a sultry day."

The judgment of historians took longer, but they came down on the side of praising Grover for audacity and courage. George F. Parker wrote in 1909, "It would be difficult to overestimate its effect. It at once lifted politics out of the ruts into which it had fallen and gave the country something real to think about. From that time forward, fiscal questions had a standing and could more easily command public interest. It was no longer complained that a speech on the tariff was dull or that an exposition of the financial condition of the country was necessarily stupid. It is probable that no document of its length ever had so wide a reading."

Robert McElroy, writing in 1923, saw Grover as "no idealist thinking free trade thoughts in a world of nations devoted to protection, but a practical, honest trustee insisting upon administration in the interest of the people."

While faulting Grover for not having delivered the message sooner, Allan Nevins wrote in 1932 that "few acts by any President have been so much acclaimed, yet it may be doubted if the precise character of the courage exhibited has been generally understood."

He described the tariff message as "a magnificent act of states-manship, magnificently executed."

Horace Samuel Merrill felt in 1957 that the tariff message confirmed the belief that Grover had "placed the nation's interest above his own and that of selfish persons in his party." But he criticized him for failing to follow up. "More was required of him," he wrote, "than to make pronouncements and issue orders."

Rexford Guy Tugwell's 1968 biography noted, "As a sound-money man, he should have also been for sound tariffs—that is, ones favored by industries and bankers. But as a Democrat, and as an honest man, he came to quite another decision. It seemed to him that, on the evidence, the low-tariff advocates were right in saying that protectionism was not necessary to support American industry and maintain high wages."

Richard E. Welch Jr., in *The Presidencies of Grover Cleveland* (1988), asserted that "a president who demanded revision in behalf of relief for consumers, a reduction of governmental subsidies to special interests, and the restraint of trusts and monopolies, is not unduly praised when given the designation of reformer." But like Merrill, Welch felt that Grover let down himself and the cause of tariff reform by believing a barnstorming tour to inspire grassroots support to be beneath the dignity of the presidential office. What was needed was a presidential campaign of public education on behalf of tariff reform. Grover left it to others to provide instruction.

The judgment of more immediate concern than that of historians about Grover's message among Democrats as 1887 ended was what effect his dramatic focus on tariff policy might have in the new year when Americans would go to the polls in a presidential election. All agreed that how the question was resolved would depend in large measure on the action taken on the message by a Congress in which Democrats controlled the House and Republicans the Senate. In a Congress in which the ranks of the parties in the two bodies were often bitterly divided on issues, party loyalty and discipline shaped the debate. Democrats backed their president's call for reductions, while the Republicans locked step against.

As the lines of debate formed in Congress, the issue was also joined in newspapers and magazines, in political clubs, around the cracker barrels in general stores, and across tables and bars in saloons. None of this bothered Grover. "If every other man in the country abandons this issue," he informed the Speaker of the House, "I shall stick to it."

★   ★   ★

Sixteen days into the new year, the first Democratic president since James Buchanan filled a seat on the Supreme Court of the United States. Upon the death of William B. Woods of Georgia, he appointed Secretary of the Interior Lucius Quintus Cincinnatus Lamar of Mississippi. Although he was widely regarded as superbly qualified, the mere fact that he was a southerner was sufficient cause for some voices to howl in protest and to carry the day in the Senate Judiciary Committee. It recommended rejection of the nomination. The issue then hung in the balance for half the year until a group of Western senators joined with those from the Northeast to repudiate the notion that no one from the former Confederacy was suitable for the nation's highest court. The Senate confirmed Lamar by a vote of 32 to 28.

That westerners backed Lamar demonstrated the high esteem

in which Lamar had been held in that region during his tenure at the Interior Department. It was an approval voiced by whites and many Indians and resulted from the interest shown by the Cleveland administration in the territorial problems and concerns of both the settlers and the people the United States government had remanded to reservations. When Grover came into office the Indian population on reservations was estimated at a little over a quarter of a million. The land assigned to them covered nearly 140 million acres, a vast portion of which was highly desirable for farming with an estimated value of $160 million. Settlers were eager to see most of this territory freed for farming and ranching in a way which would allow peaceful Indians ample living room. They argued that if every Indian family was accommodated, they would need only ten and a half million acres. At the same time this idea was being promoted, an organization called Friends of the Indians complained about the inhumane conditions imposed on those living on the reservations.

The approach of the president and his secretary of the interior was two-pronged. Congress was asked to establish a commission to visit all the reservations and suggest reforms. The two men also began looking into how the reservations system might be abolished.

The author of the proposed legislation, Senator Henry L. Dawes of Massachusetts, declared, "The law confers upon every Indian in this land a homestead of his own; and, if he will take it, makes him a citizen of the United States, with all the privileges and immunities and rights of such a citizen, and opens to him the doors of all courts in the land upon the same terms that it opens them to every other citizen . . . Two hundred thousand Indians have been led out, as it were, to a new life, to a new pathway."

A conference of Indian leaders (the Mohonk Conference) announced satisfaction. But they did not speak for all their kinsmen. The majority resented the appearance of land allotment agents to parcel out their property. More often than not, a government agent was greeted by a cloud of dust as residents of reservation villages departed in order to avoid being given a plot of ground and dubious American citizenship.

Although the intentions of Grover and his Interior Secretary were noble, the future place of the original inhabitants of what became the United States would not be settled in their terms of office. For evidence, all they had to do was read reports from the army whose soldiers had such a hard time capturing the symbol of Indian resistance to assimilation, Geronimo. In his fifteen years as a "renegade Indian," he and his small band of resisters had managed to kill more than twenty-five hundred U.S. citizens.

The policy of assimilation of Indians initiated by the Dawes Act would lapse in the four years between Grover's administrations, but upon his return to the White House he instructed the secretary of the interior in the second term, Hoke Smith, that Indian agents were to exert no undue pressure on the Indians. "The good and welfare of the Indian should be constantly kept in view," he said, "so that when the end is reached citizenship may be to them a real advantage, instead of an empty name."

There can be no doubting Grover's sincerity. He believed the Dawes Act would improve the status of Indians. The consensus of historians, including Helen Hunt Jackson, author of the landmark study of Indian policy *A Century of Dishonor*, is that he did his best to realize its goals with no expectation of political profit.

That could not be said of the ultimate Cleveland policy toward Chinese immigrants. While he had been at first sympathetic to the plight of the Chinese, most of whom had been brought into the country as laborers for building railroads in the West and subjected to abuse and violence, Grover came to the conclusion that overcoming white prejudice against absorbing Chinese into the mainstream was an impossible goal. Despite negotiations between the governments of the United States and China to work out problems of immigration, and as the 1888 presidential election season was getting under way, he backed a bill in the House to ban the return of Chinese who had left the United States. When he signed the measure into law on October 1, 1888, he said, "The experiment of blending the social habits and mutual race idiosyncracies of the Chinese laboring classes with those of the great body of the people of the United States has been proved by the experience of twenty years . . . to be in every sense unwise, impolitic, and injurious to both nations."

This unfortunate bias, which American history has proved wrong on every count, stemmed from his conviction that desirable immigrants were those who would accept American values and eagerly assimilate into American society. Like a president who would follow him, Theodore Roosevelt, he did not believe in hyphenated Americans. He believed that immigrants had to leave their nativism behind and become Americans. Were they to do so, he felt, they were entitled to all the opportunities available to native-born Americans to succeed. Consequently, when Massachusetts Republican Senator Henry Cabot Lodge won passage of a bill to bar illiterates from being let into the country as immigrants, Grover vetoed the measure. "The ability to read and write," he said, "in and of itself afford, in my opinion, a misleading test of contented industry and supplies unsatisfactory evidence of desirable citizenship or a proper application of the benefits of our institutions."

The Cleveland attitude toward blacks was not so clear-cut. He believed amendments of the Constitution gave them rights of citizenship, but he felt that, as Americans, they had no right to expect special treatment from the federal government. He'd said in his inaugural address that, in the administration of a government pledged to equal and exact justice to all men, freed slaves were not an exception. But this did not mean government owed them anything more than what it afforded to all citizens. He did not discriminate against blacks in appointments to consular and other posts. At the Piedmont Exposition in October 1887, he called for "understanding and cooperation between blacks and whites as well as the North and South" and warned of "designing demagogues" whose purpose was to endanger racial harmony.

A man of his time, he did not accept blacks as equal to whites except in citizenship of the United States. In that capacity they would receive all due respect and federal protection. But, as in the matter of the Chinese immigrants, he believed that racial differences were insuperable.

As late as 1903, six years after leaving the presidency, he told a meeting of the Southern Educational Association in New York, "I believe that neither the decree which made the slaves free, nor the enactment that suddenly invested them with the rights of citizenship any more cured them of their racial and slavery-bred imperfections and deficiencies than it changed the color of their skin." Expressing a prevailing view among most white people of his time, he saw in blacks "a grievous amount of ignorance, a sad amount of viciousness and a tremendous amount of laziness and thriftlessness."

Imbued with these beliefs, he did not appoint blacks to positions in the states of the South, took no steps to stem a rising tide of discriminatory laws (Jim Crow laws), and supported a U.S. Supreme

Court decision upholding the constitutionality of segregated schools. He spoke of black youths as "colored boys." Yet he and Frederick Douglass were not only friends, they were mutual admirers. When Grover said in his first inaugural address that all discussion of the fitness of blacks "for the place accorded them as American citizens is idle and unprofitable, except as it suggests the necessity for their improvement," Douglass commented, "It was all any friend of liberty and justice could reasonably ask."

After reading Booker T. Washington's address at the Atlanta Cotton Exposition with its advocacy of educating blacks in trades and advice to blacks against seeking social equality with the white population, Grover wrote to him, "Your words cannot fail to delight and encourage all who wish well for the race."

★   ★   ★

Having seen Lucius Lamar leave behind the territorial problems of the West to become an associate justice of the Supreme Court, Grover found himself shifting another member of his Cabinet to the Interior Department. The new secretary would be W. F. Vilas, who'd been running the Post Office Department. To replace him, Grover named "the most unselfish friend I ever had." He was Donald McDonald Dickinson of Michigan. A lawyer and a member of the Democratic National Committee, he had assisted Grover in selecting members of the Interstate Commerce Commission. Dickinson's nomination went to the Senate on January 16, 1887.

A glimpse of Dickinson's importance to Grover in preparing for the November election is found in a letter he sent to Dickinson on January 23. Headed "Confidential," it started with a hint that conspiracy was afoot. "I will work with you tonight," wrote Grover. "Come about eight o'clock."

The day after Dickinson's nomination was forwarded to the Senate, the Congress received reports from commissioners who had investigated the affairs of railroads which received aid from the government.

February also saw submission for Senate ratification of a treaty with Great Britain on the rights of American fishermen in Canadian waters, as well as duties on Canadian fish.

The treaty would almost be sunk by opponents who supported "retaliation" against both the British and the Canadians. But Grover proved unyielding. He went so far as to demand that if the treaty failed, he be given the power to "suspend by proclamation the operation of all laws and regulations permitting the transit of goods, wares, and merchandise in bond across or over the territory of the United States to or from Canada." Opposition and calls for retaliation quickly collapsed and the treaty was ratified.

The day after the nomination of Dickinson, February 21, Grover and Frances departed Washington for three days in the Florida sun. When he returned he clearly had the forthcoming campaign on his mind in a letter to James Shanahan, whom Governor Cleveland had appointed superintendent of public works in New York. Always a staunch political friend, Shanahan had written on the subject of Grover's going for a second term. Grover reverted to a familiar position on the subject of holding public office. If he were to exercise personal desires, he said, "I would insist that my public life should end on the fourth of March next . . . and be a very happy man." He continued, "But I am daily and hourly told that the conditions are such that such a course is not open without endangering the supremacy of the party and the good of the country. Occupying the position I do on this subject, having no personal ambition, willing to obey the command of my party and by my own act being in no man's way, I confess I cannot keep my temper when I learn of the mean and low attempts that are made by underhand means to endanger the results to which I am devoted. And when I see good staunch friends as you with their coats off and sleeves rolled up, I feel like taking a hand with them."

The letter ended with, "My position is this: I should personally like better than anything else to be let alone and let out; but although I often get quite discouraged and feel like insisting upon following my inclinations I shall neither go counter to the wishes of the party which I love and which has honored me nor shall I desert my friends. . . ."

A matter which he'd found discouraging was the promulgation on February 2 by the Civil Service Commission of amended rules. Demonstrating his capacity for mastering the details of complicated issues, he wrote a long letter to the commission on March 21 spelling out detailed objections to the proposed rules.

Two days later, he found himself with another vacancy to be filled on the Supreme Court, but this time it was the seat of the man who had administered his oath as president. Chief Justice Morrison R. Waite died on March 23. He had been appointed to the Court by President Grant. In pondering a replacement, Cleveland listened to numerous suggestions. Among the names was that of John G. Carlisle, the Speaker of the House. While Carlisle was a political ally and had participated in the Oak View Conferences on tariff reduction, Grover had grave misgivings about Carlisle's character. When Senator Joseph C. S. Blackburn was extolling Carlisle's qualifications, Grover interrupted him with, "Blackburn, you tell only part of the truth. You know why I won't appoint him. I won't appoint a man to be Chief Justice of the United States who might be picked up in the street some morning."

The nomination went to Melville W. Fuller. A New Englander by birth and a Chicagoan by residence, he'd been a prominent attorney and was a devoted student of the law. As to character, he was, as one observer put it, a man of singular purity. However, he was evidently a very bad poet who'd penned a long ode to Grant after Grant's death which was judged so poor that Republican newspapers gleefully printed it in its entirety. Grover had met him on the tour of the West and was impressed by his urbanity. The favorable opinion was reinforced through correspondence. By all accounts, he was the most obscure figure ever proposed for chief justice.

Whether the Senate would confirm him remained a question until July 20, when he received 41 ayes and 29 nays. A conservative with a "strict constructionist" view of the Constitution, Fuller won a reputation as the best manager of the Supreme Court in anyone's memory.

As spring moved inexorably toward another sultry Washington summer and the Congress continued in session to debate and decide upon the agenda proposed by the man occupying the White House, Republicans and Democrats turned their attention to November, when the voters of the United States would render their verdict on how well President Cleveland was conducting the business of running the country.

For the master of Oak View farm, two things were certain. First, he was assured of renomination. While old enemies in machines such as Tammany longed for a change at the top of the ticket, the Democratic rank and file understood that to turn to someone else would guarantee a Republican triumph. The second of the verities as the political season blossomed was that Grover would not again face his foe in the bitter campaign of 1884. In a remarkable expression of personal and political philosophy which would not set a precedent in American presidential history, Blaine declined to make himself available. Interviewed on the subject by a correspondent for the *New York World* who'd tracked him down in Florence, Italy, he said, "I hold I have no right to be a candidate again. A man who has once been the candidate of his party, and defeated, owes it to his party to withdraw, and not be a candidate a second time."

He also no stomach to go through "the burden and fatigue of another Presidential canvass" like the previous one. Yet unconvinced Republicans continued to beseech him to run until the door was slammed on their hopes for good in a Blaine letter from Paris on May 17. With only a month to the nominating convention in Chicago, the alternatives were John Sherman of Ohio, Chauncey Depew of New York, and Walter Q. Gresham and Benjamin Harrison, both from Indiana.

After seven votes the convention found itself deadlocked between Sherman and Gresham. Then came a telegram from Blaine, now in Scotland. It said: "Take Harrison." Obedient delegates did so on the next ballot.

Ohio-born (on August 20, 1833), Benjamin Harrison had been named for a great-grandfather who was a signer of the Declaration of Independence and a governor of Virginia. His grandfather was President William Henry Harrison. With a personality described by many as aloof and frigid as an iceberg, he was an able speaker who'd entered politics at the age of twenty-seven and handily won

Benjamin Harrison.

his first bid for office (reporter to the Supreme Court of Indiana). During the Civil War he had been in the thick of the fighting, including daring infantry charges as a colonel in the Seventieth Indiana Volunteers. His troops called him "Little Ben" even after his promotion to brigadier general in March 1865. Nominated by Republicans for governor of Indiana in 1876, he picked up a new nickname in the campaign—"Kid Gloves." He lost that election (by 5,000 votes out of 434,000) to Jimmy "Blue Jeans" Williams. As a United States senator, he had backed Cleveland's civil service reforms, but opposed Grover's vetoes of pension bills and call for tariff reductions (he favored increases). Convinced that the president had alienated so many people on an array of issues that he could not be reelected, Harrison chose to pursue a low-key campaign by remaining at his home in Indianapolis and speaking to influential groups who came to him.

The Democrats had convened in St. Louis before the Republican conclave while the man they intended to renominate remained in Washington. Because of the demise of Vice President Hendricks, they had to choose a new running mate from three contenders: Governor Isaac P. Gray of Indiana, Pensions Commissioner Chauncey F. Black of Illinois, and seventy-five-year-old and ailing Allen Thurman of Ohio. Thurman was universally liked and respected in the party and by Grover, even though his positions on the major issues of the day (silver, tariffs, and the spoils system) were opposite Grover's. That fact notwithstanding, when the delegates chose him, Grover assented.

On June 17 from Red Top, he confided his feelings on his renomination to Shan Bissell:

> *The political turmoil has not fairly begun yet. In point of fact, the campaign thus far as I see it is very quiet. I sometimes think that perhaps more enthusiasm would have been created if somebody else had been nominated after a lively scrimmage at St. Louis. I mean to be as good a candidate as I can and after the people have done their voting I shall be content and doubly so in case of success because my reluctance to again take on the burden has been fully considered, discounted, and dismissed, and because I am sure in being a candidate again I am but answering the demands of public and political duty.*

With Frances beside him, he continued, "I tell you, Bissell, I am sure of one thing. I have in her something better than the presidency for life—though the Republican party and papers do say I beat her and abuse her. I absolutely long to be able to live with her as other people do with their wives. Well! Perhaps I can after the 4th of next March."

As the Republican campaign would be conducted by the party's candidate mostly from the porch of the Harrison home in Indianapolis, the Democratic incumbent would confine himself primarily to the White House and Oak View. It was a method of running for the presidency which more than a century later must seem quaint to voters in the age of television and Internet chat rooms. It is hard to imagine a time without slickly produced TV commercials, "attack ads," sound bites, evening TV news coverage consisting of tightly managed photo ops, radio and television talk and late-night-entertainment shows with appearances by candidates as if they were stars of movies or members of a rock band, and music-video programs on which a candidate can expect to be asked what type of underwear he prefers.

Promising a campaign of "information and organization" in which every voter "should be regarded as thoughtful and responsible," Grover chose not to take to the hustings and subject himself to handshaking labor. To expound his positions to voters interested in "examining the issues involved in the pending canvass," he brought to the White House a writer who was asked to prepare a "Campaign Text Book of the Democratic Party." The book was to be completed for publication in September. The goal was to provide a history of the administration and of the personality of the man at its head.

"It was necessary to compile a complete history of every department and independent bureau or division in order to show what it had done and wherein it had adopted improved methods and so corrected abuses," wrote the man assigned this daunting task. He was George F. Parker and he left for posterity not only a unique insider's view of Grover's 1888 campaign, but a memoir of Cleveland's life, *Recollections of Grover Cleveland*, published the year after Grover's death. (No such access to a president would be repeated until 1989, when historian and biographer of Theodore Roosevelt Edmund Morris was granted unhindered access to research a biography of Ronald Reagan.) In a passage describing his work in a room across the hallway from Grover's second-floor office in the White House during "those hot weeks of July and August" of 1888, Parker provided a portrait of Grover Cleveland, who was both president and candidate:

> Gasping for air, in an oppressive atmosphere, when I would step into the hall, in the hope, generally futile, of catching some stray breath of air, it so happened once that, as I looked across the hall to the half-open door turned toward mine, I saw, reflected upon its polished surface, the hand of man busily writing.
>
> I knew that this door opened into the workroom of Grover Cleveland, President of the United States, whom I had not seen since taking up my hard task inside his official residence. So the habit was formed, when I went to work early at my daily task, of asking the watchman at what hour the President had knocked off the preceding night. I found that it was generally about three o'clock in the morning; now and then, when he had finished some severe task that he had set himself, he would stop at two o'clock.

Many of those late hours during the campaign were devoted to writing letters to persons laboring to get him reelected.

On September 14 he wrote to Chauncey Black, "The struggle

upon which we have entered is in behalf of the people—the plain people of the land—and they must be reached. We do not proceed upon the theory that they are to be led by others who may or may not be in sympathy with their interests. We have undertaken to teach voters, as free, independent citizens, intelligent enough to see their rights, interested enough to insist upon being treated justly, and patriotic enough to desire their country's welfare. Thus this campaign is one of information and organization."

That task was to be placed in the hands of surrogates. While the top of the ticket remained in Washington, the second man on the Democratic slate, vice presidential nominee Allen Thurman, took to the stump. Unfortunately, his efforts flagged because of age and faltering health. Nor did others fare much better in educating voters on an issue which emerged as the dominant one. On the subject of tariffs the Republican campaigners painted Cleveland and the Democrats as free traders who would sacrifice American laborers and farmers to foreign interests, especially to those of the British. Anti-Cleveland posters distributed by Democrats showed Grover against the backdrop of the Union Jack. Harrison was shown all but wrapped in the Stars and Stripes.

Republicans also stoked fears, warning that abandoning protective tariffs would result in higher taxes, lower wages, and unemployment. A Democratic victory, they declared, would mean a continued attack on veterans' pensions and retreat from and reversals in federal power in favor of the states. Instead of rising, the standard of living of Americans would slip into decline.

All of these Republican tactics were bolstered by campaign organization and leadership which the Democratic Party lacked, starting at the top. The result was more effective work by the Republicans at the grass roots, especially in the East. Of special concern was New York. The state with the most electoral votes (36), it would also be deciding whether to continue the administration of Democratic governor David B. Hill. Unfortunately, Grover and Hill had become so estranged politically that Grover refused to give Hill a formal endorsement. His enunciated rationale for this was that he felt it was not his business to meddle in the affairs of the party at the state level.

"The exercise of such judgment in the formation of tickets &c &c," he wrote to one of his New York managers, "must be left to those in whose hands party organization has placed it."

This attitude displeased Hill and his supporters and unnecessarily divided the state party as Republicans were reaping the fruits of sowing seeds of discontent among usually Democratic Irish voters. They successfully portrayed Cleveland on the tariff question as a lackey of Great Britain "employed by Ireland's cruel enemy to aid her work of enslavement."

Testing the political winds, the *New York Herald* hoisted a storm warning on a national scale. "The Democratic organization is weak," the newspaper said on August 10. "The Republicans began with an aggressive campaign and are forcing the fighting in every State. . . . While the Republican canvass shows animation the Democratic canvass droops and hangs."

The situation grew bleaker in September, but Grover remained planted in the White House. On September 29 he wrote blithely to Governor Isaac P. Gray of Indiana: "One or two quite rash Indianians have informed me lately that though they did not contemplate defeat in their State, the organization of the party there was not as close and complete as it ought to be. But these reports have caused me no uneasiness, since I have been assured that you have undertaken to look to this matter. I only want to remind you that there will be, later in the campaign, an attack made upon your forces that will be exceedingly dangerous unless all our men are in line, and touching elbows. I think the feeling is quite general in these parts that you are the best reliance for that thorough organization that appears to me to be indispensable to success."

Governor Gray's challenge was formidable. The Republican presidential candidate was from Indiana and had pledged his party to carry it. To help Harrison redeem that vow, the Indiana Republicans spared no expense. They paid $15 per vote (not in silver or greenbacks, but in gold).

The magnitude of bribery was surpassed in New York, but only because there were more voters available and Tammany Hall had raised the practice of buying ballots to an art.

As the campaign continued into October, Grover's thoughts wandered on one occasion to its end. He responded on October 15 to a letter from William A. Fisher which invited him to go duck hunting. Grover wrote enthusiastically (and a little wistfully), "I need hardly tell you how much I appreciate your effort to put me in the way of a little recreation, with freedom from official cares and labor. . . . I know I should enjoy the shooting very much, though I am not sure I should do myself any great credit. If you will let me know when the ducks are fat and plenty and tame and obliging, I will make a supreme effort to accept your invitation."

Stoic, solid, stolid, and still sticking to the White House and Oak View, he left the closing weeks of campaigning and his fate in the hands of those he trusted, and to the hearts and minds of the American voters he'd hoped to educate and inform in a belief that their intelligence would lead them to see their rights and interest them enough to insist upon being treated justly, and patriotic enough to desire their country's welfare. On Tuesday, November 6, 1888, he wrote to Dr. Ward, "This is Election Day and at the hour I write (4 P.M.), the people have determined who they will have for their next president. You know how I feel in the matter and how great will be the *personal* compensations of defeat. I am very sure that any desire I may have for success rests upon the conviction that the triumph of my party at this time means the good and the prosperity of the country. You see I am in a good mood to receive the returns whatever they may be."

The key to the outcome proved to be the states adopted as the homes of the two candidates, Harrison's Indiana and Cleveland's New York. In 1884 Grover had carried both. But now they went into Harrison's column. Of the losses the worst was New York. Although the national tally of the popular vote gave the Democrats a margin of victory of 90,000, Grover's votes in New York fell short of those given to Hill. The governor received a plurality of 19,171. Harrison won by a margin of 14,000, thereby throwing New York to the Republicans and ensuring him a lopsided win in the Electoral College (233 to 168).

When Navy Secretary Whitney broke the bad news to Grover and Frances in the White House, the president said, "Well, it's all up."

As analysts of the outcome concluded that he'd lost because of his stand on tariffs, Grover told a friend he had no regrets. "I would rather have my name to that tariff measure," he said, "than be President."

On Christmas Eve he wrote to the Massachusetts Tariff Reform Association, "Temporary defeat brings no discouragement; it but proves the stubbornness of the forces of combined selfishness, and discloses how great is the necessity of redoubled efforts. . . . In the track of reform are often found the dead hopes of pioneers and the despair of those who fall in the march. But there will be neither despair nor dead hopes in the path of tariff reform, nor shall its pioneers fail to reach the heights. Holding fast to their faith and rejecting every alluring overture and every deceptive compromise which would betray their sacred trust, they themselves shall regain and restore the patrimony of their countrymen. . . ."

A few days after Christmas a Cleveland loyalist, William B. Hornblower, called at the White House to pay his respects. He found Grover alone, sitting at his desk. Amenities of greeting and expressions of consolation regarding the defeat completed and accepted, Grover spoke of the issue which had evidently been the cause of the loss. Recalling that advisers and friends had asked him not to send Congress the tariff message, he said, "They told me that it would hurt the party; that without it, I was sure to be re-elected, but that if I sent that message to Congress, it would in all probability defeat me; that I could wait till after the election and then raise the tariff question. I felt, however, that this would not be fair to the country; the situation as it existed was to my mind intolerable and immediate action was necessary. Besides, I did not wish to be reelected without having the people understand just where I stood on the tariff question and then spring the question on them after my reelection. Perhaps I made a mistake from the party standpoint; but damn it, it was right. I have at least that satisfaction."

Hornblower responded, "Yes, Mr. President, it was right, and I want to say to you, that not only was it right, but that the young men of the country are with you and four years from now, we mean to put you back in the White House."

9

★

No Happier Man

The loss of the election was not a personal matter, Grover said to a reporter from the New York *Herald*. "It is not proper to speak of it as my defeat. It was a contest between two great parties battling for the supremacy of certain well-defined principles. One party has won and the other has lost—that is all there is to it."

Jubilant Republicans interpreted the outcome differently. They sang:

> Down in the cornfield
> Hear the mournful sound
> All the Democrats are weeping—
> Grover's in the cold, cold ground!

With four months remaining of his term, he was not a political corpse yet. However, in the colorful vernacular of American politics he was a lame duck. Although the Constitution required him to report to Congress on the state of the union, the message of

December 1888 amounted to nothing more than a formality. The only legislative agenda that mattered would be set by the new president. Writing to Harrison on February 15, Grover informed him that, according to custom, he would issue a proclamation to convene the Senate in a special session on March 4, 1889, the day Harrison would take office.

On February 22 Grover granted a retrospective interview to correspondents of *The New York Times* and the *Baltimore Sun*. "The animating spirit of the Administration was administrative reform," he said. "Not exclusive attention to any one phase of improvement in that service, but a wholesale ventilation and stirring up of all the branches of that service, the lopping off of useless limbs, the removal of the dead wood, and such a renewal of the activity by the introduction of new blood as the necessities of the service should demand."

Two weeks after the presidency passed from his hands to Benjamin Harrison's, Grover would mark his fifty-second birthday. By all measures, except for his assertions that he was tired of shouldering the daily burdens of office and was glad to surrender them, he remained as vigorous in body and mind as the bachelor who'd arrived in Washington four years earlier. Now, of course, he was married, and while he wasn't poor, he had to plan earning a living. Some newspapers claimed that he left the White House with a "private fortune." But he exited in no better financial shape than on the day he'd entered. Asserting that "a man is apt to know too much in my position that might affect matters in the least speculative," he had not played the stock market. When he did buy stocks he insisted that they not be acquired on margin, but paid for in full, and he held on to them.

To support himself and Frances after leaving Washington, he

arranged to be "of counsel" in the distinguished New York law firm of Bangs, Stetson, Tracy and MacVeagh. In that capacity he would have an office, use of the library, law clerks, and stenographers in carrying out duties as a court-appointed referee. The deal also guaranteed him no work during summers.

The move to New York meant not only finding a place to live there, but disposing of Oak View. The initial arrangement was to rent it. But he spelled out certain conditions in a long letter to the caretaker, Patrick Kiernan. The tenants would be permitted use of his road wagon and "all the horses, cows and other stock and animals upon the place." Any calves could be sold for veal, with an exception. "Any calf born of 'Grace,' the Jersey cow from Philadelphia," he insisted, "is not to be disposed of without consulting me." The farm would ultimately be sold for $100,000, a nifty profit. The area where it stood would become a Washington suburb in the twentieth century and known as Cleveland Park.

A daunting task of a different sort facing Grover and Frances was their move out of the White House. After four years, despite his policy of not accepting gifts of intrinsic value, the attic was crammed with an odd assortment of objects. Among the jumble were thousand of photographs, including scores of pictures of children who had been named after him and Frances, and many photos of children sent by proud parents who had heard that Mr. Cleveland loved children. Gallons of patent medicines and lotions had been donated by citizens concerned about the president's health. The superstitious had sent rabbits' feet and other good-luck charms. The chief executive's reported fondness for cigars had brought boxes of them. Press coverage of his fishing vacations had resulted in an unrelenting cascade of rods, flies, sinkers, hooks, and lines. Knowing their president was a hunter, kindred souls had sent guns, cartridges, belts, game baskets, duck decoys, and stool pigeons. Would-be authors and poets forwarded copies of their works. A Michigan prospector provided a gold nugget with a request that the government buy the land on which it was claimed to have been unearthed. From Utah had come a letter accompanied by "a suit of endowment garments such as are worn by the High Priests of the Mormon Church." The trove of gifts amounted to more than three thousand items, including a bust of President Garfield carved from soap, a silver-plated shoe from the famous racehorse Nancy Hanks, and a not-very-good oil painting of roses with a note attached by string which suggested, "You might feel like sending me $100 and we will be quits."

What to keep and which items were to be thrown out were Frances's decisions, she worked the hours of sorting them into a schedule of going-away parties and small luncheons for relatives, friends, and a good many Democrats who feared they would not soon have another opportunity to see the inside of the White House. On February 15 she arranged for a get-acquainted dinner for the Harrison family. The following day it was her last ladies' entertainment, a luncheon in honor of the sister of President Arthur. And on March 4, a day of thunder and heavy rain, as her husband and the incoming president departed in a carriage for the inauguration ceremony at the Capitol, she said good-bye to the White House staff. Each received an autographed picture. But as she got into a carriage to go to the Capitol she voiced a final order for one of them, Jerry Smith. "Now, Jerry, I want you to take good care of all the furniture and ornaments in the house and not let any of them get lost or broken, for I want to find everything just as it is now, when we come back again."

Puzzled, Smith asked when that might be.

With the smile that had enchanted official Washington and captivated the press, she replied, "We are coming back just four years from today."

For the time being, she and her husband would reside in the Victoria Hotel on Madison Square at Broadway and Fifth Avenue. Five weeks after leaving office, Grover wrote to Bissell, "You cannot imagine the relief which has come to me with the termination of my official term. There is a good deal which seems to result from the Presidency and the kindness of people in a social way which keeps me in remembrance of Washington life, but I feel that I am fast taking the place which I desire to reach—the place of a respectable private citizen."

In an April 19, 1889, letter to William F. Vilas, he complained. "The way I am being pelted by real estate men puts me in mind of office-seeking four years ago, and to make it more pleasant, the newspapers occasionally state that I am looking at some property in the country, which immediately lets loose a steam of offers of that kind of habitation. I shall move very quietly and deliberately and hope to, in time, suit myself."

He asked, rhetorically, "What shall be done with our ex-Presidents?" The answer, he speculated, might be one which had been recommended by Henry Watterson, editor of the *Louisville Courier-Journal*. "Take them out and shoot them."

George F. Parker wrote of Grover's transformation in lifestyle, "It was his first experience of life in a great city. The whole environment was strange to him. He accepted few invitations, made only two or three speeches—mainly in reply to conventional welcomes."

One of these was on April 27 to the New York Democratic Club. "I come to you with no excuses or apologies," he said. "No man can lay down the trust which he has held in behalf of a generous and confiding people, and feel that at all times he has met, in the best possible way, the requirements of his trust; but he is not derelict in duty if he has conscientiously devoted his effort and his judgment to the people's service. . . . We know that we have espoused the cause of right and justice. We know that we have not permitted duty to country to wait upon expediency. We know that we have not trafficked our principles for success. We know that we have not deceived the people with false promises and pretenses. And we know that we have not corrupted or betrayed the poor with the money of the rich."

★   ★   ★

The search for a house ended with the purchase of 816 Madison Avenue. Near Sixty-eighth Street, the four-story redbrick and brownstone dwelling offered numerous windows, an elegantly arched doorway, a facade with twin upper-floor turrets, and an oak-paneled drawing room. Grover and Frances furnished it simply with cheerful rugs, good pictures, comfortable chairs and sofas, and an onyx clock for the mantlepiece. On a black pedestal stood a life-size marble bust of the lady of the house. When Illinois friends suggested he make his home in Chicago, he replied, "I am now happy and contented as a resident of New York City, and am daily the grateful recipient of the kindness and consideration of her citizens. You have a wonderful City and I am glad the people of Chicago cannot monopolize the pride, due to every American, arising from her prosperity and growth. But New York State and New York City are very dear to me and I should not know how to entertain the thought of living elsewhere."

Yet he did not venture out much to partake of New York's

amenities and diversions. Going to the theater was an indulgence to be enjoyed sparingly. He preferred to stay at home in the evening playing cribbage with friends. He left home in the morning to walk a formidable way downtown to his office at 45 William Street. This trek was his only exercise. Invited by friends to take up golf, he declined. His sports were fishing and hunting. When a relatively new friend, editor Richard Watson Gilder, invited him to spend some time at Gilder's home on Cape Cod, Grover immediately asked about the quality and quantity of scaly creatures found in nearby Buzzards Bay. Informed that there was an abundance of bluefish and sea bass, he accepted Gilder's invitation for an early summer visit.

What would become a close friendship between Grover and Gilder had begun at Frances's graduation from Wells College. Gilder had given the commencement address and afterward had escorted Frances to the White House and been introduced to the president. But their first lengthy conversation did not occur until December 1886, when Gilder and his wife and young son were invited to call at the White House. The two men sat talking until about eleven o'clock. The subject which bound them was the issue of international copyright. Grover had touched on it in a previous State of the Union message and Gilder wanted him to deal with it once more. Grover informed him that the forthcoming message would be strictly on the matter of tariffs.

The relationship which evolved between Gilder and Grover would result in a volume of reminiscences by the former, *Grover Cleveland: A Record of Friendship*. Published the year after Grover died, the book provided a wealth of insights into Grover, beginning with his move to New York and the four years out of office and continuing through his second presidency and on to his

816 Madison Avenue, as it was in Cleveland's time.

retirement and death. Gilder wrote, "The book of one's life is divided into few or many volumes: some may be unhappy, some full of romance and the joy of life. Mr. Cleveland's question about the fishing possibilities of the Marion waters proved to be the opening of a volume brimming with unalloyed pleasure for a little group of friends."

Early in the first summer of Grover's forced retirement from the presidency he took Gilder up on the invitation, occupying a small cottage near Gilder's. He became so enamored of the area around Buzzards Bay that by the time the summer of 1891 rolled around, he'd bought several acres with a cottage on a small peninsula. He named the site Gray Gables.

His Cape Cod neighbors quickly discovered that the man who made a pleasure of business as president was determined to make a business of pleasure. Gilder observed this one day while he and Grover were fishing. When Gilder's attention wandered off into a daydream, he found himself rebuked. "If you want to catch fish," Grover chided, "attend strictly to business."

But the ex-president was not always so deadly serious about his angling. On one occasion he poked fun at himself. In a letter to Gilder on June 9, 1890, he wrote, "I started the fishing branch of the firm business today and am glad to report that the season promises well. I found here a feeling of depression in the trade and on every side there seemed to be the greatest apprehension for the future. I determined to test the condition and am entirely satisfied that if the industry is properly cared for and prosecuted with zeal, industry, and intelligence, satisfactory returns may confidently be relied upon." This diligence to business paid off handsomely. He caught twenty-five fish.

Afternoons and evenings at Gray Gables often involved friendly conversations in which Grover's new coterie of friends and neighbors learned that he was, as Gilder noted, "one of the very raciest of talkers and raconteurs." One new associate, the famous actor Joseph Jefferson, expressed his view that Grover had missed his vocation. Instead of entering politics, he should have gone on the stage. "With a few familiar friends," Gilder wrote, "he was the soul of good company; not dominating the conversation, but doing his

Gathered around the hearth at Gray Gables are (left to right) *Frances's mother, famed actor Joseph Jefferson, Mrs. Jefferson, Cleveland's close friend R. W. Gilder, Frances, and Mrs. Gilder.*

share of repartee and story-telling, with all the aids of wit, a good memory for detail, and, when necessary, the faculty of mimicry."

Noticeably lacking in the Cleveland circle at the Marion cottage were politicians. Nor were they in abundance in his Madison Avenue house. Old associates and visitors from out of town were usually greeted at his William Street office. Few came to his residence. Gilder found this remarkable. "Here he was, living in the city in which existed the largest and most thoroughly disciplined political machine in his party, the strongest political organization in the country. [He] might easily have permitted himself to cultivate some sort of 'pleasant relations' with the leaders of the machine. But nothing of the kind was going on."

Neither did he take advantage of his sudden freedom from

official duties to travel, except for Gray Gables for the fishing, Adirondacks outings with Dr. Bryant and others, and one trip to Buffalo in the summer of 1891 for a couple of speeches. Both avoided politics, as did others he made in his first year out of office. He declined an invitation from Chauncey F. Black to discuss politics in a speech in Philadelphia. He claimed that "duty and inclination dictate that I should, as much as possible, assume a modest position, free from any imputation of arrogating to myself special influence or control."

None of this kept his supporters from longing for his return to the political arena, and as soon as possible. When some went so far as to express their hope that he might run for president, he attempted to dissuade them by predicting that the outcome would be another party defeat. But if there was anything which might draw him back into the fray, it was what was going on regarding tariffs and other issues close to his heart in a Republican-controlled Congress under a Republican president about whom Grover had mixed feelings. Having been a president, he empathized with Benjamin Harrison's dilemmas in seeking to balance public duty and private opinion on one hand, and partisan demands on the other. But he watched with dismay as Harrison allowed a spendthrift Congress to pillage the Treasury surplus through extravagant appropriations and to be dissipated further by granting unjust and unwarranted veterans' pensions. So much money was being spent that the legislative session of 1889–1890 was called the "Billion Dollar Congress."

Grover wrote to his former interior secretary, William F. Vilas, of his amazement that "such retrogression could be made in so short a time" regarding their policy concerning Indians and public lands and concerning advances in civil service reform. He said that the people "who occupy" Washington were "fast running off the rope which I believe is bound to get about their necks."

His prediction proved correct. In the 1890 congressional election the Republicans suffered a crushing defeat. Voters handed Democrats an overwhelming majority in the House (235 to 88). In Grover's opinion the outcome constituted vindication of his policies of frugality in government and tariff reduction. Consequently, the possible return of Grover Cleveland to the political stage did not seem quite so fanciful an idea.

A week after the election he traveled to Columbus, Ohio, to attend a birthday banquet for his former vice presidential running mate, Allen Thurman. He used the occasion to attack a new protective tariff act authored by William McKinley. The audience greeted him and the tough remarks warmly. A month later, a Democratic victory celebration at Madison Square Garden gave him an ovation. January 8, 1891, found him in Philadelphia for the Jackson Day banquet of the Young Men's Democratic Association. The subject of his address was "The Principles of True Democracy," but its scope included assailing the Billion Dollar Congress. The McKinley Act was "an unjust tariff which banishes from many humble homes the comforts of life, in order that palaces of wealth [and] luxury may more abound."

The following month brought a Cleveland public protest on the passage by the Senate of a free-coinage-of-silver measure. It had won approval with the assent of many Democrats. Alarmed by this, Grover decided to speak out. Warned that he risked damaging himself politically, he would hear none of it. He said, "I am supposed to be a leader of my party. If any word of mine can check these dangerous fallacies, it is my duty to give that word, whatever the cost may be to me."

The opportunity came his way in an invitation to speak to the Reform Club of New York on February 10. He declined to attend the group's dinner meeting, but not the chance to express himself on silver. He did so in the letter he sent to E. Ellery Anderson, stating he would not be able to attend the event and proceeding to express his gladness "that the business interests of New York are at last to be heard" on a subject which he believed to be "the greatest peril" if "the scheme embraced in the measure now pending in Congress, for the unlimited coinage of silver," were adopted.

Grover's friends and allies, including Dan Lamont, were shocked, dismayed, and convinced that by focusing on silver he had thrown away any chance of a successful return to the presidency. Lamont pleaded for another letter which "would set the party back on the tariff question and away from the silver issue." Lamont proposed that "at the very outset in your letter you can in three or four sentences set the silver position aside as one on which neither party is united . . . and then take in the tariff question as the issue on which the parties divide, and give them [Democrats] something on that which could be used as a campaign leaflet."

Grover demurred, telling Shan Bissell he never felt happier than when he'd "thrown the presidency away." He said, "It seems to me that a weight has been lifted off and a cloud removed. At any rate, no one can doubt where I stand."

Taking the stand against silver, he said, had been much less difficult a decision than vetoing the Five-cent Fare Bill as governor. He told Gilder, "I am confidently looking for a return to common sense and conservative ideas in certain quarters."

That appeared to be so in the House. It voted down the Senate bill and for the moment, the free-silver issue receded. At the same time, enthusiasts for a second Grover Cleveland presidency interpreted what was now being called "the silver letter" as a signal from its author that Grover had emerged from the house on Madison Avenue and Gray Gables and back into an active role in the nation's politics. George F. Parker was one of these hopefuls, but he found "no organization, no plan, no money, for promoting the third nomination." Yet somehow the movement began to take on something like form—not from any open approval on the part of the man chiefly involved, but by his silence. He found that prominent men from outside or distant states began to ask whether he thought Mr. Cleveland might accept an invitation to speak at some Democratic celebration or banquet. Others dropped into his office to ask Parker to arrange for them to see the man who was keeping his own counsel. Parker wrote of this period of rising hopes, "I bore no official or personal relation to him [but] before long, however, I was supposed, in the mind of such persons, to be a sort of assistant or secretary, so that the reputation of managing a campaign for a Presidential nomination was thrust upon me."

★   ★   ★

George Parker directed his attention and efforts to persuading his prospective candidate to consider the hated press not as an enemy but as an asset. Toward that end Parker compiled a book of Cleveland addresses and papers for the years 1882 through 1891 and sent copies to newspapermen and editors. By encouraging Grover to make himself more available to the press, Parker created a new breed in the world of politics—the press secretary.

It was a formidable task. The organs of the "fourth estate" of the 1890s flaunted political affiliations not only on their editorial pages, but also in their news coverage. They were not interested in political objectivity and impartiality and placed no restraints on attacking opponents for traits having nothing to do with their qualifications for office.

In Cleveland's case, the easiest aspect to assault was his physical appearance. The perennial Cleveland antagonist Charles Dana peppered the *Sun* with the phrases "elephantine economist" and the "Stuffed Prophet." *The Washington Post* reported that Grover did not attend the theater because he was "too big and fat" to fit into the seats. Cartoonists delighted in exaggerating his size.

Resigned to ingrained opposition from powerful city newspapers, Parker concentrated on reaching the press on a broader scale and reaped a good deal of success. His strategy was to set up interviews with local businessmen and other leading citizens who would promote the ideas of the unofficial Cleveland-for-president movement. What the reporters did not know was that what these individuals had to say was guided and coordinated. "The note running through these interviews," Parker wrote in his book of memoirs, "was insistence upon the importance of Mr. Cleveland's nomination to the revival of business." He boasted that newspaper editors or owners never so much as suspected that they were being controlled from New York.

A hundred years before America's political lexicon included the term "spinmeister" and decades before the coining of the phrase "public relations," Parker reflected on being a manipulator and proudly noted, "One often hears of the pride which comes from the exercise of open power. But no one can exaggerate the pleasure that follows as the effect of working entirely behind the scenes when he finds his devotion to a single object thus effectively promoted by men and influences both unseen and unknown."

With these efforts afoot, the prospective candidate could not easily dismiss from his mind the possibility that his enemies within the New York State Democratic Party might not be ready to fall into step with the movement. From Gray Gables on July 3, 1891, he wrote to Dan Lamont, "My information and belief is that Tammany Hall will not aid us. They don't like me—never did and never will—and they will not help any movement with which my name is associated."

On the same day, in response to a letter from Gilder which enclosed newspaper clippings of an unflattering nature, he accepted them as "indices of the meanness and malice of men and politicians," and went on to say that he was "wondering when the bluefish will be about and biting." He next reported that he had put up "a nice flagstaff" with a "fine large flag with 44 stars upon it which early tomorrow morning will be flung on the breeze—if there is any."

Of his summer retreat he wrote, "We are all the time happy in our Gray Gables and its improvement. Every day something new is brought to light which would, if done, add to its beauty and convenience."

While Grover was penning these letters on politics, fish, and improvements at Gray Gables, he was looking forward to an event in the fall which would excite more of his fellow Americans than anything he might have to announce in the realm of politics.

Frances was pregnant.

★   ★   ★

The "blessed event" occurred in the Madison Avenue house a few minutes after midnight, October 3, 1891. The "little strong, healthy girl" he described in a letter to Parker was named Ruth.

To Shan Bissell, who was also an expectant father, he wrote, "I who have just entered the real world, and see in a small child more of a value than I have ever called my own before—fame, honor, place, everything—reach out my hand to you and fervently press the wish—the best my great friendship for you yields—that in safety and joy you may soon reach my estate."

Public delight and attention by the press over Ruth's birth became a nationwide phenomenon the equal of which would not be found in American political history until the birth of a son to President-elect and Mrs. John F. Kennedy on November 25, 1960. The popular nickname for John F. Kennedy Jr. would be "John-John." When thrilled Americans in 1891 immediately gave the Clevelands' daughter the name "Baby Ruth," a shrewd candy manufacturer immortalized it on the wrapper of a chocolate-covered peanut bar which would remain a popular candy-counter item to this day for people with a sweet tooth, who believe it was named for a baseball hero of the twentieth century, Babe Ruth.

Friends and associates of the ex-president soon remarked among themselves that the birth of Ruth had the same effect on Grover as had his wedding to Frances. He appeared to brim with happiness and contentment. He exclaimed in a letter to Dr. Joseph Bryant on December 31, "The Clevelands are at present the healthiest and happiest family in the world." To his friend George S. Hornblower, whose own little girl had sent Ruth a doll, he wrote, "I scarcely do anything just now but read the kindest messages of congratulation and receive in every possible way manifestations of the kindness which pervades the people of the land."

Kindness they offered in abundance, but would they also cast their ballots for him in 1892?

*   *   *

As the new year dawned, he certainly seemed ready and willing to seek those votes. While George Parker masterminded the press coverage of what appeared to be a popular groundswell for Cleveland, the strategy for winning the nomination on the first ballot was the result of the work of the former navy secretary, William

While living in New York, the Clevelands became the parents of a daughter, Ruth.

Whitney. "Doubt no longer existed or was possible," Parker recalled. "It was not only public sentiment to which appeal would be made, but by this time the most effective, because . . . a machine had been constructed—exclusively a Cleveland machine, having only the smallest connection with anything that was in existence at the close of the first term, or with the official organization of the party in even so much as one State."

A majority of the workers had never seen their candidate in person. Hardly any of them had spoken to Parker or Whitney. They were lawyers, doctors, businessmen, financiers, farmers, and clergymen. "I doubt that one in five of them has ever voted in a primary or was known to the local management of his party," Parker observed. "While thousands of people were engaged, lovingly and devotedly, in this task they were unaware of what others were doing, there was no commanding general, and, when it was all over, there was left no distinctively Cleveland machine which could be used again. There were no agents traveling here and there, no central newspaper dominated for both the profit and the glorification of the candidate—there was nothing but attachment to a man and a cause."

The official call for the convening of the Democratic National Convention went out early in February 1892. At the same time, Grover accepted a long-standing invitation to address students at the State University of Michigan at Ann Arbor on February 22, George Washington's birthday. His topic was to be "Sentiment in Our National Life." But another event on that date concerned Grover and his backers more than what he planned to say to the students. In an unprecedented move, the New York Democratic Party chairman, Edward Murphy, called a convention for the twenty-second to elect delegates at large for the national convention to be held on June 21. Grover and his forces interpreted the goal of this "snap convention" to be a device to ensure that the state's delegation would go to the national convention under the unit rule and be committed to Grover's old nemesis and now United States senator David B. Hill. The maneuver backfired. Democrats who had not been able to attend the snap convention because of snow-blocked roads howled in protest. The *New York World* denounced the tactic as a "midwinter folly" that was illogical, undemocratic, and unwise. Democratic newspapers across the state echoed the sentiment.

When the call for the snap convention was made, Grover was on his way back to New York from a hunting trip to Joseph Jefferson's plantation in Louisiana. When the train stopped in Baltimore, newspaper reporters thronged the railroad station. They located the former president having breakfast in a Pullman car. The *World* correspondent described for his readers a man whose face "was the picture of innocent merriment." Asked for a statement on the snap convention plan, Grover replied, "The State committee has selected a historic day. I hope the weather will be fine."

As the snap convention was meeting and following the Murphy/Hill script, Grover kept his appointment in Ann Arbor. The speech was a reverent appreciation of "the father of the country." But near the conclusion he told the students, "Interest yourself in public affairs as a duty of citizenship, but do not surrender your faith to those who discredit and debase politics by scoffing at sentiment and principle, and whose political activity consists in attempts to gain popular support by cunning devices and shrewd manipulation."

The students applauded their approval loudly and long.

Hill's endorsement by the snap convention notwithstanding, George Parker interpreted the rigged outcome as a plus for

Grover's candidacy. "From that moment the nomination campaign took on new color," he wrote, "and an activity began which, within a short time, was to involve the entire country." Meanwhile, New Yorkers for Cleveland set about arranging their own convention to name an alternative delegation. They proudly called themselves "Anti-Snappers." Headquarters for the rebellion was established at No. 57 Broadway. In charge of the propaganda campaign was Parker, who prepared a memorandum outlining action to show the Democrats nationwide not only that Grover Cleveland could carry the essential state of New York in November, but that no other candidate could.

On May 1, with Whitney in command of the campaign and Parker's information apparatus in full swing, Grover wrote to Lucius Lamar. After noting that he had passed through months that were "trying and perplexing," he slipped into his frequently gloomy mood:

> *The office of President has not, to me personally, a single allurement. I shrink from everything which another canvass and its result involve. I know what another election means, and I know the dark depth that yawns at the foot of another defeat. I would avoid either if I would consult alone my comfort, my peace, my desire. My discomfort arises from a sense of duty to honest people and devoted friends. . . . One thing I know. Forces are at work which certainly mean the complete turning back of the hands of the dial of Democracy and the destruction of party hopes. Is it ordained that I am to be the instrument through which Democratic principles can be saved—whether party supremacy immediately awaits us or not? If folly is to defeat us in any event, ought I be called upon to place myself under the falling timbers?*

244

As Grover wrote to Lamar the boom for Hill was rapidly deflating. He lost votes for convention delegates in Rhode Island and Massachusetts to Cleveland slates, followed by Georgia, widely believed to be Hill's strongest southern base. Evidently, nothing stood in the way of Grover's being nominated.

Meanwhile, Benjamin Harrison, the "human iceberg," had a moment when it appeared that presidential incumbency was not a guarantee of renomination. Suddenly in his path stood his own secretary of state, James G. Blaine. The man who had asserted four years earlier that no one who had been defeated for president was entitled to try again had changed his mind. The bid proved unavailing. The Republican convention in Minneapolis reaffirmed Harrison on the first ballot.

When Democrats convened in Chicago, the delegates found Whitney's well-oiled machine in place at the Palmer House and, with great efficiency and confidence, selling the proposition that Grover Cleveland was the only Democrat who could be elected. At five in the afternoon of June 22, nominations began. There were three contenders: Grover, Hill, and Horace Boies of Iowa. At the end of the call of the roll of states just before dawn on the twenty-third, with the New York delegation solidly behind Hill, the Cleveland column counted 10¼ more votes than the required 607. The victory was flashed by special wire to Gray Gables as Grover was unconcernedly hanging fishing lines for drying.

Chosen as his running mate was Adlai E. Stevenson, an ex-
congressman from Illinois (his grandson would run twice for president against Dwight D. Eisenhower in the 1950s). Because he was a free-silver proponent, his nomination was viewed as a conciliation to that faction of the party, as well as a chance to woo voters in agrarian Illinois at a moment when issues of importance to

farmers were being given voice by a newly organized political movement.

Launched in May 1891, the People's, or Populist, Party held its nominating convention thirteen months later and chose as its candidate James B. Weaver. The platform favored free and unlimited coinage of silver, government ownership of the railroads and telegraph and telephone systems, revocation of land grants to the railroads, a graduated income tax, postal savings banks, direct election of U.S. senators, a single term for the president and vice president, ballot initiatives and referendums, recall elections, and improvements in conditions of laborers.

As the presidential race got under way in a mood of civility and calm which earned it praise as the cleanest, quietest, and most creditable in the experience of the post–Civil War generation, the last of these issues shattered the quietude of the presidential campaign.

★   ★   ★

Like the July 1863 battle at Gettysburg, which had marked a turning point in the Civil War, a bloody drama unfolded on the steamy morning of July 1, 1892, at a steel plant owned by Andrew Carnegie. In the town of Homestead on the banks of the Monongahela River a few miles upstream from Pittsburgh, the plant had operated since 1889 under terms of an agreement on wages with a labor union. The Amalgamated Association of Iron and Steel Workers was part of Gompers's AFL, with a membership of about a quarter of a million. As its collective bargaining agreement with Carnegie's Homestead operation neared expiration in June, the company had insisted that wages be cut back. The goal was to break the union. This plan culminated in a notice written by Carnegie which asserted that "there has been forced upon the Firm the question Whether its Works are to be run by 'Union' or 'Non-Union.'" The notice decreed it "will be necessarily Non-Union after the expiration of the present agreement."

As the industrialist departed for a vacation in his native Scotland, he left the dictum in the hands of Homestead's manager,

The 1892 strike at Andrew Carnegie's Homestead steel plant was broken up by armed Pinkerton guards backed by the Pennsylvania militia.

Henry Clay Frick, with orders to Frick to post it at Frick's discretion. The manager not only did so with pleasure, he locked out all union workers and hired three hundred men from the Pinkerton Detective Agency at $15 a week per man to keep them out. When the small private army arrived at the plant on barges to take up posts, they were met by five thousand angry steelworkers. Shots were fired and a ferocious battle got under way. When it ended with the Pinkertons routed, ten men were dead and more than sixty had been wounded. But in the next phase of the struggle the union men found themselves in a confrontation with the Pennsylvania militia. At the request of Sheriff William H. McCleary, the governor of Pennsylvania, Robert E. Pattison, ordered eight thousand troops to Homestead to guard the plant. Under their protection, Frick succeeded in smashing the union by employing unaffiliated laborers.

Expressing outrage at the Homestead affair, Grover said it showed "the tender mercy the workingman receives from those made selfish and sordid by unjust governmental favoritism." He denounced the "exactions wrung from [labor] to build up and increase the fortunes" of capitalists and said workers "have the right to insist on the permanency of their employment."

The remarks were made in a nomination acceptance speech before twenty thousand party faithful at Madison Square Garden. It was his only major public appearance of the campaign. Rather than go on a speaking tour, he chose to spend the summer at Gray Gables. But stacks of correspondence to be answered afforded him little time for relaxation.

On July 24 he griped to William Vilas about the press's attention, "You know I am watched like a suspected criminal."

On the twenty-ninth of July, with the memory of the Homestead bloodshed nagging him, he wrote to Carter H. Harrison, editor of the *Chicago Times*, "I am thinking a good deal lately about the relations between labor and capital and the conditions and prospects of our laboring men." With the letter went the text of his congressional message on labor, along with a plea to Harrison for his newspaper's endorsement.

When asked by another editor for a photograph of Mrs. Cleveland which he wished to reproduce in a publication called *Once a Week*, Grover replied, "I am exceedingly anxious to shield her as much as possible from any notoriety, and especially as is connected with a political campaign. The *New York World* has lately published a number of her pictures, and notwithstanding good intentions, has greatly annoyed her and myself; and I ask you as a special favor to forego carrying out your design."

From Gray Gables on September 16 went a note to Richard Watson Gilder: "My judgment is decidedly in favor of making my headquarters here for some time to come. I *know* it would be good politics for me to go to New York for good until nearly the end of the campaign, but I don't seem to be running things much. Take my advice, my dear friend, and *never run for President.*"

He closed the letter with, "Mrs. Cleveland and the BABY are as well as possible and both would send love if they were awake. I wish you were here to fish with me."

Gray Gables saw a steady flow of visitors, some of whom added the spot to an itinerary which took them first to nearby Fall River to take in the scene of a murder case which provided Americans in the summer of 1892 more excitement than the presidential campaign.

The suspect was a "spinster" named Elizabeth Borden who stood accused of hacking to death her father and stepmother. Neither the horror of the grisly double murder nor Elizabeth's controversial acquittal prevented widespread singing of a macabre ditty:

> Lizzie Borden took an axe
> And gave her mother forty whacks;
> When she saw what she had done
> She gave her father forty-one.

Another woman attracting attention during the campaign, though nowhere nearly as much as Lizzie, was Mary Ellen Lease. Campaigning for the Populist ticket, the attractive, thirty-seven-year-old Irish-American from Wichita, Kansas, exhorted farmers to "raise less corn and more hell." Fond of excoriating the wealthy and the powerful, she claimed that "Wall Street owns the country" and that the "great common people" were slaves to the master monopoly. Among her complaints: "The West and South are bound and prostrate before the manufacturing East." "The parties lie to us." "Kansas suffers from two great robbers, the Sante Fe Railroad and the loan companies." And "Over 10,000 shop-girls in New York are forced to sell their virtue for the bread their niggardly wages deny them." Her demands were "money, land, and transportation," abolition of national banks, and "the power to make loans direct from the government."

Except for the Populists' call for an end to high tariffs, the man who believed government was not in the business of supporting the people found nothing appealing in Mrs. Lease's program and rhetoric. Especially offensive to him in Populist propaganda was the upstart party's contention that there was no difference between Republicans and Cleveland Democrats. The Populist paper, *National Economist*, had declared on May 14, "It is universally known that the entire body of economic legislation enacted by the Republican party during the period of its ascendency had been dictated or inspired by interests localized within the plutocratic circle which comprises New York, New Jersey, and Pennsylvania. It has not perhaps been so generally recognized that the species of Democracy known as Clevelandism seeks to go beyond the Republicans in the direction of compliance with the grasping demands of the moneyed and monopolistic interests in the same circumscribed section."

These affronts notwithstanding, and appreciating that the popularity of the Populists in Colorado, Idaho, North Dakota, Wyoming, and Lease's Kansas posed a threat to the Republican strength in those states, Clevelandites chose not to enter a slate of presidential electors in them. The party threw its support to Populist electors in hopes of keeping the states out of the Harrison column. It was shrewd politics, but in hindsight it was unnecessary. Grover won the presidency in a landslide the like of which had not been seen since Lincoln was reelected in 1864. The Democrats found themselves blinking in amazement at carrying New York, New Jersey, Connecticut, and Indiana, and almost winning all the electors in the Republican bastions of Ohio and Michigan. The final popular vote for Grover was 5,556,000. Harrison earned 5,175,000. Weaver had 1,041,000. The Electoral College tally was 277 for Cleveland and 145 for Benjamin Harrison.

★　★　★

George Parker saw in the man whom he had helped reelect as president the most striking civilian figure to occupy the White House since the days of Lincoln. "He attracted notably the attention of students of history, and, though not college-bred, college professors and young men fresh from their studies had turned to him in a wonderful way. After all the political vagaries of the preceding twenty-five years, here was a man about whom nobody could make any mistake. He had been brave enough to send to Congress his celebrated tariff message of 1887, though he saw that it might, as it undoubtedly did, defeat him for re-election. So, in 1892, his renewed declaration, shortly before the convention, for the gold standard, might defeat his renomination; but he gave it forth against the protest of friends. All knew . . . that a choice of Cleveland would be a declaration for (1) old-fashioned Democratic ideas of the Constitution; (2) economies; (3) merit as the ultimate test for appointment to office; (4) tariff reform; (5) the gold standard. His party, knowing that he stood for all those things, nominated him; and because the people also stood firmly for them, they elected him."

Newspaper editor Lawrence Godkin, who in the paternity scandal of the 1884 campaign had expressed preference for Grover's private unchastity over Blaine's public corruption, also attributed Grover's 1892 triumph to the "young voters who have come to the stage since the reign of passion and prejudice came to an end, and the era of discussion has opened. If the canvass has consisted largely of appeals to reason, to facts, to the lessons of human experience, it is to Mr. Cleveland, let us tell them, that they owe it. But they are indebted to him for something far more valuable than this— for an example of Roman constancy under defeat, and of patient reliance upon the power of deliberation and persuasion on the American people. Nothing is more important, in these days of boodle, of cheap bellicose patriotism, than that this confidence in the might of common sense and sound doctrine and free speech should be kept alive."

All that Godkin and Parker said was true, but what is remembered about the election of 1892 is that for the only time in history, American voters elected a president to serve a second, nonconsecutive term. On election night in a house he had acquired on West Fifty-first Street in New York City, Grover accepted the results somberly. "It is a solemn thing," he had often said, "to be President of the United States." Now he told those who'd gathered round him, "We must hear, above victorious shouts, the call of our fellow countrymen to public duty, and we must put on a garb befitting public servants."

10

⚜ ★ ⚜

As Sound as a Dollar

Struggles between labor and capital so vividly demonstrated by the Homestead incident and other clashes, along with the discontent in agrarian America being exploited by the Populists, might not have seemed to the people of the United States of that time to be manifestations of a significant change in the nature of their nation. Like the Lizzie Borden murder trial, they were merely current events to be read in newspapers and talked about in parlors of homes or during Saturday marketing. Ordinary people are usually too busy with their lives to notice that they are in the midst of changes which will be judged by later generations as historic. Yet the voters who'd chosen to send Grover Cleveland back to the White House lived in an America which had been transforming itself even in the four years since he'd been voted out of office in 1888.

It was a process of both a revolutionary and an evolutionary nature that had been going on since the last shot had been fired in the Civil War. That farmers in the West complained about the power of railroads was because "the iron horse" had expanded rapidly westward. Places considered remote frontiers before the war had been linked not only by steel rails but by telegraph lines. What had been market towns had blossomed into cities. Improved transportation and communication ~~to and~~ with those places brought even more expansion and with it a demand for products of industries reliant upon the availability of finances, thereby magnifying the power of banking institutions and investment resources which were in the hands of a few men answerable to no one and able to control politicians and, therefore, government. The consequence of such concentration of wealth was class division, which in turn required organization of workers into unions led by men such as Samuel Gompers. The year 1890 had witnessed more strikes than any other time in the century. For farmers who had no one to strike against, the only recourse was grassroots political action advocated by the likes of Mary Ellen Lease and the formation of Farmers' Alliances.

It was a period of unrest which Cleveland-era historian Horace Samuel Merrill called "the pentecost of politics" and which formed the foundation of a Cleveland victory that carried in on its coat-tails a House of Representatives and a Senate controlled by Democrats for the first time since the presidency of James Buchanan. So overwhelming was the triumph that the *New York Herald* saw the Republicans "fallen to pieces."

How unified were Democrats? Not very. One needed only to look at the top of the ticket. Grover was gold standard; his running mate, now Vice President-elect Stevenson, was free silver. That fault line extended throughout the party leadership and rank and file. Another formed around tariffs. The same divisions extended across a post-Civil War country that would have been mostly unrecognizable to Lincoln and his successors in the years of Recon-struction. As Grover prepared for a second administration he was the inheritor of an economic system which had already begun a transformation when he was a nineteen-year-old lad called "Big Steve" arriving in Buffalo, New York, in 1855 without a clue as to what he might make of his life.

★   ★   ★

Conditions on March 4, 1893, went a long way toward dispelling a widely held belief that wherever Grover went he would find fine "Cleveland weather." When he again placed his left hand on the Bible his mother had given him as a boy, with a bookmark inserted at the Ninety-first Psalm, verse 12 ("They shall bear thee up in their hands, lest thou dash thy foot against a stone"), the crowd in front of the Capitol stood in snow and a cold drizzle. The oath was administered by Chief Justice Fuller. The inaugural address was brief, much to the relief of the shivering audience. But that evening during a reception in the White House library above the Blue Room, the climate turned warmer. "There gradually stole upon some of us the suspicion something was wrong," wrote Gilder. "Upon investigation it was found that electric light wires had set the silk covering of the east wall of the Blue Room on fire. A lad-der was quickly brought and the fire was extinguished before much damage was done. The family and guests did not let the incident mar the pleasure of the evening, and no publicity was given the occurrence."

In the twenty-twenty hindsight of history, if one believes in auguries, the bad weather and the fire could be interpreted as ill omens. But as Gilder observed the twenty-second president of the

United States inaugurated as the twenty-fourth, he found Grover in "a hopeful and even elevated state of mind." In those around him there was "a decided feeling of elation because of the popular vindication of his lonely and courageous stand, especially in the matter of sound money."

Discussion of the currency had taken up much of his inaugural address. He promised tariff reform in the interests of the people,

President Cleveland at the start of his second term.

restraints on trusts, and maintenance of the gold standard. At the moment he spoke, the Treasury's reserves amounted to a perilously low $100,982,410, a sum which had been sustained only after the Harrison administration had borrowed $6 million from New York banks. This dire situation was a result of the Sherman Silver Purchase Act. It required the government to purchase four million ounces of silver a month at market price and required that silver coinage and paper money (greenbacks) be redeemable for gold. Grover was urged by gold-standard business leaders and members of his new Cabinet to seek its immediate repeal.

Named to the Cabinet were Walter Q. Gresham, secretary of state; John G. Carlisle at the Treasury Department; Richard S. Olney, attorney general; J. Sterling Morton (the father of Arbor Day) to run the Department of Agriculture; Hoke Smith, resuming his post as secretary of the interior; Hilary A. Herbert, secretary of the navy; and longtime friends Wilson "Shan" Bissell as postmaster general and Dan Lamont as secretary of war.

"Although it was not a strong cabinet," Richard E. Welch Jr. wrote in his analysis of the Cleveland presidencies, "it would prove to be a loyal and unified cabinet. In his official family, Cleveland would find the solace of agreement and friendship, but he would receive no criticism or correction when those offerings might have served him better than unanimity. Few of its members had played an important role in party politics, and they would have little influence with party members in Congress. In the coming battles over the currency and the tariff, they would not be able to furnish the political finesse their chief both lacked and disdained."

If through that wonder of technology which since the Civil War had captured America's imagination and countless images of individuals there could have been available to the members of the Cabinet a photograph of the state of the country's economy, the president's men would have looked at an unsettling panorama. From Atlantic to Pacific they could have counted sixty million countrymen, fifteen times the population a hundred years earlier. The vast majority of them lived on farms with costs of production going up and the prices paid for their produce continuing on a downward spiral that had been proceeding for a decade. A farmer's profit margin was so slender and his land and everything on it were so deep in debt that, like the Texans who had been denied federal funds to buy seed to recover from a drought, the next climatic calamity meant being wiped out. Manufacturers whose survival depended on selling wares to them were so overstocked that one business group, the National Association of Stove Manufacturers, complained there were too many stoves and not enough people to buy them. Protective tariffs kept prices on foreign-made goods so high that few could afford them, resulting in a decline in imports. Much of the revenue that was collected through customs levies and in other payments to the government was received not in gold but in greenbacks and silver certificates. And Congress had been on a four-year spending spree, doling out revenue faster than it came in from all sources.

All of this would quickly beset the Cabinet and the man who had vindicated his wife's promise of March 4, 1889, to the household staff at 1600 Pennsylvania Avenue that the Clevelands would be back to take up residence again in exactly four years.

Upon Frances's return she found significant changes. As the inauguration-night fire in the library above the Blue Room demonstrated, gas lighting had been replaced by electricity. One tele- phone had become several, requiring an operator. An immediate alteration in White House routines and in the layout of the residence quarters of the Executive Mansion was the devoting of one of the chambers to Baby Ruth.

Soon after the Clevelands returned to the White House, a letter arrived for the child from Mark Twain. It began, "My Dear Ruth," and went on to explain, "I belong to the Mugwumps, and one of the most sacred rules of our order prevents us from asking favors of officials or recommending men to office, but there is no harm in writing a friendly letter to you and telling you that an infernal outrage is about to be committed by your father in turning out of office the best consul I know (and I know a great many) just because he is a Republican and a Democrat wants his place. I can't send any message to the President, but the next time you have a talk with him concerning such matters I wish you would tell him about Captain Mason [Frank Mason, consul general in Frankfort, Germany] and what I think of a government that so treats its efficient officials."

The reply from Grover stated, "Miss Ruth Cleveland begs to acknowledge the receipt of Mr. Twain's letter and say that she took the liberty of reading it to the President, who desires her to thank Mr. Twain for his information, and to say to him that Captain Mason is not to be disturbed in the Frankfort Consulate. The President also desires Miss Cleveland to say that if Mr. Twain knows of any other cases of this kind he will be greatly obliged if he will write him concerning them at his earliest convenience."

Another Republican whose job was on the line was Theodore Roosevelt. As a reward for campaigning for Harrison in 1888, he had been appointed a member of the U.S. Civil Service Commission. As a member of the New York State Legislature, he had worked well with Governor Cleveland, but he had no expectation of being reappointed to the commission by a Democrat, no matter how warm their past relationship.

"When I leave on March fifth," he remarked, "I shall at least have the knowledge that I have certainly not flinched from trying to enforce the law during these four years, even if my progress has been at times a little disheartening."

When he picked up rumors that Grover Cleveland harbored no grudge against him for his campaigning against a fellow reformer, Roosevelt was surprised and delighted, but dubious. As the prospect of his being offered reappointment grew more likely, Harrison's secretary of the navy, Benjamin Tracy, urged TR to accept. "Well, my boy, you have been a thorn in our side during four years," he said. "I earnestly hope that you will remain to be a thorn in the side of the next Administration."

To the satisfaction of reformers and Mugwumps such as Mark Twain, Roosevelt accepted reappointment and served in the post for two years. When he resigned in March 1895 it was not because he was displeased with Grover, or the president with him. He accepted appointment by a reform mayor of New York to the city's board of police commissioners with virtual carte blanche to clean up and reform the largest and most corrupt police department in the country. When his three fellow commissioners elected him head of the board, he heard himself addressed as President Roosevelt, which sounded good to those like Senator Henry Cabot Lodge, who envisioned the day when Roosevelt would surely inherit that "higher kingdom."

That Roosevelt had a future, Grover also did not doubt. He told Gilder, "Don't make any mistake; your friend Roosevelt is a good deal of a politician."

Yet between 1889 and 1893, the only time the young Republican with the promising future received an invitation to dinner at the White House was when it came, not from the president of his party, but from Democrat Grover Cleveland.

With Daniel Lamont now running the War Department (presumably with an eye toward avoiding embarrassments to his president and friend such as the Confederate battle-flags flap), a new confidential secretary was required. Grover chose Robert Lincoln O'Brien, a young man who had acted in that capacity during the campaign. He found much to do, including assisting Grover in dealing with another onslaught of office seekers and visits by congressmen and senators, each with a favorite candidate for whatever job needed filling. These demands on presidential time became so great that Grover issued an executive order that sent a shock wave through the capital:

> The time which was set apart for the reception of Senators and Representatives had been almost entirely spent in listening to applications for office, which have been bewildering in volume, perplexing and exhausting in their iterations, and impossible of remembrance. A due regard for public duty obliges me to decline, from and after this date, all personal interviews with those seeking appointments to office, except as I on my own motion may especially invite them. Applicants for office will only prejudice their prospects by repeated importunity and by remaining in Washington to await results.

Dispensing with an abundance of job seekers and their allies proved an easy matter, but the pressing problems of the shortage of gold in the U.S. Treasury, tariff reform, and other aspects of a troubling and silver-surplus-troubled economy could not be handled with the stroke of a pen and the issuance of a press statement. Neither could the president, simply through words, quell a rising tide of apprehension among Americans about the soundness of dollars in their pockets and in banks, all of which they were assured had the backing of the U.S. Treasury's store of gold, which would never be permitted to fall below $100 million.

On April 20, as a result of foreign and domestic demands for conversions of silver for gold, it did just that. Unfortunately, Secretary of the Treasury Carlisle was sloppy in the wording of a statement, approved by the president, that was intended to be a reassuring signal as to the health of the national coffers. Carlisle said the Treasury would meet demands for payments in gold "so long as it has gold lawfully available for the purpose." As a result of this ambiguous declaration, nervous Americans and foreign investors jumped to the conclusion that the abandonment of the gold standard was in the offing, and sooner rather than later.

Informed of Carlisle's remark, an unofficial Cleveland adviser, financier Francis Lynde Stetson, advised Grover in an urgent message from New York on the night of the twenty-second. "The situation here tonight is such that I do not feel it consistent with my personal regard for you and your Administration to withhold the expression of my opinion . . . upon the financial question. Gold today has gone to a premium. . . . There is a general feeling of alarm, not among Republicans alone, but among your warm and sincere supporters, and this feeling is not confined to Wall Street, but is affecting the mercantile community, which is unable to obtain the necessary banking accommodations, and consequently feels not merely alarmed but a severe pinch. The situation is such that no careful observer will be astonished at a pronounced and serious panic at any moment."

Grover issued a statement to reassure doubters that he had no intention of taking the government off the gold standard and that demands for payment of government notes in gold would be honored.

In the world in April 1893 there existed few more careful observers of Wall Street and the general national economy than the man who had broken the back of the Homestead steelworkers' union. Rather than panicking, Andrew Carnegie had found reassurance. He wrote to Grover on April 22 that he believed that "the decision to pay notes in gold saved this country from panic" and had reassured foreigners who "had taken alarm and begun to withdraw their capital in gold." But Carnegie urged further action.

"Unless all doubt is put to rest," he went on, "there is still great danger of the country being drained of its gold. Had Secretary Carlisle's statement been unequivocal, this trouble would not have arisen. All excitement can be allayed and the crisis safely passed by a simple declaration from you. If I might suggest, somewhat like the following: 'As long as I am President of the United States, the workingman is going to be paid in as good a dollar as the foreign banker is.' "

Carnegie also proposed that such a statement would be "good politics."

The president's response came the next day. He issued the following statement to the United Press:

The inclination on the part of the public to accept newspaper reports concerning the intentions of those charged with the management of our national finances seems to justify my emphatic contradiction of the statement that the redemption of any kind of Treasury notes, except in gold, has at any time been determined upon or contemplated by the Secretary of the Treasury or any other member of the present Administration. The President and his Cabinet are absolutely harmonious in the determination to exercise every power conferred upon them to maintain the public credit and to preserve the parity between gold and silver and between all financial obligations of the Government.

Unhappily for Grover and innumerable others, this attempt to keep a spark from flaring into the flames of financial panic failed. On May 4, three days after Grover had traveled to Chicago to open the World's Columbian Exposition, a firm which appeared to be one of the steadiest in the nation, the National Cordage Company, went into bankruptcy, causing the already jittery stock market to take a nosedive.

Back in Washington, Grover awoke on May 5 not only to this painful news from Wall Street, but with a tender swelling in the roof of his mouth. Dismissing the ache as probably an inflammation caused by a bad tooth, he went to work as usual. On his agenda was preparation of the announcement banning congressmen and senators from using the occasion of White House receptions to lobby him on behalf of office seekers. Also on his desk was a stack of letters, formal resolutions passed by various groups, and newspaper editorials urging him to convene a special session of Congress to repeal the Sherman Silver Purchase Act. While he understood the reasoning behind these pleadings, he did not wish to rush the matter. Preferring instead to build up the gold reserve while allaying fears through expressions of confidence in the soundness of the currency, he decided that a call for a special session could wait until the end of July.

★ ★ ★

On the White House calendar in May and June was a series of dinners, receptions, and other social events, averaging several a week. The faltering economy notwithstanding, protocol and custom demanded that the president and his charming wife make themselves available to be seen and greeted. State receptions were mobbed. Daytime events held by Mrs. Cleveland for "the ladies" attracted so many attendees, including men, that there was not enough space to accommodate all of them at once.

To bring order out of the chaos, visitors to receptions were organized into lines. And to speed the process of greeting the president, Mrs. Cleveland, and others arrayed to meet the guests, each visitor gave his or her name to a presidential assistant, who then whispered it to Grover and each of the others in turn. One of the callers was a man named Decker. But when he found himself in front of the president, Grover gave his hand a quick shake and said, "Happy to meet you, Mr. Cracker." Passed on to Frances, he heard, "Happy to meet you, Mr. Baker." Next came Mrs. Whitney, who said, "Happy to meet you, Mr. Black."

On Easter Monday of 1893 the coincidence of the traditional egg roll on the south lawn and one of the ladies' receptions brought two thousand visitors into the mansion while twenty thousand children and their parents thronged the grounds and left them a trampled and muddy ruin. But the highlight of the spring socials was European royalty in the person of the Infanta Eulalia of Spain.

The visit by the daughter of the king of Spain was intended as a goodwill gesture at a time when a noisy segment of American public opinion was calling for the United States to intervene in the Spanish colony of Cuba to assist Cuban rebels in kicking the

Spaniards out. Accompanied by her consort, Prince Antoine, and nineteen Spanish nobles, the Infanta swept into the Executive Mansion on May 22 and was received in the Red Room. The following evening she was honored with a state banquet in the East Room. Official Washington had not become quite so excited over a woman since Frances Cleveland's debut as first lady in 1886.

Yet as fascinating as the lady of Spain was, she could not hope to surpass the first lady in the attention of Washingtonians and the people's eyes and ears in the nation's capital in the form of the press.

Frances Cleveland with Ruth (right) and Esther,
the first child born in the White House.

All of them discovered that the beautiful twenty-one-year-old girl who had captured their hearts and a president's seven years earlier was a more mature and self-confident woman of twenty-eight. Some keen observers of her fuller figure speculated that Baby Ruth might soon have a sibling.

They were right; a second daughter, Esther, would enter the world on September 9, adding another distinction to the Cleveland presidency—the first child born in the White House. When the arrival was announced a sizable segment of the American public expressed disappointment that Ruth had not been given a little brother. Frances wrote to Mrs. Daniel Manning of Esther, "She is a sweet baby, looking much as Ruth did at her age, with dark eyes

During Cleveland's second term, he and Frances frequently escaped to a house in Washington called Woodley.

and hair. All here are pleased that she is a girl, however disappointed the nation may be."

As in his first term, Grover did not welcome the spotlight on his private life, especially in view of the fact that the nation's "First Family" had indeed become a family. Once again he looked for a place where they could escape constant scrutiny. Not having shared Frances's confidence on March 4, 1889, that the Clevelands would be returning to the White House on March 4, 1893, he'd sold Oak View. After failing to acquire the house of Admiral David D. Porter at 1710 H Street as a retreat, he leased an estate near Oak View. Called Woodley, it was owned by Oak View neighbor Philip Barton Key. Although the Clevelands did not own Woodley, they came to regard it, like Oak View, as their true home in Washington.

Fleeing to Woodley provided private citizen Grover Cleveland a welcome respite from constant public scrutiny, but as June neared its close there was no place where *President* Cleveland could go to escape the deepening crisis in the economy, accompanied by a rising clamor for action. As a result, a month sooner than he'd planned, he issued a call for Congress to convene in a special session on August 7 to take up repeal of the silver-purchase law.

The announcement was made on June 30 while Grover was on his way out of Washington for a visit to New York City. The declared purpose of the excursion was to board the yacht *Oneida*, owned by one of Grover's circle of friends, Commodore E. C. Benedict, for a leisurely cruise up to Grover's summer retreat, Gray Gables, at Buzzards Bay.

The real reason, noted by Daniel Lamont on a draft of the special-session declaration, was "on account of illness."

The secretary of war had joined a conspiracy of silence a few days after the White House physician had examined the sore spot on Grover's palate. He'd found a lump the size of a quarter dollar and declared it malignant. To be sure, he sent a tissue specimen to Dr. William H. Welch of Johns Hopkins Hospital in Baltimore, who confirmed that it was cancerous. When Grover's friend and fishing companion Dr. Bryant reported the finding to Grover, he advised, "Were it in my mouth, I would have it removed at once."

Grover's preference was to wait until Congress had convened. Bryant retorted that he could not assume responsibility for any delay. Grudgingly, the president consented to surgery, but only if his condition be kept secret. He insisted that the public's awareness that their president was ill might cause a panic. Accepting

Cleveland's longtime friend and fishing companion Dr. Joseph Bryant, who helped arrange for Cleveland to undergo his operation for cancer of the mouth aboard the yacht Oneida.

Grover's demand, Bryant coordinated the arrangements with Lamont. On June 20 he reported that he'd enlisted the services of Dr. W. W. Klein, a Philadelphia surgeon and one of the most distinguished medical men in the country. Others recruited were Dr. E. G. Janeway, a general physician, and Dr. Ferdinand Hasbrouck, a dentist, both of New York. The procedure would be carried out aboard the *Oneida* as she sailed up the East River from Pier A. Reporting to Lamont, Bryant couched the next recommendation in code: "I think our friend should go aboard on Friday night or at all events early Saturday."

The conspiratorial atmosphere thickened in another message to Lamont on June 20. "Do you not think there should be a cipher code, which can be used? It seems to me that this will be especially important in case anything unfavorable happens. If anything springs a leak 'it may not be amiss. . . .'"

The Oneida *was owned by Commodore E. C. Benedict, shown with Cleveland and Frances at an earlier date.*

The date agreed upon for the president to be in New York was June 30. He arrived that evening in the company of Secretary of War and Mrs. Lamont and Dr. Bryant, with no one observing them thinking anything was afoot other than the beginning of a presidential vacation. No one knew that a team of doctors was already on board the yacht. Certainly, nobody watching from Pier A could have suspected that the president was in New York for a grim purpose. He settled into a deck chair, lit a cigar, and chatted until midnight as though he were a man without a care. And while the yacht remained dockside within sight of Bellevue Hospital through the night, whatever worries he might have had in mind didn't keep him from getting a good night's sleep without need of a painkiller or sedative. Nor was he distracted from reading the morning newspapers and eating a full breakfast as the yacht got under way. The only person on board who exhibited any anxiety about the secrecy surrounding the operation was Dr. Bryant. He joked to the captain, "If you hit a rock, hit it good and hard, so that we will all go to the bottom!"

The procedure took place in the saloon, stripped of all furnishings except an organ, which was bolted to the floor. A chair for the patient was placed against the mast. The initial anesthetic was nitrous gas. But when it failed to put Grover to sleep, ether was used. Thirty-one minutes after it took effect, the operation was over. In that brief but tense time, as the *Oneida* plied the waters of the East River at half speed, the dentist pulled two upper left bicuspids and the surgeon removed the entire left upper jaw from the first bicuspid to just beyond the last molar, and part of the palate.

Three days later, the president was on his feet. When the yacht docked at Buzzards Bay on July 5, he went ashore unassisted and walked to Gray Gables. On the seventeenth, a small piece of palate tissue was examined and removed as a precaution. Declaring the surgery a success, the doctors judged the patient to have been as docile and courageous as anyone in their experience. In due course a rubber prosthesis was fitted to form an artificial jaw, which proved undetectable.

Yet one newspaperman, E. J. Edwards, who wrote articles for the *Philadelphia Press* under the pseudonym "Holland," published a story claiming that President Cleveland had had part of his jaw removed. Although no one appeared to believe the account, the White House issued a denial. It was bolstered by a letter from one of Cleveland's Buzzards Bay neighbors to another Philadelphia paper, *Public Ledger*. L. Clarke Davis attested, "I have seen the President at intervals since he first came to Buzzards Bay this summer, passing hours and days in his company and in the boat fishing with him. I passed all of last Monday with him, fishing, and I have never seen him in better health, never stronger, physically or mentally, and I consider him in both respects the healthiest man I know of."

So successful was the lie (the term "cover-up" was for a political and journalistic future which no one in 1893 could possibly have imagined), and so good was everyone involved at preventing the "leak" which had worried Dr. Bryant, that a full account of Grover's cancer and its concealment would not be revealed for a quarter of a century.

There were clues that all had not been well with the president; he looked a little thinner, a bit wan, with a tendency to tire, and he was not as even-tempered as usual—but there were ample reasons to explain this in a president who had to deal with an economy which in that summer had gone from what journalists of the day and future historians concurred in calling "The Great Panic of 1893" into a full-scale depression.

The special session of Congress convened as ordered on August 7. Awaiting them was a message from the president. Repeal of the Sherman Act, he said, would result in erasing all doubt that the government intended to remain solvent. Without mentioning gold, he warned that if the wholesale buying of silver continued, the result would be an economy based on it, with disastrous effects on America's financial standing in the world. He blamed no one for getting the country into such a perilous predicament. But to continue on such a course, he said, would be ruinous.

With the issue laid before it, Congress began debating in an atmosphere of suspense. In the House of Representatives, with its constitutional responsibility to originate all money bills, the oratory on both sides of the issue from both sides of the aisle was often eloquent. But not until the sixteenth did it truly soar in the person of a Democratic congressman from Nebraska who was so highly appreciated as a speaker that he'd earned the nickname "Boy Orator of the Platte." Intending to speak for only an hour in the cause of silver, William Jennings Bryan went for three. The question was not just gold versus silver, he declared, but "the corporate interests of the United States, the moneyed interests, aggregated wealth and capital, imperious, arrogant, compassionless" on one side and on the other "an unnumbered throng, those who gave to the Democratic party a name and for whom it has assumed to speak. Workworn and dust-begrimed, they make their mute appeal, and too often find their cry for help beat in vain against the outer walls, while others, less deserving, gain ready access to legislative halls."

When the roll was called on August 28, repeal passed overwhelmingly—239 to 108. The Senate would debate for two months before passing it 48 to 37. By all accounts, Grover had won a remarkable victory through lobbying and the power of his personal influence. Said the *New York World*, "Praise is due first to the Administration of Grover Cleveland, which has stood like a rock for unconditional repeal."

No less glowing in praise was the *Times*, stating that "between the lasting interests of the nation and the cowardice of some, the craft of others, in his own party, the sole barrier was the enlightened conscience and the iron firmness of Mr. Cleveland."

Unfortunately for Grover, his party, and the country, the victory halted neither the depression nor the gold drain. In January 1894 the reserve stood at only $65 million. When "silver congressmen" sought to force the Treasury to turn its silver bullion cache into coinage (a tactic known as seigniorage), the bill passed the House and Senate speedily. Grover just as quickly vetoed it with the argument that overvalued silver dollars were a dangerous form of inflation. With the amount of gold on hand continuing to slide and public confidence following it downward, Grover seized upon an 1875 law which he interpreted as empowering the president to unilaterally float a bond issue. He vowed to use such authority "whenever and as often as it becomes necessary to maintain a sufficient gold reserve and in abundant time to save the credit of our country."

He would do so twice between February and November 1894, with disappointing results. Meanwhile, there came a day in April when all Grover had to do to find Congressman Bryan's work-worn and dust-begrimed legions was to look through the White House windows.

11

Think of It!

On the ninth of March 1894, one year and five days into his second nonconsecutive term as president, Grover penned a letter to his friend and ally Charles H. Fairchild that was a mixture of personal worry about his friend's health, expression of disappointment over Fairchild's opposition to a nomination to the post of internal revenue collector, and an occasion for the writer to voice a familiar complaint.

"Necessarily I have passed through a sort of hide-thickening process," Grover wrote, "but in the midst of the various attacks from quarters not unexpected, I am desirous of holding, if I can, the friends whose encouragement and support I not only need but *desire*."

On March 18 he wrote to Don Dickinson, thanking the postmaster general for recalling that the date was the president's fifty-seventh birthday. Again he took the opportunity to grumble. He told Dickinson, "These are days of especial perplexity and depression and the path of public duty is unusually rugged; therefore it is that any proof of continual confidence and affection of friends is intensely welcome. I thank you from the bottom of my heart."

Exactly what a citizen by the name of Jacob Coxey was doing on those dates isn't known, but there is no doubt that the Ohioan was a very disgruntled fellow. A short, bespectacled man with a wife (Lucille), a daughter (Mame), and a son, Jacob, called "Legal Tender," Coxey was a silverite and Populist with an idea which he believed was the solution to the country's economic mess. The way out of the depression, he had proposed in a petition to Congress, was for the U.S. government to issue $500 million in irredeemable paper money for highway construction. The scheme also included a provision by which local governments wishing to make public improvements would be allowed to deposit with the Treasury Department notes equal to their face value. In 1894 these were not only bold and daring suggestions, but extremely radical (so much so that his dream of federally financed public projects wouldn't attain respectability until President Franklin D. Roosevelt proposed a Public Works Administration to deal with the unemployment of the Great Depression of the 1930s).

That the Congress of 1894 would approve such a plan and send it to the White House to be signed into law by a man who'd said the government does not support the people was indeed a far-fetched notion. The Congress wasted no time in dismissing Coxey's petition.

Undeterred and undaunted, Coxey decided to organize like-minded folks for a march from Ohio to Washington, D.C., and confront the nation's leaders with "a living petition." The start of American history's first "march on Washington" was set for March 25 in Massillon, Ohio. Coxey called his followers the "Army of the Commonwealth of Christ." Fascinated and bemused headline writers christened it "Coxey's Army." A good many newspaper editors viewed its foot soldiers, counted in the thousands at the outset and picking up others along the way, with alarm. They predicted the marchers would find upon their arrival in the capital that they'd walked into a bloodbath.

The trek took more than a month, but when Coxey's footsore, bedraggled, and exhausted army appeared on the capital's streets on May 1, it numbered less than five hundred and was vastly outweighed by amused spectators and wary ranks of armed policemen. What the marchers did not know as they headed along Pennsylvania Avenue toward Capitol Hill was that they'd also been observed by plainclothes Secret Service agents who had gotten orders from Attorney General Olney, on orders from the president, to trail them all the way.

As the marchers approached the Capitol, the weather was pleasant and the lawns around the building lushly green. But when they ventured to cross them, they found themselves swarmed by police and placed under arrest, and in some instances clubbed by officers, for the misdemeanor of treading on the grass. Coxey's valiant effort to break through the police cordon to read aloud the "Coxey Good Roads bill" resulted in his being hauled off to jail. A week later, a court found him guilty of trespassing and sentenced him to twenty days and a five-dollar fine.

An unintended consequence of Jacob's exercise in political protest was the addition to the general American lexicon of a derisive phrase, "like Coxey's Army," not heard much lately but once quite common and meaning a large group, as in, "The people descended on the place like Coxey's Army." Unfortunately, and perhaps sadly reflecting on the state of teaching of history in pub-

Led by Ohio farmer Jacob Coxey, the "Army of the Commonwealth of Christ" marched to Washington, D.C., in April 1894 to demand government relief from an economic depression.

lic schools, most persons who might still use or hear the phrase more than likely have no idea of its colorful origin.

Although Coxey's Army of the Commonwealth of Christ had its moment of fame in the spring of 1894, its leader and members headed back to their homes having failed in their mission. What many Americans had begun calling "the Cleveland depression" persevered unabated. In the ensuing months of 1894 and into 1895 and 1896, banks continued to fail and other financial institutions went under. Fifteen thousand businesses turned belly-up. Farm foreclosures rose. Some railroads found themselves in receivership. Unemployment in Pennsylvania climbed to 25 percent, to more than a third of the labor force in New York, and to a staggering 43 percent in the State of Michigan. The numbers of homeless became so vast in New York City that police stations were turned into shelters. Across the country tens of thousands of desperate men hit the roads in search of jobs that were not available. Thousands who had been attracted to Chicago in the expectation of finding work at the Columbian Exposition found themselves both disappointed and stranded. Other Americans who were lucky enough to have jobs saw their wages slashed.

Many of these frantic people blamed their plight on the president and a few of them vented their ire by sending threatening letters. They alarmed Frances so much that she pleaded with her husband to increase the number of White House guards. When the roster was raised from two to twenty-five patrolmen and two sergeants, some citizens were shocked and outraged.

A Washington newspaper reported, "Mr. Cleveland not only keeps off the sidewalks; he seldom goes driving—and when he does he is under the protection of two detectives who follow the White House carriage in another vehicle."

A nasty joke also circulated. Upon seeing a man on his hands and knees on the White House lawn, the president demanded to know what he was doing. The man replied, "I'm hungry and I have to eat grass." Grover responded, "Go around to the back yard. The grass is longer there."

★   ★   ★

By New Year's Day 1895, the gold reserve had dropped to a new low ($45 million). This was an unexpected consequence of the Treasury's offering of bonds in an effort to bolster the gold reserve. Ironically, those who bought the notes had cashed in their silver certificates to pay for them. One observer said, "Peter paid Paul, and the gold reserve was not increased in the process." Consequently, a third bond issue was devised in which the sale would be made privately on the condition that half of the gold in the purchase had to come from overseas sources and half from the buyers' own stash of gold. The intended purchasers were the Wall Street banking houses of August Belmont and the country's most famous, and arguably the public's most detested, financial tycoon.

Born in Hartford, Connecticut, in 1837, John Pierpont Morgan had studied mathematics in Germany and in 1857 had begun a Wall Street ascent that by 1861 enabled him to lend $20,000 to an unscrupulous arms dealer who bought obsolete carbines from the War Department for $3.50 each and resold them to the government for $22. Morgan had also profited through Civil War gold speculation. In the postwar railroad-building frenzy, he emerged as a major player while at the same time becoming a significant dealer in federal securities. When the 1880s brought rampant and unrestrained competition and resultant financial difficulties in the railroading business, he provided fresh capital and reorganization through a process that came to be called "Morganization."

Two popular stories made the rounds of the country and helped make J. P. Morgan a legend in his own time. When an admirer of Morgan's yacht, *Corsair*, asked Morgan how much it had cost, Morgan replied, "If you have to ask, you can't afford it." Another young man applied to Morgan for a loan and was refused, but Morgan said, "I'll let you be seen walking down the street with me on my way to lunch." It was enough to ensure the youth credit elsewhere.

Grover had come to know Morgan socially during his first administration and in the next four years in New York. His impression of Morgan was of a successful businessman who had a capacity for doing great things. His admiration was tempered by "watchfulness" when, on the snowy evening of February 7, 1895, Morgan and a young associate arrived at the White House for a meeting with Treasury Secretary Carlisle, Attorney General Olney, and the president.

Grover would recall his approach to Morgan as a situation requiring "the most careful handling." George F. Parker recounted a retrospective interview held in 1907 in which Grover recalled, "Acting for the Government, I was put into the position of seller, dealing, almost wholly in the view of the public, with another man who stood in relation of buyer; and we all know how different is the point of view. I had not gone far, however, before my doubts disappeared. I found that I was in negotiation with a man of large business comprehension and of remarkable knowledge and prescience. In an hour or two of preliminary discussion I saw he had a clear comprehension of what I wanted and what was needed, and that, with lightning-like rapidity, he had reached a conclusion as to the best way to meet the situation. I saw, too, that, with him, it was not merely a matter of business, but of clear-sighted, far-seeing patriotism. He was not looking for a personal bargain, but sat there, a great patriotic banker, concerting with me and my advisers measures to avert peril, determined to do his best in a severe and trying crisis."

Whatever his motivations, Morgan agreed to buy bonds, and to bring other bankers with him in the deal. The syndicate they formed would pay $65,117,000 in gold for $62,515,000 in 4 percent bonds.

Morgan and his associates also pledged themselves to "exert all financial influence and make all legitimate efforts to protect the treasury of the United States against the withdrawal of gold." They kept their part of the deal, but they also offered bonds they'd bought at 104$\frac{1}{4}$ for sale on the open market. The value shot to 118, giving the syndicate a profit of $7 million.

Not surprisingly, conflicting points of view were voiced regarding the Cleveland-Morgan bond deal. Morgan admirers claimed that the banker had personally saved the good faith and credit of the United States. Grover's supporters hailed their president for doing the same. Cleveland opponents on Capitol Hill and elsewhere found him a hypocritical betrayer of his often-expressed wish to maintain a separation between the government and the banking industry. Other detractors falsely accused Grover of being in cahoots with the moneymen and personally profiting from the deal.

★   ★   ★

Even before the Morgan bonds sale, congressional Democrats had experienced the wrath of an electorate which blamed the depression on the Cleveland administration's anti-silver policy. As a result, with the approach of the elections of 1894, many Democrats did everything possible to run away from the gold-standard defender in the White House. Alabama senator John T. Morgan (no relation to J. P.) declared, "I hate the ground the man walks on." Assessing the state of "Cleveland Democracy" in the South, Senator Zebulon Vance asserted that if the voters had known in 1892 what 1893 and 1894 held for them, Cleveland would not have garnered a single electoral vote south of the Potomac. South Carolinian Andrew Harles said the rural citizens of his state hated Cleveland with a "regular proletarian hatred."

Grover exclaimed to his Secretary of State, "Think of it! Not a single man in the Senate with whom I can be on terms of absolute confidence."

Criticism of Grover frequently became viciously personal. Ben Tillman of South Carolina asserted that the heart of Judas when he betrayed Christ had not been blacker than the "scoundrel" Cleveland's. He added, "He is an old bag of beef and I am going to Washington with a pitchfork and prod him in his fat ribs." This bravado earned for Tillman the nickname "Pitchfork."

Discerning fertile ground to be plowed in the states of the old Confederacy in the congressional elections, Populists rushed into the fray. When they proved successful, one observer predicted the ultimate disappearance of the Democratic Party. The three-year-old party elected 6 United States senators, 7 seats in the House, 21 state executive posts, 150 state senators, and 315 state representatives.

Voters had handed the Democrats a humiliating defeat. A former Cleveland man, Thomas Watson cracked, "Never since the Wonderful One Hoss Shay went to pieces in one comprehensive, simultaneous and complete smashup has there been such an all-around catastrophe as that which had happened to the Democratic party." It lost control of the House of Representatives. The Republican majority would be 244 to 104, a loss for the Democrats of 115 seats. And the finger of blame for the debacle was pointed at the man in the White House.

The arrangement with J.P. Morgan three months later only served to sour public opinion even more. As Allan Nevins succinctly stated in his 1932 Cleveland biography, "By hundreds of thousands, hard-handed Americans believed that Cleveland and [Treasury Secretary] Carlisle had sold the credit of the republic to Morgan and the Rothschilds, and had pocketed a share of the price. Their vituperative anger was additional evidence of a sectional and class bitterness that now made even armed revolution seem far from impossible."

For the target of so much reviling rhetoric and blame-placing for the depression, the issue of gold versus silver was but one ingredient of a prescription for restoring an ailing economy. Hand in hand with holding to the gold standard and stemming the flow of gold from the Treasury went a continuing attack on what Grover believed to be another cause of economic distress.

★   ★   ★

The Cleveland fiscal policy was a three-legged stool: opposition to federal paternalism (the government does not support the people); the gold standard; and reduction, if not elimination, of protective tariffs, which he believed hurt the American consumer while provoking tariff retribution by foreign governments against American exports. In pursuit of tariff reduction in December 1893, he collaborated with Congressman William L. Wilson of West Virginia in authoring a bill intended to ease tariffs in a manner which would not cut import duties so severely that the government's chief source of revenue would be imperiled. He soon learned that the distance between the White House and the floor of the House of Representatives was a road littered with the remains of good intentions. When the Wilson tariff bill came out of the Ways and Means Committee for a vote on February 1, it had an amendment to close an anticipated tariff revenue gap of 15 percent by imposing a 2 percent tax on personal incomes over $4,000.

Grover was not happy about the income tax, but he conceded that without it the bill faced an uphill struggle to gain passage by the House. And there would be an opportunity to change the measure when it came before the Senate. The bill cleared the lower chamber 204 to 140.

Its fate was now in the hands of the Senate's Finance Committee. Among the members were individuals with their own agendas, based either on the business interests in their states or on their personal political and economic philosophies. Many senators insisted on protections for the products manufactured or grown in their states. An objector to the income tax provision in the House bill was Grover's longtime rival David Hill, who vowed never to vote to impose such a levy on the workers of New York. The result after five months of haggling and bitter wrangling was a measure so transformed in its character by more than six hundred amendments that it was promptly derided as a "mongrel" with few differences between it and the McKinley Tariff Act in that it imposed import duties on everyday necessities. Passed by the Senate by a vote of 39 to 34 with a dozen senators abstaining, it moved to a committee for reconciliation with the House version.

Displeased with the measure as it was being mangled in the Senate committee, Grover had expressed his feelings in a letter to Congressman Wilson. While obviously heartfelt, it was more than a little intemperate in warning every "true Democrat and every sincere tariff reformer" that the bill in its present form "falls far short of the consummation for which we have labored." Abandonment of that cause, he warned, "means party perfidy and party dishonor."

If there can be specified one common and abiding trait among members of the U.S. Senate from its first session in 1789 to the dawn of the third millennium, it must be pride in themselves and the institution they boastfully proclaim to be "the greatest deliberative body in the world."

What the Senate as a whole, as well as individual members, has never countenanced is an insult and a scolding lecture from the chief executive of a coequal branch of government. Therefore, the president's use of "perfidy" and "dishonor" had the effect, in Allan Nevins's colorful language, of a "brickbat thrown into a nest of hornets."

The Democratic senator who had championed the Cleveland-Wilson Bill and whose name was on the final version, Arthur Pue Gorman, took to the floor of the Senate to speak stingingly of Grover's letter as the most extraordinary, unprovoked, and unwise communication ever written by a president. He termed it the product of dishonesty and duplicity.

Against this ominous background, an effort by Congressman Wilson to prevent acceptance of the Senate version of the bill in the conference committee was doomed to fail. When the bill was presented to the House on August 13, it passed 182 to 106, with only twelve Democrats voting nay.

The question which buzzed in the stifling air of a capital August like Nevins's disturbed hornets was whether the man who had shown himself to be a prolific user of the veto as a mayor, governor, and president would prove true to form. Once the measure reached his desk he had ten days to act. In mulling the decision, he certainly lived up to a reputation for protracted deliberation which some Cleveland observers found akin to those of Shakespeare's Hamlet. To veto or not to veto was pondered at the White House for two weeks. The decision was reached on the very last day before Wilson-Gorman would become law without his approval.

In a letter dated August 27, 1894, and sent to Congressman T. C. Catchings, the president again demonstrated his gift for analyzing complex legislation. Through fifteen paragraphs which in Robert McElroy's biography take up three and a half pages, he provided point-by-point objections to the bill before him, along with a sometimes eloquent dissertation on where he stood and why, not only on the issue of the tariff, but as a member of the Democratic Party, a committed reformer, and a fervent disciple of government "founded in patriotism and upon justice and fairness toward all interests." A reading of the letter more than a century later provides insights into the man who wrote it and into the anguish with which he did so. The following phrases stand out:

"I do not claim to be better than the masses of my party. . . ."

". . . there are provisions of this bill which are not in line with honest tariff reform . . ."

"The trusts and combinations—the communism of pelf—whose machinations have prevented us from reaching the success we deserve . . ."

"When we give our manufacturers [tariff-free] raw materials we unshackle American enterprise and ingenuity, and these will

open the doors of foreign markets to the reception of our wares and give opportunity for the continuous and remunerative employment of American labor."

"The million of our countrymen who have fought bravely and well for tariff reform should be exhorted to continue the struggle, boldly challenging to open warfare and constantly guarding against treachery and half-heartedness in their camp."

"Tariff reform will not be settled until it is honestly and fairly settled in the interest of a patient and long suffering people."

Within twenty-four hours after Grover completed the letter, the Wilson-Gorman Bill went into the statutes without the presidential signature.

But that was not the end of it. After engaging in a period of deliberation, the United States Supreme Court, on May 20, 1895, in deciding the case of *Pollock v. Farmer's and Trust Company*, ruled that the 2 percent income-tax provision of the law was unconstitutional.

12

✦

Derailments

When eighteen-year-old Stephen Grover Cleveland arrived in Buffalo, New York, in 1855 and sidetracked plans to seek his future in Cleveland, Ohio, another young man from central New York was just setting his equally adventurous feet in Chicago, Illinois. At age twenty-four, George Mortimer Pullman had been partners with his brother in a cabinetmaking business in Albion, a small town on the Erie Canal. When plans were announced for widening the canal, requiring the demolition of several brick buildings, George saw an alternative. Why not just move the structures, intact, from their present sites to new ones? After proving to one dubious but desperate owner that it could be done, he quickly landed contracts to shift others. With no more such work available in Albion, and hearing that the rapidly growing city of Chicago was intent on raising its entire business district from its soggy foundations to a new street level, he headed west.

The challenge awaiting him in Chicago was formidable. The brick Tremont House hotel was an impressive four stories high—

the tallest structure in the city—and smack in the middle of the area which was to be elevated through landfill. Confident in his ability to save buildings from destruction, Pullman talked the owners out of their plan to tear down the hotel and build a new one, and convinced them that he could save Tremont House by jacking it up to the new street level. The bold scheme involved stationing twelve hundred men in the cellar with five thousand jackscrews and lifting the hotel a half turn of a screw and an inch at a time. The job went so smoothly that life in the hotel proceeded undisturbed. As one amazed witness observed, "Not a chambermaid blinked an eye and not a piece of crockery was broken."

Pullman's success made him an instant celebrity, attracted similar projects, and left him enough well off financially—in a booming city which was determined to become the mecca of the country's expanding railroad network—to spend some of his money tinkering with an idea to design and build a sleeping car.

He was not the first to tackle the problem. The story of efforts of several designers to build and put a sleeper into service is told in detail in several histories of American railroading, including *The Story of American Railroads* by Stewart H. Holbrook (1947). What others in the competition did not have was Pullman's luck in the form of an exploratory look at his car, the Pioneer, in early 1865 during a visit to Chicago by the wife of the president of the United States. By all accounts, Mary Todd Lincoln was enchanted with the car's beautiful appointments and comfort. Therefore, when the funeral train carrying the body of her assassinated husband stopped at Chicago on its way to the Lincoln burial place in Springfield, Illinois, Mrs. Lincoln requested that Pullman's Pioneer be attached to the train for her use. Pullman's reputation as a sleeping-car builder was later enhanced when President Ulysses

S. Grant rode the Pioneer from Detroit to his old home in Galena, Illinois.

Pullman soon started building other kinds of luxurious cars which transformed trains into hotels on rails. But a condition of Pullman's leasing of his sleeping, dining, and drawing room cars by the nation's expanding railroads with long-distance services was that the operation of the cars, including the hiring of porters, be under control of the Pullman Palace Car Company. This meant that someone who boarded a train with Pullman cars in Boston would reach his destination, no matter how far away, having been in the care of persons trained not by the railroad but by the Pullman company employees. Because Pullman headquarters was located in Chicago, training was conducted there. In 1881 these activities were concentrated in a "company town." Built on the outskirts of Chicago and named Pullman, it was praised by some as a "model town" and criticized by social reformers as a throwback to a feudal system in which wages, rents, and everything else were strictly controlled by the employer/landowner.

Certainly, no one questioned that the lord of the fiefdom was George Pullman, or that he was determined that no one would challenge him as king of sleeping cars. Anybody who dared to compete met ruthless resistance and ended up surrendering by being bought out or being broken in costly litigation. The result was that by 1894 the Pullman Palace Car Company was a monopoly with a capitalization of $36 million and holding surplus profits of about $25 million. In the previous fiscal year it had paid shareholders, including mercantile mogul Marshall Field, $2.5 million in dividends.

Yet as the "Cleveland Depression" deepened and the company claimed to be suffering from a loss of business, it joined other industries in slashing workers' wages. It did not, however, lower the rents in the company town. To do so, or to share the firm's surplus with employees, George Pullman would later assert, "would have amounted to a gift of money to these men."

When a committee of Pullman workers appealed to Pullman in May 1894 that either wages be raised or rents be cut, they were refused and three of them were fired.

★ ★ ★

The act outraged a man who had been born in the same year that Pullman had arrived in Chicago and Grover Cleveland had been persuaded by his uncle to suspend his plan to go to the namesake city in Ohio and try his luck in Buffalo. The son of Alsatian immigrants, Eugene Victor Debs entered the world in Terre Haute, Indiana, on November 5, 1855. His father had been a shopkeeper. Like Grover at about the same age, Eugene had to leave school to bolster the family finances. He took a job in Terre Haute railroad shops and then as a locomotive fireman. In 1875 he help found the local lodge of the Brotherhood of Locomotive Firemen.

Despite being a railroad man, he'd opposed a series of strikes in 1877. Three years later, he had changed his mind and come to the conclusion that concerted action by the workers would be required if labor conditions were to be improved. In 1878 he became editor of the union publication and the Brotherhood's treasurer and grand secretary. He also tried his hand at politics. He was Terre Haute city clerk (1880–1884) and won election in 1885 to the lower house of the Indiana legislature. By this time he was confirmed in a belief that the surest way for laborers to organize unions was by craft lines. This view changed during an 1885 strike against the Chicago, Burlington and Quincy Railroad. He decided the proper track for labor in the railroad industry was solidarity *across* craft lines. Giving up his $4,000 annual salary from the firemen's brotherhood, he formed a union open to railroad workers of all crafts. He called it the American Railway Union. Within a year its membership reached 150,000 in 465 locals. The men fired by Pullman in 1894 were members. When the national convention of the A.R.U. met in June, the recourse chosen was exactly the concept which Grover Cleveland had envisioned as a proper role of government in disputes between labor and capital—arbitration.

The union delegates also set a deadline. Unless the Pullman Palace Car Company adjusted the grievances by June 26, the A.R.U. would direct its membership to refuse to handle Pullman cars and equipment.

That Pullman employees were members of a national union of railroad workers struck Grover as very odd. He would write in *Presidential Problems*, published in 1904, "The employees of the Pullman Palace Car Company could not on any reasonable and consistent theory be regarded as eligible to membership in an organization devoted to the interests of railway employees; and yet, during the months of March, April, and May, 1894, it appears that nearly 4,000 of these employees were enrolled in the American Railway Union. This, to say the least of it, was an exceedingly unfortunate proceeding, since it created a situation which implicated, in a comparatively insignificant quarrel between managers of an industrial establishment [a railway car builder] and their workmen, the large army of the Railway Union."

This immediately thrust the A.R.U. into conflict not only with Pullman, but with railroads contracted with Pullman. These rail companies were not a group of disorganized and unrelated operations; they had a kind of union themselves. Eight years previously, the heads of twenty-four of them, either centered in Chicago or terminating there, had formed the General Managers' Association to coordinate operations. At the heart of these activities were switchmen. These men handled the coupling of Pullman cars to trains. The General Managers' Association had decided to pay wages on an agreed scale, then proposed that similar scales be imposed by all member railroads. This proposal was regarded by unions as unacceptable. Now, with the A.R.U. threatening to pull its members off their jobs over an issue which did not involve the railroads directly, the association backed Pullman.

When the Pullman Palace Car Company cut workers' wages, their union's leader, Eugene Debs, called a strike which shut down railroads all over the Midwest, resulting in bloody clashes.

When June 26 passed without Pullman compliance with the union's demand, Debs gave the order for the boycott. He later described the effect this way: "The employees, obedient to the order of the convention, at once refused to haul Pullman cars. The switchmen, in the first place, refused to attach a Pullman car to a train, and that is where the trouble began; and then, when a switchman would be discharged for that, they would all simultaneously quit, as they had agreed to do. One department after another was involved until the Illinois Central was paralyzed, and the Rock Island and other roads in their turn."

What had started as a dispute affecting a single firm and four thousand workers mushroomed into a capital-versus-labor crisis affecting many thousands more in twenty-seven states and territories. It was also a genuine threat to a nation of millions of people grown increasingly dependent on the flow of goods by rail, and it happened in the midst of an economic depression which Americans largely blamed on the president and his stubborn defense of the gold standard and demands for lower tariffs.

Having left orders with appropriate executive departments to keep the White House informed concerning developments in Chicago, and with Frances and the girls having gone to Gray Gables, Grover had traveled to Chesapeake Bay to do some fishing with friends. He returned to the Executive Mansion late on June 27 and went to bed. Perusing the morning papers at breakfast, as had been his lifelong custom, he read with alarm that the union ultimatum and its rejection by the Pullman company had precipitated a strike which one paper reported had "assumed the proportions of the greatest battle between labor and capital that has ever been waged in the United States."

Reports to Grover from Attorney General Olney painted a bleak

Attorney General Richard Olney.

picture. The number of walkouts in Chicago was estimated at 20,000, and Debs's union headquarters figured another 40,000 men had quit or struck elsewhere. Freight and passenger traffic to and from Chicago was at a halt. The Post Office Department found its operations hampered or forced to halt all over the West. While interruptions of freight and passenger service were undoubtedly a grave development, and certainly an inconvenience to citizens, it was the latter disruption, in Grover's view, as well as that of Olney and others, which posed a challenge to the government. To let the situation go on without federal intervention was not an option.

In the days leading up to the strike, the government had not been idle. It anticipated that if there was trouble, Chicago would be the center of it. "In these circumstances," Grover noted in his 1904 account of the Pullman strike, "it would have been criminal neglect of duty if those charged with the protection of governmental agencies and the enforcement of orderly obedience and submission to Federal authority, had been remiss in preparations for any emergency in that quarter."

Accordingly, when the U.S. attorney reported on June 30 that on the previous night a group of strikers had stopped mail trains in the suburbs of Chicago, the U.S. marshal requested that he be authorized to employ a force of special deputies on trains to protect the mails and to "detect the parties guilty of such interference." With the president's approval, Attorney General Olney gave the order for "prompt and vigorous" action. He also designated Chicago attorney Edwin Walker to act as special counsel for the government in any subsequent legal proceedings.

On July 1 the U.S. attorney in Chicago advised Olney that he was preparing to ask a federal court to issue an injunction against the union. He also reported that there was movement of very little mail, that the marshal was using all his forces to prevent riots and obstruction of tracks, and that the four hundred men on hand to do all this were an inadequate number. The message also requested one hundred riot guns.

Further inflaming the crisis were newspaper stories filled with what Illinois governor John Peter Altgeld termed exaggerated, distorted, and often baseless information. On July 1 the *Chicago Tribune* headline blared "Mobs Bent on Ruin." The next day the U.S. attorney reported to Olney that Judges Peter S. Grossup and William A. Woods had signed an injunction ordering the union to "refrain from interfering with or stopping any of the business of the railroads in Chicago engaged as common carriers." Debs's union was also told to cease persuading employees to stop work. The U.S. attorney then announced that the injunction extended to all union members and disobedience could subject individuals to arrest.

On the afternoon of the issuance of the injunction, a crowd of union members in the town of Blue Island, Illinois, demonstrated their opinion of the court order by attacking a federal marshal and 125 deputies, one of whom was stabbed. In a veritable state of panic, the marshal telegraphed Olney: "In my judgment it is impossible to move trains without having the Fifteenth Infantry from Fort Sheridan moved here at once. There are 2,000 rioters here and more coming."

Subsequent news accounts of the situation in Blue Island over the next few days were at odds with the marshal's report, but they came too late. Olney, in a message to the U.S. marshal in Chicago,

Illinois governor John Peter Altgeld.

299

offered assurances that if it became necessary, troops would be used "promptly and decisively." Chicago immediately responded with an alarming assertion that "people engaged in trades are quitting employment today, and in my opinion will be joining the mob tonight, and especially tomorrow, and it is my judgment that the troops should be here at the earliest possible moment."

For Grover the situation demanded a straightforward answer to a simple question: "Did the people elect Eugene Debs or Grover Cleveland president?"

On July 2 he held a meeting of his Cabinet. It followed a conference with General Nelson Miles. The commander of the army's western department, which had hunted and caught Geronimo, had advised that deploying troops in Chicago would be premature.

Artist rendering of federal troops breaking up the Pullman strike.

This view was endorsed by Secretary of War Dan Lamont. But that opinion was outweighed by the telegram from the man on the scene asking for troops. At 3:30 in the afternoon, Lamont walked next door to the War Department and commanded soldiers from Fort Sheridan to move immediately to Chicago.

They arrived on July 4, causing some residents to assume that the infantry, cavalry, and units of artillery were there for an Independence Day celebration. The U.S. attorney told the press, "We have been brought to the ragged edge of anarchy, and it is time to see whether the law is sufficiently strong to prevent this condition of affairs. If not, the sooner we know the better."

He wasn't alone in spouting dangerous words. Hotheaded and growing hotter, Eugene Debs warned, "The first shots fired by regular soldiers at the mobs here will be a signal for civil war. I believe this as firmly as I believe in the ultimate success of our course. Bloodshed will follow, and ninety percent of the people of the United States will be arrayed against the other ten percent. And I would not care to be arrayed against the laboring people in the contest, or find myself out of the ranks of labor when the struggle ended."

Supervising the troops was General Miles, as each day the number of soldiers increased and rumors swept the anxious city that once all the railroad property was torched, the mobs would set fire to department stores and homes of millionaires. Expectations of full-scale civil war seemed anything but far-fetched.

Like a self-fulfilling prophecy, the simmering crisis exploded into warfare on the seventh. A mob attacked the soldiers. When the battle ended, seven men had been killed. The next day, without notice to Altgeld, Grover put the city under martial law, banning all unlawful assemblages and vowing, "There will be no vacillation in the punishment of the guilty."

Two days later, a grand jury indicted Eugene Debs and others on seventy-one charges, including obstructing the mails.

To defend himself, Debs turned to a Chicago lawyer who would bestride the stage of the American system of justice in federal and state criminal and civil courts for forty years.

★   ★   ★

At the outset of the Pullman strike, thirty-seven-year-old Clarence Seward Darrow rushed to Debs's cause, quitting a lucrative position as legal counsel to the Chicago and North Western Railroad. Born in Kinsman, Ohio, on April 18, 1857, he had studied law at the University of Michigan, clerked in a Youngstown law firm, and was admitted to the bar in 1878. He'd been practicing law in Chicago since 1887 and had been a partner of the man who was governor of Illinois during the Pullman strike and rioting, John Peter Altgeld.

Although Grover felt justified in using troops, the irate governor disagreed in a tart letter to the president. He wrote, "Surely the facts have not been correctly presented to you in this case or you would not have taken the step; for it is entirely unnecessary and, as it seems to me, unjustifiable. Waiving all questions of courtesy, I will say that the State of Illinois is not only able to take care of itself, but it stands ready today to furnish the Federal Government any assistance it may need elsewhere."

Grover retorted that in order to keep the mails moving, "and upon abundant proof that conspiracies existed against commerce between the States," it had been clearly "within the province of the Federal authority" to send in troops. There had been no intention, he told Altgeld, "of thereby interfering with the plain duty of the local authorities to preserve the peace of the city."

Who was right?

As in most historical controversies, each was. And both were wrong. Clearly, Grover could not permit mobs to interfere with the legitimate governmental responsibility to ensure that the people's business be carried out. He could not countenance interference with the mails. But he also had a duty under the Constitution to at least consult with the governor before sending federal troops. While the president may be rightly criticized for acting too swiftly, Governor Altgeld can be correctly charged with being slow to grasp the situation. Regarding the obtaining of the injunction, historian Allan Nevins concluded that while it was a proper tactic under the circumstances, it was improperly drastic in its terms. It was right to outlaw the physical obstruction and violence, but wrong to effectively outlaw a strike. Richard E. Welch Jr., in his book *The Presidencies of Grover Cleveland*, agreed. He concluded, "Cleveland permitted the judicial and the military force of the federal government to be used in a manner that was of exclusive benefit to one party in a labor-management dispute."

A result was Grover's enemies' portrayal of him as a strike-breaking lackey of capitalists and a hypocrite in his espousal of a need for federal evenhandedness in disputes between capital and labor. The ordering of the army to end the crisis by moving against the strikers and the use of force against Coxey's Army were coupled by critics with governmental ineffectiveness in dealing with the continuing depression to characterize the Cleveland administration's policy toward the workingman as at best indifferent. At worst it was cruel.

This assessment of the president's actions was not shared by most of the public. In the weeks following the federal intervention Grover's popularity soared. At the height of the crisis, when Debs predicted a new civil war, few Americans dismissed his words as empty rhetoric. Fear of anarchy was real. The arrival of the army and the arrest of Debs and others were greeted with a nationwide sigh of relief. Americans might disagree with some of Cleveland's policies, but after the show of force in Chicago they could not accuse him of being a weakling president.

One newspaper writer with a high opinion of himself as a poet wrote:

> The railroad strike played merry hob,
>   'The land was set aflame;
> Could Grover order out the troops
>   To block the strikers' game?
> One Altgeld yelled excitedly,
>   "Such tactics I forbid;
> You can't trot out those soldiers," yet
>   That's just what Grover did.

Had the Cleveland response to the strike been justified by facts? Had it been legal? These questions would be sorted out in judicial and quasi-judicial proceedings. There would be a formal investigation into all aspects of the strike, and a trial of Eugene Debs et al.

To conduct the investigation, Grover appointed a three-man commission. Its brief from Grover was to "visit the State of Illinois and the city of Chicago and such other places in the United States as may appear proper [in order to] make careful inquiry into the causes of any pending dispute or existing controversy, and hear all persons interested therein.

While Debs and the others awaited trial, the commission heard 109 witnesses and compiled these facts: costs to railroads for destroyed property and hiring of guards of at least $685,308; loss of earnings as a result of interruptions of train service, $4,672,916; wages lost by 31,000 Pullman employees, estimated at $350,000; individuals shot and killed, 12; persons arrested by police on charges of murder, arson, burglary, assault, intimidation, riot, and lesser crimes, 515; indictments on federal charges of obstruction of the mail, conspiracy in restraint of trade, and conspiracy to injure, threaten, or intimidate, 71.

In placing fault for this tragedy, the commission found that conditions created at Pullman enabled "the management at all times to assert with vigor its assumed right to fix wages and rents absolutely, and to repress that sort of independence which leads to labor organizations and their attempts at mediation, arbitration, strikes, etc."

But the real blame for the disorders, declared the commission, had to rest with "the people themselves and with the government for not adequately controlling monopolies and corporations, and for failing to reasonably protect the rights of labor to redress its wrongs."

Grover could find some consolation in this endorsement of the federal board to arbitrate labor-capital disputes he'd proposed to an indifferent Congress. Yet he could not ignore the sting of the report's rebuke of his personal and political philosophy of non-intrusion by government in the way American business conducted its business. Cleveland biographer Rexford Guy Tugwell properly noted that in the president's not having moved to restrain business and pushing harder for government attention to labor's complaints, history had caught up with Grover "and he had not been ready."

Official placement of culpability on the Pullman company and on the government dereliction of responsibility in redressing imbalances in the capital-labor equation proved immaterial to the plight of Eugene Debs and the others. They still awaited trial for contempt of court for their defiance of the injunction and resistance to legitimate authority. They had obviously done both. On December 10, 1894, they were sentenced to jail for six months. But the issue of greater moment for Debs and his lawyer, Clarence Darrow, was not defiance of the injunction, but what authority the federal government, or any government, had to seek such a restraint and a court to grant it. To challenge the constitutionality of those actions, Darrow applied for a writ of habeas corpus on the grounds that the facts of the case did not constitute disobedience to the injunction because the injunction was improper. He argued the issue before the United States Supreme Court on March 25 and 26, 1895. The next day the justices, as noted in an earlier chapter, ruled otherwise.

The decision affirmed that the U.S. government "may remove everything put upon highways, natural or artificial, to obstruct the passage of interstate commerce, or the carrying of the mails" and that it was "equally within its competency to appeal to the civil courts for an inquiry and determination as to the existence and the character of any of them, and if such are found to exist or threaten to occur, to invoke the powers of those courts to remove or restrain them, the jurisdiction of the courts to interfere in such matters by injunction being recognized from ancient times and by indubitable authority."

In terms of Debs and the others, the Court ruled, "Such an

injunction having been issued and served upon the defendants, the Circuit Court had authority to inquire whether its orders had been disobeyed, and when it found that they had been disobeyed, to proceed . . . and to enter the order of punishment complained of."

Debs served the six months and left confinement to find his A.R.U. destroyed, but himself in the role of a national hero in the cause of organized labor. The son of a middle-class shop owner would later claim that he'd spent the six months reading and reflecting on Socialism and emerged committed to its principles. In 1896 he supported the candidacy of William Jennings Bryan, but three years later he organized the Social Democratic Party. In 1901 it merged with a similar party to form the Socialist Party of America. Debs was its candidate for president five times. In 1905 he was a founder of the Industrial Workers of the World (known as the Wobblies). For opposition to United States involvement in World War I he was indicted again, this time under the Espionage Act, and was sentenced to ten years. Confined to the nation's toughest prison (the Atlanta federal penitentiary), he was again the Socialist candidate for president in 1920 and got 920,000 votes. The man who won, Warren G. Harding, commuted his sentence in 1921. Still expounding Socialism, Debs died five years later in Elmhurst, Illinois, at the age of sixty-one. (1926)

While Debs carried the banner of Socialism into the twentieth century, his lawyer in the Pullman strike built a career and reputation as a defender of "the underdog." Arguably the most famous defense attorney of the twentieth century, Clarence Darrow represented the United Mine Workers union in a 1902 strike in which President Theodore Roosevelt turned to ex-president Grover Cleveland as a conciliator. Three years later, Darrow would again defend coal miners, including William "Big Bill" Hayward, against a charge of murdering a former governor of Utah. In 1911 he appeared for the defense in the bombing of the offices of the *Los Angeles Times* in which twenty people were killed. But his most famous cases came in the 1920s. He defended the "thrill kill" child murderers Nathan Leopold and Richard Loeb, saving them from the death penalty, in 1924. The next year he found himself cross-examining William Jennings Bryan on whether the Bible was to be taken literally in all aspects. The titanic confrontation between the country's two greatest public speakers in the case of Tennessee schoolteacher John Scopes was the dramatic high point of the "monkey trial." The issue was whether Scopes was free to teach that humans, rather than being created by God, were the result of evolution as theorized by the English naturalist Charles Darwin.

There's no doubt that these later cases were far more sensational, and therefore better known generally, than the prosecution of Eugene Debs. Leopold and Loeb and the Scopes trial rank high on lists of cases each of which in its time was deemed "the trial of the century." But few trials of an individual in any century of American history proved to have a more immediate and continuing significance. Grover looked back to the Pullman strike and wrote that "the inherent power of the Government to execute the powers and functions belonging to it by means of physical force through its official agents, and on every foot of American soil, was amply vindicated."

He was right. Therefore, he was entitled to claim in his customary language that his personal conscientiousness and courage had marked out a path "now unchangeably established, which shall hereafter guide our nation safely and surely in the exercise of the important functions which represent the people's trust." His dramatic and telling intervention in the Pullman strike restored a popularity which the continuing economic depression had severely eroded.

Events overseas would presently bolster Grover's reputation as a defender of principle.

★   ★   ★

In establishing the presidency, the framers of the Constitution appreciated that the conduct of foreign affairs could not be vested in a legislature. It required one pair of hands on the wheel of state. The founders of the Republic also recognized that in the execution of foreign policies the armed forces of the United States needed a commander in chief.

Since President George Washington had advised in his farewell address against "foreign entanglements," his successors had given lip service to the admonition. While expanding the nation geographically at the expense of European states and neighboring Mexico, presidents had used a doctrine enunciated by President James Monroe to warn world powers against pursuing designs for new colonies and preservation and expansion of existing ones in the Western Hemisphere. But no country which spanned a continent and conducted business across oceans that formed its eastern and western boundaries could remove itself from international affairs which touched on its vital interests, and possibly posed a threat to its security.

Consequently, when the people of the United States looked across the Pacific Ocean in the 1880s and 1890s, they could not miss the strategic importance of the islands of Hawaii and Samoa. In the latter, the concern was the possibility of a takeover by Germany, resulting in the dominance of lucrative mid-Pacific trade routes between the United States and the Orient by the German navy. Under a treaty of 1878, the United States had pledged itself to recognize and defend the independence of Samoa.

In 1886, as Germany exhibited an interest in displacing the Samoan king, Malietoa, with a monarch amenable to German control, the Cleveland response was to call for a conference among Great Britain (which also had a stake in the future of the island), Germany, and the United States in Washington. But the meeting adjourned without resolving anything. A few months later, Germany flexed its muscles by deposing Malietoa and replacing him with a more compliant ruler, Tamasese. The United States protested and called another conference. But events in Samoa chose their own course in the form of a bloody rebellion in which twenty Germans were killed. When Germany threatened to go to war with Samoa, Grover sent three warships to the island while at the same time signaling the Germans that a diplomatic solution was desired. Next, nature played a hand by means of a typhoon which sank most of the ships in the German and American fleets and took a total of fifty lives.

All sides agreed to meet again, this time in Berlin. Before the conference got under way, however, Grover was turned out of office. The outcome of the conference was an agreement that Samoa would be subject to a tripartite protectorate, a deal agreed to by Harrison's administration.

Back in office in 1893, Grover viewed the arrangement as not only immoral, but exactly the kind of entangling alliance Washington had warned against. But the deal had been made and, under the law, he could do nothing to change it.

Regarding Hawaii, Grover also inherited the policy of the Harrison presidency, but with a different attitude toward accepting and continuing it. In his view, the Hawaiian Islands were of far greater importance to the United States than Samoa, not merely because Hawaii was closer to the American mainland, but because the islands were, in his words, "in the highway of Oriental and Australasian traffic" and "virtually an outpost of American commerce and a stepping-stone to the growing trade of the Pacific."

In this outlook he had numerous supporters, but none more vitally interested in Hawaii than a colony of Americans who lived there under the rule of Queen Liliuokalani. The leader of the American community was a wealthy planter, Sanford B. Dole. In 1893, before Grover began his second term, and with the collaboration of Harrison's consul in Hawaii, John L. Stevens, the Americans formed a secret Committee of Safety and promptly deposed the queen. Under the guise of "protecting" American lives and property, Stevens ordered Marines from the U.S.S. *Boston* to seize government buildings. He then unilaterally "recognized" the "Provisional Government" and proclaimed Hawaii a United States protectorate.

Leaving the Stars and Stripes flying behind them, a delegation of Americans sailed for the United States. When they arrived in Washington, D.C., on February 3, 1893—a month and a day before Grover would take the presidential oath—the Harrison administration welcomed them warmly and quickly sent the Senate a treaty annexing Hawaii.

Unfortunately for Dole and his cohorts, the Senate didn't act as swiftly as hoped. The treaty was still in committee when Grover took over the White House. With his sense of morality and justice offended, the new president withdrew the treaty and nine months later renounced annexation. He told the Congress, "The United States cannot be properly put in the position of countenancing a wrong after its commission any more than of consenting to it in advance.

The status of Hawaii, he declared, was a matter to be left to "the extended powers and wide discretion of the Congress."

The House and Senate passed a resolution mandating the status quo. Hawaii would not be annexed, but neither would Queen Lil-iuokalani be returned to her throne. Tacked onto the decree was a warning to foreign powers not to interfere in Hawaii.

When Grover accepted Congress's will, Dole lost no time in proclaiming the Republic of Hawaii, which Grover also accepted. Sometime later, he greeted Dole as a great and good friend and offered best wishes for Dole's "personal prosperity." With that, Hawaiian annexation was put on hold, but only for a span of four years. The islands would become a possession of the United States as an ancillary bonus of the Spanish-American War of 1898.

The secretary of state during these problems in the Pacific was Walter Q. Gresham, a man who wholeheartedly agreed with Secretary of the Treasury Carlisle's outlook on the world as a vast market for United States goods not only in Europe and Asia, but in Central and South America. Like Grover, they were convinced that exports were key to solving the economic depression, and so they were for low tariffs and vigorous exploitation of international trade. When the free flow of U.S. goods was threatened by a revolution in Brazil in which the port of Rio de Janeiro was blockaded, Gresham, on orders from the president, refused to recognize the rebels and sent ships to Rio harbor to ensure unhindered passage of U.S. merchant vessels to trade with the established government. However, in disputes between Britain and Nicaragua, which was not important to American traders, Grover, Gresham, and Carlisle saw no reason to become involved.

This was not the reaction in 1895 to the heating up of a long-simmering dispute between Great Britain and Venezuela, considered a vital U.S. trade partner. The heart of the issue was the boundary between Venezuela and British Guiana. The disagreement had been going on for more than half the century. Grover's concern was twofold. He feared an outbreak of war (with implications of a disruption of trade), and he suspected that Great Britain's obstinacy in not settling the matter diplomatically masked an intent to expand its colonial territory. If true, would this represent, as claimed by some vociferous Americans (who proudly called themselves jingoes and advocated the exertion of American power in the world generally and in the Western Hemisphere in particular), a direct, unacceptable challenge to the Monroe Doctrine?

Unsure of the answer, Grover convened his Cabinet in May 1895 to discuss the matter. The talks ended with Grover asking Gresham to look into the issue and write a report. Before Gresham could do so, he became ill with pleurisy and died on May 28. Grover replaced him at the State Department with the man who had been at the storm center in the Pullman strike, Richard Olney. Grover told him to review Gresham's work on the report, make whatever revisions he deemed appropriate, and present it for review.

It was ready on July 2, when Grover was ensconced at Gray Gables. Because Olney had a home nearby, he delivered it personally, only to find Grover seemingly distracted and uninterested. He left the report and went home to wait for a response. It came a few days later in a note from Gray Gables which explained Grover's behavior on the second. Not even the possibility of going to war with the British in defense of the Monroe Doctrine had been more important to him in the first week of July than the news he announced to Olney. At the time he'd brought the report, Frances was expected at almost any moment to have a baby. Born on July 7, Marion Cleveland, the father proudly told Olney, was strong, plump, and loud-voiced.

As to Olney's paper on Venezuela, Grover exclaimed in writing, "It's the best thing of the kind I ever read, and it leads to a conclusion that one cannot escape if he tries—that is, if there is anything in the Monroe Doctrine at all . . . you place it, I think, on better and more defensible ground than any of your predecessors—or *mine*."

The Olney document so forcefully asserted the Monroe Doctrine that Grover called it "your twenty-inch gun." The position paper stated that the United States government was entitled "to resent and resist any sequestration of Venezuelan soil by Great Britain." It was sent to Ambassador Thomas F. Bayard in London for delivery to the government of Her Majesty Queen Victoria.

The prime minister, Lord Salisbury, took his time in sending a response. It was handed to Olney on December 7 by Britain's ambassador, Sir Julian Poncefote. In no uncertain terms Lord Salisbury dismissed the extension of the Monroe Doctrine to include the boundary squabble as a "novel prerogative."

Grover found this claim and its school-headmaster-to-dull-student tone offensive and sent both it and Olney's letter as addenda to a special message delivered to Congress on December 17. In an example of typically blunt language reminiscent of his veto messages as mayor, governor, and president, he asserted:

> If a European power, by an extension of its boundaries, takes possession of the territory of one of our neighboring Republics against its will and in derogation of its rights, it is difficult to see why to that extent such European power does not thereby attempt to extend its

system of Government to that portion of this continent which is thus taken. This is the precise action which President Monroe declared to be "dangerous to our peace and safety," and it can make no difference whether the European system is extended by an advance of frontier or otherwise.

The message asked Congress for money for establishment of a commission to "make the necessary investigation" and report its findings. If it found an inherent threat of aggression in the British policy, Grover continued, it would be the duty of the United States to resist by every means in its power "a willful aggression upon its rights and interests."

He warned, "There is no calamity which a great nation can invite which equals that which follows from a supine submission to wrong and injustice, and the consequent loss of national self-respect and honor, beneath which are shielded and defended a people's safety and greatness."

Congress was ecstatic in its support. An appropriation of $100,000 for the commission was passed with breathtaking speed. A leader of the jingoes, Senator Henry Cabot Lodge, was reported by a correspondent for the London *Times* to be bubbling with delight. *The Washington Post* found in the message a call to arms. It said, "The jingoes were right after all, and it is not to be the fashion henceforth to sneer at patriots and soldiers."

Most editors rallied behind Grover. One senator anticipated a benefit beyond defending the Monroe Doctrine. "War would be a good thing even if we get whipped," he said, "for it would rid us of English bank rule." Wall Streeters, fearing a run on gold, had a spasm of jitters.

Ambassador Bayard found all this terribly troubling. He thought the president's faculties had become unsettled. But he found a glimmer of hope that Europeans would pay more heed to the United States' concerns about South America. Evidently, the message got through to Salisbury. He opened a door to a diplomatic resolution, but it was a back door. During months of talks through a series of intermediaries, Britain signaled she was amenable to a settlement providing for arbitration which would save face all around. But by the time a treaty was ready for ratification in February 1897, Grover was in the final weeks of his term. (The arbitration panel established by the treaty would not meet until October 3, 1899.)

Five years later, Grover wrote, "I hope there are but few of our citizens who, in retrospect, do not now acknowledge the good that has come to our nation through this episode in our history. It has established the Monroe Doctrine on lasting foundations before the eyes of the world; it has given us a better place in respect and consideration of the people of all nations, and especially of Great Britain; it has again confirmed our confidence in the overwhelming prevalence among our citizens of disinterested devotion to American honor, but by no means least, it has taught us where to look in the ranks of our countrymen for the best patriotism."

If Grover had wished to look for an individual who drew inspiration from the handling of the Venezuelan affair, he would have found him at 300 Mulberry Street in New York City, presiding over the commissioners who were running the police department. During the height of the crisis, Theodore Roosevelt sent Grover a letter of enthusiastic congratulations. In the missive Roosevelt proposed that the United States also "drive the Spaniards out of Cuba."

Grover demurred. But TR would have his way three years later. In the 1898 undertaking by the United States to wrench Cuba from beneath the heel of Spain, he was fated to become a hero of mythic proportions by leading a charge up San Juan Hill (he called it "my crowded hour"). His bravado in the Spanish-American War catapulted him into the governor's mansion in New York. Just two years later, because of an assassin's bullet in September of 1901, he realized Henry Cabot Lodge's dream and came into the higher kingdom of the presidency.

That something more awaited Roosevelt, Grover had never doubted. George F. Parker in his memoirs quoted Grover's earliest assessment of Roosevelt as follows: "When I was Governor, he was still a very young man and only a member of the Assembly, but it was clear to me, even thus early, that he was looking to a public career, that he was studying political conditions with a care that I had ever known any man to show, and that he was firmly convinced that he would some day reach prominence."

As the election year of 1896 dawned, Grover Cleveland, following an extraordinary series of events through four decades, helped in no small measure by "Cleveland luck," found himself not at the beginning of a political career, but in its twilight. As historian Richard E. Welch Jr. noted, "a man of little charisma, less eloquence, and limited imagination and intellectual powers" had been the dominant figure in United States politics for more than a decade. He'd authored no laws and often failed to win congressional acceptance for legislative proposals, but he had an undoubted hold on the public imagination and was seen by friend and foe alike as a strong president.

Now the hour was coming for him to go. But what was there for an ex-president to do?

13

✦

Written on Their Hearts

In early summer of 1896, as the Democratic Party prepared for its first presidential nominating convention since 1884 at which Grover Cleveland was not a contender, the resident of the White House and Gray Gables had the continually vexing matter of gold and silver on his mind. On June 16 he wrote to his dentist, Dr. Kasson C. Gibson, "This morning about an hour ago, there came out of a tooth in my right under jaw, next to the dead tooth you fixed up, a piece of gold about the size of a pea. This indicates how completely I have been on the gold standard. I've got the gold in my possession. What shall I do with it?"

The same day, in an open letter published in the *New York Herald* and addressed to "the Democratic voters," it was silver which upset him. Having heard of a movement within the party to adopt a free-silver platform, he said he refused to believe "that when the time arrives for deliberate action there will be engrafted upon our

Democratic creed a demand for the free, unlimited and independent coinage of silver. I cannot believe this, because I know the [Democratic Party] is neither unpatriotic or foolish, and because it seems clear to me that such a course will inflict very great injury upon every interest of our country which it has been the mission of our party to advance, and will result in lasting disaster to our party organization."

As Grover was the leader of gold-standard Democrats, the champion of the cause of free silver was William Jennings Bryan, whose candidacy for the Democratic presidential nomination Grover viewed as fraudulent. "His mind, training and imagination," he said, "all combine to make of him a Populist, pure and simple. He has not even the remotest notion of the principles of [the Democratic Party]."

If he felt so strongly about keeping the nomination from Bryan, why didn't he make himself available? The short answer is that he was, to use a term from the following century, burnt out. In March of 1896 he'd marked his fifty-ninth birthday, with more than thirty of those years spent in politics. In the previous three years he'd undergone a secret cancer operation and lived thereafter in the shadow of possible recurrence while losing sixty pounds. He'd endured scorn from those who blamed him and his policies for the relentless economic hard times. He'd found himself despised by most of the nation's farmers for not yielding on free silver and dealing with an often obstructionist Congress. He'd ordered U.S. soldiers into action against American citizens for the first time since the Civil War, defied the popular will to oppose the Americanization of Hawaii, taken the country in the direction of a possible third war with the British, and read scurrilous items about himself in unfriendly newspapers nearly every day.

In spite of all this, as the letter to his dentist showed, he'd retained a sense of humor. It was still there a few months after he left office when a friend visited him with a fine setter dog. When it ran to Grover and all but jumped in his lap, the friend tried to pull it away. "No, let him be," Grover said. "He at least likes me."

And regarding running again, there was always the example of Washington and each of the presidents since who'd followed his example in eschewing a third term.

Consequently, and with Grover's warnings about choosing a free-silver candidate and platform notwithstanding, the Democrats picked the orator from Nebraska who was no longer a boy (he was thirty-six), but still had the rhetorical flair to coin a New Testament analogy to depict the workingman being sacrificed on a cross of gold. Disgusted by the nomination of Bryan, Grover found little to like in the Republicans' nomination of the author of the McKinley Tariff Act. The only saving grace in William McKinley, now governor of Ohio, was that he was pro gold standard.

Grover was not alone in expressing dismay at the two parties' nominees. Rebellious anti-silver Democrats bolted the party and formed their own. Claiming to be "true Democrats," they called themselves the Gold Party and begged Grover to carry their standard. He declined the offer. Unable to vote for Bryan and the Republican McKinley, Grover cast his vote for the new party's slate of Senator John W. Palmer and Simon B. Bruckner. When McKinley won the election, Grover welcomed Bryan's defeat.

The handing-over of power from a Democrat to a Republican was not an unpleasant event. They met at the White House on the evening before McKinley's inauguration. Also present was George F. Parker, who took notes and later reported Grover's account of the conversation.

*In the 1896 presidential race, Cleveland favored Republican William McKin-
ley over "free silver" Democrat William Jennings Bryan.*

I was struck by the feeling of sadness which characterized this interview on both sides. The one question on Mr. McKinley's mind was the threatened war with Spain. He went over with me, carefully, the steps I had taken to avert [it], emphasized his agreement with the policy adopted, and expressed his determination to carry it out so far as lay in his power. . . . In parting he said [to Grover]: "Mr. President, if I can go out of office, at the end of my term, with the knowledge that I have done what lay in my power to avert this terrible calamity, with the success that has crowned your patience and persistence, I shall be the happiest man in the world."

The men would meet again (for the last time) for the next day's ceremonial ride to the Capitol for McKinley's inauguration.

The moments before the president-elect's arrival at the White House found Frances saying tearful good-byes to the staff. She and Grover had not liked living in the Executive Mansion and had spent a great deal of time at Oak View in the first term and at Woodley and Gray Gables in the second, but she could not forget that she had been married in the White House or that in 1889 she had made a promise to return in 1893. Or that her second child had been born there. It was a hard place for her to leave.

Not so for her husband. Awaiting McKinley's appearance, Grover sauntered through the corridors and stately rooms, no doubt pondering why and how his popularity had plummeted among much of the public and his party had rejected his policies. Pausing in the Red Room, he peered at a painting of himself by the renowned portraitist Eastman Johnson. Presently turning away, he directed William Sinclair to remove it and store it in the attic, saying he saw no reason to impose his image on the new president.

★   ★   ★

On November 8, 1896, Grover had contacted an acquaintance, Professor Andrew F. West, about the New Jersey town of Princeton, seat of a Presbyterian college. He wrote, "Mrs. Cleveland and I, naturally enough, are casting about for a resting place where we can settle with our three babies after the fourth of next March. Somehow for the last few days the idea has entered our minds that we might be very satisfied and comfortable at Princeton."

He was interested in buying a house "in which I can live and die ... having plenty of room and a fair share, at least, of the conveniences of modern existence" which could be maintained cheaply. He also specified the need for a healthy and comfortable climate ("especially in the winter") and good schools nearby.

Grover found much to like about West. Weighing 240 pounds and with a character at least as stubborn as Grover's, he was a professor of Latin. The newcomer to town was evidently so fond of West that when he found the house he was seeking he named it "Westland." Quickly settling in, he resumed his daily routine of rising between seven and eight, reading the newspapers, assessing the morning mail, and going to work in a second-floor study. He just as speedily fit in among the academics, who were doubtless impressed with having a former president of the United States as a neighbor. The man they came to know was unlike the one who had been president. The stiffness of manner noted by denizens of the political universe was displaced by a charming mellowness.

As president, he had sedulously declined offers of honorary degrees. But when he was invited by Princetonians to receive a doctorate of law, he cheerfully agreed. The would-be scholar of Clinton, New York, who had been forced by a scarcity of money to go

Cleveland's Princeton home.

to work, boasted in a June 19, 1897, letter to Richard Olney at Buzzards Bay: "You needn't put on any airs because you are settled on Cape Cod. I'll open up there myself in a few days—and I've got a degree that I'm going to bring with me." He added that when the degree had been bestowed in Latin, the presentation was "to my certain knowledge faultless."

Students took a liking to him and created an annual tradition of congregating to serenade him on his birthday. On October 18, 1897, they happily celebrated the birth of a boy whom Grover and Frances named Richard Folsom Cleveland. The proud father wrote to a friend that everyone said "the buck" looked like his father. "That, of course, is nonsense," he continued, "but just as soon as his mother is well enough to be about, I should be glad to have your unbiased judgment on that question."

The letter also stated, "I must have some money pretty soon, and I suppose I must sell something." Among items he considered disposing of were shares of Chicago Gas, which, unfortunately at that moment, were below par. Yet he and Frances were far from broke. Daniel Lamont estimated Grover's worth in 1897 at over $300,000. This moderate fortune in 1897 terms had come from savings from his law practice, his salary as president (pensions for the nation's chief executives were in the distant future), and the sale of Oak View. With a good deal of his wealth tied up in stocks, he frequently worried about the availability of cash. To garner more he agreed to write for magazines on issues of his presidency and current events. He also assembled a book, *Presidential Problems*, setting out his policy and thinking during the four crises (Richard Nixon's *Six Crises* was half a century away) of his two terms: "The Independence of the Executive," on the matter of his claim of executive privilege in the battle with Congress over removal of officials; "The Government in the Chicago Strike of 1894"; "The Bond Issues"; and "The Venezuelan Boundary Controversy" (published in 1904). A series of articles on hunting and fishing were later assembled in a book, *Fishing and Shooting Sketches*.

On the retirement of presidents he said, "Something ought to be done. As it is now, nothing seems to be *dignified* enough for them. Now there was Harrison; he went into law. The first time he got up to argue a case in court everybody laughed; it seemed so queer. I know how it is. I went back to law myself when I left Washington the first time. I walked into supreme court and there on the bench sat two judges I had appointed myself. No, it doesn't do . . . So a fellow has to remain a loafer all the rest of his life simply because he happened to be president. It isn't right. It isn't fair."

Asked why he didn't write about the subject, he retorted, "I'd

In August 1901, the author of the recently published book Fishing and Shooting Sketches *demonstrated that he knew his subject well. Cleveland wrote: "If we catch a fish we shall add zest to our recreation. If we catch none, we shall still have the outing and the recreation—more healthful and more enjoyable than can be gained in any other way."*

like to—I'd like to very well, only they'd say I was trying to feather my own nest."

Urged to write an autobiography, he hesitated. He wrote to Richard Watson Gilder that he hoped his circle of friends would continue to have faith in him whether his autobiography was written or not. He added poignantly, "I want my wife and children to love me now and hereafter to proudly honor my memory. They will have my autobiography written on their hearts where every day they may turn the pages and read it. In these days what else is there that is worth while to a man nearly sixty-eight years old?"

In the same conversation he said, "I honestly think, my dear Gilder, that there are things in my life and career that if set out, and read by the young men of our country, might be of benefit to a generation soon to have in their keeping the safety and the mission of our nation; but I am not certain of this, for I am by no means sure that it would be in tune with the vaudeville that attracts our people and wins their applause. Somehow I don't want to appear wearing a fur coat in July.

Events which commanded his interest, if not his pen, included the outbreak of hostilities with Spain over Cuba which he had worked to avoid and which began with the sinking of the battleship *Maine* in 1898. He was also distressed that McKinley's administration acceded in the annexation of Hawaii. In a December 3, 1899, letter to Booker T. Washington lauding the work of the Tuskegee Institute, he expressed no alteration in his thinking concerning the black population. But he was at the same time a little prescient on the subject of future racial violence. He wrote, "It has frequently occurred to me that in the present condition of our free negro population in the South, and the incidents surrounding them, we cannot absolutely calculate that the future of our nation will be always free from dangers and convulsions, perhaps not less lamentable than those which resulted from the enslaved negroes less than forty years ago. Then the cause was the injustice of the enslavement of four millions, but now we have to deal with eight millions, who, though free and invested with all the rights of citizenship, still constitute in the body politic a mass largely affected with ignorance, slothfulness, and a resulting lack of appreciation of the obligations of citizenship."

In a speech to the Southern Educational Association in New York City on April 14, 1903, he spoke of "the white man's burden" and called for toleration and consideration of "the feelings and even the prejudice or radical instinct of our fellow-countrymen of the

South, who in the solution of the negro problem must, amid their own surroundings, bear the heat of the day and stagger under the weight of it."

Occasional speeches were not without a touch of drollery. Addressing the Medical Association of New York on February 15, 1890, he declared, "I have no doubt that it is very funny for people to caricature doctors as playing into the hands of undertakers, and to represent lawyers as being on such good terms with the evil one as to preclude the last chance of their salvation."

As retirement did not keep him from speaking out, neither could private citizenship insulate him from his old nemesis, the press. He maintained an aversion to being interviewed. When he did grant a reporter some time, he expected what was said to be off the record. When a correspondent kept urging him to go on the record concerning McKinley's Caribbean policy, particularly on the subject of what was to be done with Puerto Rico (taken by the United States in the Spanish-American War), Grover exclaimed, "That, sir, is a matter of too great importance to discuss in a five-minute interview, now rapidly drawing to its close."

Mellower though he seemed, he still showed flashes of impatience. When a friend decided to demonstrate "a new way to cut your cigar, a more hygienic way," Grover silently watched the procedure, then picked up a cigar and trimmed it in his accustomed unhygienic manner by biting off the end.

He resisted efforts by doctors and concerned friends to get him to exercise by going for walks. He preferred, as always, to exert himself no more than what was required to hook a fish.

Doing just that on a small lake in the Berkshires on September 6, 1901, he learned that President McKinley had been shot while greeting the public at the Pan-American Exposition in Buffalo.

Speaking a week later at a memorial service in Princeton's Alexander Hall, Grover saw "a most serious lesson" for the nation. The shock of it is so great that it is hard at this time to read this lesson calmly. We can hardly fail to see, however, behind the bloody deed of the assassin, horrible figures and faces from which it will not do to turn away. If we are to escape further attack upon our peace and security, we must boldly and resolutely grapple with the monster of anarchy.

With the death of McKinley—the third assassination of a president in Grover Cleveland's lifetime—the dandy known in the New York State Legislature as "the Dude" when Grover was the governor at last came into the higher kingdom foreseen by Henry Cabot Lodge. Within weeks of becoming the twenty-sixth president of the United States, Theodore Roosevelt again found an ally in "the Big One."

Four months before Roosevelt assumed office, coal mine owners had rejected arbitration in a dispute with the United Mine Workers of America. The result was a strike by 140,000 workers, led by their union president, John Mitchell. The work stoppage in the Pennsylvania coal fields continued into autumn and seemed more than likely to carry on into winter. Mindful that he now presided over a nation dependent upon the uninterrupted flow of anthracite to keep industries and railroads operating and for warming homes, schools, and hospitals, Roosevelt welcomed an appeal from the union for the federal government to get involved by establishing a commission to resolve the issues of pay and working conditions. When the owners, led by George F. Baer, refused to agree, Roosevelt felt pressure to follow the course Grover had taken in Chicago and employ troops to maintain order and protect property while the coal companies brought in strikebreakers. Unlike

Theodore Roosevelt.

Grover in the Pullman strike, Roosevelt doubted he had such authority unless the governor of Pennsylvania asked for federal intervention. He chose, instead, to invite Mitchell and coal company presidents to a meeting at the White House on October third. They convened at eleven in the morning. To Roosevelt's dismay, he found the owners unwilling to accept arbitration. When the conference broke up in the afternoon, they exited with a boast that they'd "turned down both the members and the President."

After reading of the collapse of the talks in newspapers while on a train from Gray Gables to Princeton, Grover sent a letter to Roosevelt. He wrote, "I am so surprised and 'stirred up' by the position taken by the contestants that I cannot refrain from making a suggestion. . . . Has it ever been proposed to them that the indignation now being launched against both their houses might be allayed by the production of coal in an amount, or for a length of time, sufficient to serve the necessities of consumers, leaving the parties to the quarrel, after such necessities are met, to take up the fight again where they left off 'without prejudice' if they desire?"

It was an idealistic proposal, but utterly impractical because it was an impossible request. Miners were not prepared to work at unacceptable wages; owners were not interested in having to take them back. But more important to Roosevelt than what the letter proposed was that it came from Grover. It handed Roosevelt moral support, blunted criticism from Democrats, and undercut the argument that Cleveland's handling of the Pullman strike provided an acceptable precedent to follow. If Grover was now against using force, why should Roosevelt employ it?

Roosevelt saw a way to modify Grover's idea. Rather than invoke troops to protect the mines, he would send soldiers to run them and keep coal flowing while the issues underlying the strike were investigated by a presidential commission . . . with Grover Cleveland a member.

When asked if he would participate in *an inquiry*, Grover assented. He then sold all his coal mine stocks, losing $2,500. But when the owners grudgingly surrendered to pressure to accept

Roosevelt's plan, they made it clear that they could not accept as a member of the arbitration commission "the dangerous radical" Cleveland.

Having gotten what he wanted, Roosevelt wrote to Grover to inform him he would not be participating. In fact, Grover had agreed to take part in an investigation, *not* as an arbitrator.

Roosevelt's shrewd use of the name of Grover Cleveland had an unexpected effect on the peace and quiet of retirement from public life which Grover had come to cherish. Speculation ran rampant that he was amenable to running for president in 1904. Among newspapers weighing the likelihood, *The New York Times* thought that "at the proper time the reformer from Buffalo will enter the field."

Grover thundered in reply to that story and others of similar content: "To be thus pictured as an old Brahmin seated in the background and aspiring to manage things my own way is alike distasteful to me and absolutely false as to my true position."

While this was transpiring, Grover accepted a position as a trustee of Princeton University, and awaited the birth of his fifth child. Born on July 18, 1903, the boy was named Francis Grover. In a telegram announcing the birth to Mrs. John Grier Hibben, wife of the future president of Princeton, he joked that "a tramp boy" had trespassed upon the premises and was "first seen and heard about 10 o'clock A.M." The wire continued, "The shameless naked little scoundrel weighed over nine pounds. [His brother] Richard was very much tickled as long as he thought it was something on the doll line, and was quite overcome with laughter when he found it was a real baby. . . . The dear mother is as well, apparently, as possible; and seems to me very self-conceitedly happy—as if she thought she had done a good job."

Cleveland in academic robe in his role as a trustee of Princeton.

To Buzzards Bay neighbors, he followed a different line:

"It may possibly be that some of you are aware of a very recent event in my household which has increased by one the present population of the town of Bourne, and has also added another to the future fishermen in Buzzards Bay. The newcomer was weighed on the scales I use for weighing the fish I catch; and he registered nine pounds and a half. That's not a wonderful weight for a child. For a fish it would be all right and among fishermen no explanation need be made. But it was not a fish that was weighed, and others besides fishermen have an interest in the truthfulness of all that pertains to the vital statistics of Bourne Township. Therefore I take this opportunity to say that nine and a half pounds registered on my fishing scales honestly means nine pounds—no more and no less. The extra half pound is a matter of special and private arrangement between me and the scales. By this statement I satisfy all my conscientious scruples and disdain any attempt to gain credit for half a pound more increase in population than I am entitled to."

Grover's happiness was dimmed in the autumn when he returned to Princeton by the death of Wilson (Shan) Bissell. He saw in Shan's demise a "reminder that the shafts are flying."

Still floating in the political atmosphere were speculation and outright assertions that he was about to return to politics as a candidate for president. He shot down that prospect in a letter of November 25, 1903, for publication by newspaper editor St. Clair McKelway. He wrote, "I have not for a moment been able, nor am I able now, to open my mind to the thought that in any circumstances or upon any consideration, I should ever again become the nominee of my party for the Presidency. My determination not to do so is unalterable and conclusive."

Trusting that the letter would stop the talk, Grover enjoyed Christmas at Westland with Frances, Ruth, Esther, Marion, Richard, and five-month-old tramp trespasser Francis, and looked forward to watching the presidential campaign from the sidelines as Theodore Roosevelt hoped to show that having become president in 1901 as a result of assassination, he could claim the White House on his own in 1904.

The new year did not start well for the Clevelands. On January 2, Grover noted in his diary, "Ruth is a little sick with tonsillitis."

Cleveland's retirement home was named Westland. Seated with him on the steps are (left to right) *Esther, Francis, Mrs. Cleveland, Marion, and Richard. Baby Ruth died of diphtheria in 1904 at age twelve.*

On the third: "Ruth still sick, but better."

January 6: "Doctor said this morning Ruth had diphtheria."

At two in the morning on the seventh, the twelve-year-old was "not so well." Two doctors were called, but before the second arrived, around three o'clock, Ruth died.

She was buried the next day (January 8). On the tenth, Grover wrote in his diary, "I had a season of great trouble in keeping out of my mind the idea that Ruth was in the cold, cheerless grave instead of the arms of her Saviour." The thought was expressed again on the eleventh. "It seems to me I mourn our darling Ruth's death more and more. So much of the time I can only think of her dead, not joyfully living in Heaven."

Four days later, he was feeling better as he wrote, "God has come to my help and I am able to adjust my thought to dear Ruth's death with as much comfort as selfish humanity will permit."

A letter to a friend on February 20 stated, "It seems so long since we buried Ruth, and yet it is only six weeks yesterday. We are becoming accustomed to her absence. For the rest of it we have not a shadow of doubt that all is well with the child."

Although never one to become a member of a church congregation, he had not wandered from his father's religion. Three years after Ruth's death he wrote to Rev. Calvin Dill Wilson, "I have always felt that my training as a minister's son has been more valuable to me as a strengthening influence and an incentive to be useful than any other incident of my life."

★   ★   ★

In April 1903 Grover Cleveland had been out of office for six years and had long reconciled himself to having exited the White House as an extremely unpopular figure, perhaps the most unpopular man in the United States. When friends proposed that he write about his two terms, or at least collect and publish his papers and speeches, he asked dubiously, "Who would want to read them?"

Yet he hadn't been completely abandoned. Some groups proved interested in having him speak to them. Letters expressed encouraging notes about his handling of one issue or another. And there was all that speculation that if he decided to run again, he might find a welcoming reception. But nothing surprised and pleased him quite so much as what happened on the last day of April in a city he had been warned to avoid in the summer of 1887 by members of the Grand Army of the Republic who were irate about the plan for the return of Confederate battle flags.

In the spring of 1903 the people of St. Louis were not interested in remembering the Civil War. Their hearts were set on celebrating the hundredth anniversary of the biggest land deal in the history of America, and possibly the world—President Thomas Jefferson's acquisition from France of almost all the territory west of the Mississippi. To mark the occasion, they extended an invitation to all Americans to "Meet me in St. Louis" at the Louisiana Purchase Exposition. One of those they asked to attend was Grover.

As a private citizen and a president whom he thought Americans considered a failure, he expected no more than cursory applause for no more reason than that he was, like him or not, an ex-president. Americans always showed their respect to someone who'd held the presidency, if only out of deference to the office. Besides, the crowd at the exposition had the current president to cheer, the enormously popular hero of San Juan Hill.

The energetic Rough Rider "Teddy" Roosevelt received a fittingly presidential greeting, but when Grover was introduced and rose to speak, the crowd erupted in a tumultuous ovation which went on and on like rolling thunder.

Evidently, Grover Cleveland was not the anathema he supposed himself to be. When his book, *Presidential Problems*, was published by the Century Company in October 1904, it was not ignored, but widely read. His presence was also welcomed when he spoke in New York City on October 21 on behalf of the Democratic candidate for president, Alton G. Parker. When the Republicans nominated Roosevelt, Grover had written to Richard Olney (who'd been a presidential hopeful himself), "Did you ever see such a boyish, silly performance as the Republican National Convention which has just adjourned? Perhaps Lodge & Co. think they can safely calculate on the stupidity of the people to elect 'Teddy.' "

Parker proved woefully inadequate. A landslide of votes went to the man on a horse who'd charged up San Juan Hill.

Now president in his own right, Roosevelt made Grover an offer of a position around which there could be no controversy. On June 17, 1905, he asked Grover to assume the presidency of a commission in charge of the commemoration of the English settlement in 1607 of Jamestown, Virginia. He assured Grover that the position would demand "little work," but that "your name and position would be an immense strength" for the undertaking. No one dared suggest that Grover was too radical for the post.

The value of the Cleveland name also appealed to a man with a middle name that seemed more than fitting for someone who held a controlling interest in the Equitable Life Assurance Society. In May 1905 Thomas Fortune Ryan had paid $3,500,000 for 502 shares of one of three firms which dominated the lucrative insurance business. The companies (Equitable, Mutual Life, and New York Life) were in fact huge reservoirs of cash which its officers felt free to plunder by any means that secured windfall personal profits. Unfortunately for them, the New York State Insurance Department had launched an investigation. What Ryan hoped to achieve in wresting control of Equitable was to save the firm by reorganizing it, starting with a revolution in how the boards of directors of insurance companies were chosen. Ryan proposed to turn Equitable into a "mutual company" in which policyholders elected a majority of its board (28 of 52 seats). The others would be designated by a three-man panel that would serve as trustees. The plan was endorsed by the insurance department. The three trustees Ryan proposed were men of unimpeachable reputation: George Westinghouse, Justice Morgan J. O'Brien, and Grover Cleveland.

In accepting the offer, Grover pledged to the policyholders that the new directors would be "such persons as are imbued with conservative views of management, and who will regard as distinctly violative of duty the use of funds of the Society directly or indirectly in the promotion, underwriting, or syndicating of new and uncertain enterprises, or the investment of such funds in speculative stocks and securities." He kept his word, and in 1907 accepted an offer to head an insurance-industry watchdog organization, "The President's Association of Life Insurance Companies."

When Grover took on the responsibilities as a trustee of Equitable, he was sixty-nine years old. Among the many birthday gifts he received was a bottle of scotch drawn from the same vat reserved for the British royal family. The presenter was Andrew Carnegie. "Despite all fanatical medical advice," Grover wrote in a thank-you letter, "I insist upon it that a man at the age of sixty-nine, a man should know himself of at least one thing that meets his physical condition."

This was an admission that he was not in the best of health and that he might not live to celebrate his seventieth. But he did, and the nation which he'd believed had turned its back on him in 1896 joyfully marked the milestone with him. The mayor of New York ordered flags flown to honor a private citizen, an unprecedented gesture. Mark Twain was on record as saying Grover's character elevated him to the status of George Washington. The president of Princeton, Woodrow Wilson, wrote him expressing "the admiration and affection" of everyone at the university. At the Cleveland birthplace in Caldwell, New Jersey, a bronze plaque was put up.

Three months after his seventy-first birthday, suffering from gastrointestinal disease, kidney disorders, and heart failure, he was taken secretly by car from a seaside hotel in Lakewood, New Jersey, to Westland. At 8:40 on the morning of June 24, 1908, he said on his last breath, "I have tried so hard to do right."

14

Fur Coat in July

Grover Cleveland spoke again, posthumously, in the September 1908 edition of *American Magazine*:

"A sensitive man is not happy as President. It is fight, fight, fight all the time. I looked forward to the close of my term as a happy release from care. But I am not sure I wasn't more unhappy out of office than in.

A term in the presidency accustoms a man to great duties. He gets used to handling tremendous enterprises, to organizing forces that may affect at once and directly the welfare of the world. After the long exercise of power, the ordinary affairs of life seem petty and commonplace. An ex-President practicing law or going into business is like a locomotive hauling a delivery wagon. He

New York Times *headline.*

341

ROOSEVELT WIRES HIS CONDOLENCE

Abandons Plan to Go to New London and Will Attend the Funeral To-morrow.

MRS. ROOSEVELT GOING, TOO

They Will Make the Trip to Princeton and Return by Special Train.

PRESIDENT'S PROCLAMATION.

OYSTER BAY, L. I., June 24.— This proclamation was issued by the President immediately on hearing of Mr. Cleveland's death:

A PROCLAMATION.
The White House,
June 24, 1908.
To the People of the United States:

Grover Cleveland, President of the United States from 1885 to 1889 and again from 1893 to 1897, died at 8:40 o'clock this morning at his home in Princeton, N. J. In his death the Nation has been deprived of one of its greatest citizens.

By profession a lawyer, his chief services to his country were rendered during a long, varied, and honorable career in public life. As Mayor of his city, as Governor of his State, and twice as President, he showed signal powers as an administrator, coupled with entire devotion to the country's good, and a courage that quailed before no hostility when once he was convinced where his duty lay. Since his retirement from the Presidency he has continued well and faithfully to serve his countrymen by the simplicity, dignity, and uprightness of his private life.

In testimony of the respect in which his memory is held by the Government and people of the United States, I do hereby direct that the flags on the White House and the several departmental buildings be displayed at half staff for a period of thirty days, and that suitable military and naval honors, under the orders of the Secretaries of War and of the Navy, be rendered on the day of the funeral.

Done this twenty-fourth day of June, in the year of our Lord one thousand nine hundred and eight and of the Independence of the United States of America the one hundred and thirty-second. THEODORE ROOSEVELT.

By the President.
ALVEY A. ADEE,
Acting Secretary of State.

New York Times
headline.

has lost his sense of proportion. The concerns of other people and even his own affairs seem too small to be worth bothering about.

I thought I was glad when Mr. McKinley came to Washington to be inaugurated, and I took a drink of rye whiskey with him in the White House and shook hands with him and put my hat on my head and walked out a private citizen. But I miss the strain, the spur of constant thinking, the consciousness of power, the knowledge I was acting for seventy million people. \\

No moment demands more concentration in the minds of the living on the deeds of the dead than a funeral. At Grover Cleveland's on June 26, 1908, a Presbyterian minister closed the service with these lines from Wordsworth's poem "The Character of the Happy Warrior":

Who, if he rise to station of command,
Rises by open means; and there will stand
On honorable terms, or else retire. . . .

Twenty years earlier, in the heat of his failed campaign to stay in the White House, Grover had phrased the sentiment as a question: "What is the use of being elected or re-elected unless you stand for something?"

How well had he done? Shakespeare warned in *Julius Caesar,* "The evil that men do lives after them; the good is oft interred with their bones." But not immediately, and certainly not when Americans bury a president. Praise for "Grover the Good" flowed like a mighty river, and none of it more graciously than from those who had been his severest critics.

The newspaper which had been persistently anti-Cleveland, the *New York Sun*, said in an editorial, "In the long perspective the three most conspicuous features of Mr. Cleveland's public career perhaps are these: his steadfast fidelity to the cause of civil service reform, his readiness to go to war with the strongest naval powers in defense of the principle that is part of the Monroe Doctrine, and his courageous but strictly constitutional application of Federal force in the case of the Chicago railway riots in 1894."

The *New York World's* editorial saw a public career that was "a demonstration of political courage" and cited the wording of President Theodore Roosevelt's statement on Grover's death in which he noted that Cleveland "quailed before no hostility when once he was convinced where his duty lay."

Said Roosevelt's protégé, himself a future president of the United States, William Howard Taft, "Throughout his political life he showed those rugged virtues of the public servant and citizen, the emulation of which by those who follow him will render progress of our political life toward better things a certainty."

New York governor and future Chief Justice of the United States

NO EULOGY OVER MR. CLEVELAND

The ex-President Laid at Rest with the Simplest of Rites, as He Had Wished.

WORDSWORTH POEM READ

"Such a Man," Says Dr. Van Dyke, as He Finishes It, "Was Our Friend."

BARELY 5,000 IN STREETS

President Roosevelt and Three Governors Beside Bier—Troops There, but Solely to Aid Police.

Special to The New York Times.

PRINCETON, N. J., June 26.—Characteristic of the life he had lived since his retirement from the Presidency was the burial here this afternoon of Grover Cleveland. Simply, modestly, in dignified retirement, he passed the last eleven years of his distinguished life, and simply, modestly, with the quiet dignity that marked the man and with no show of pomp or circumstance, his body was borne to the grave.

Not a note of music, not a word of praise for his achievements or of description of his worth, not even a phrase in recital of who he was or what he had done, was uttered. Ministers of his religion read from their ritual its simple but beautiful burial service, and one, his old and close friend, read parts of a century-old poem. Then the friends and distinguished men who had gathered to do him this last honor followed his body to the cemetery, listened there to the conclusion of the burial service, and went their way. Over the solemn hush that rested upon the village rose only the mellow tones of the bell of Old Nassau tolling the passing of the great man.

New York Times *headline.*

343

Charles Evans Hughes said, "The fame of Grover Cleveland is secure because of the ruggedness, the simplicity of his character, and because of his inflexible determination in executing his honest judgment."

A political adviser to Theodore Roosevelt and other Republicans, former secretary of state and future United States senator Elihu Root, declared, "With high and unquestioning courage he stood always for what he believed to be just and honest and best for his country. With unconcealed scorn and wrath he stood against all sham and chicanery."

In the earliest memoir by a friend, *Recollections of Grover Cleveland* (1909), George F. Parker wrote, "With those whom he trusted and who understood him he was the most genial of companions and the staunchest of friends. He recognized in full the dignity of his office and required of others and of himself the observance of its obligations, but he abhorred needless display and empty ceremonial. He sought to accomplish his ends by straightforward methods, and once having made up his mind as to his duty, he was unflinching in his discharge of it."

A slender reminiscence also published in 1909 was entitled *Mr. Cleveland, A Personal Impression.* A Buzzards Bay neighbor after Grover left office for good, its author, Jesse Lynch Williams, wrote, "The quality which impressed one most on becoming acquainted with Mr. Cleveland was not his greatness—one anticipated that; but his genial kindliness and his quiet, pervasive humor. He even had charm. I had pictured him, as many perhaps still see him, a gruff old warrior, resting after his battles, brooding over the past; silent, except when stirred occasionally to pronouncing a polysyllabic profundity; august, austere, a personage difficult to know and impossible to love. I expected to admire him, but it never occurred to me that one might like him; still less that he might care to be liked by those among whom he had cast his lot."

In the introduction to the next year's *Grover Cleveland: A Record of Friendship*, Richard Watson Gilder spoke of "large traits of his character, and those important public services which far transcended partisan accomplishment, have made their impress upon the American people and the world." At a memorial meeting marking what would have been Grover's seventy-second birthday, held in New York's Carnegie Hall in March 1909, Gilder had read a poem he'd composed for the occasion. The second stanza went:

> The people! Never once his faith was dimmed
> In them his countrymen; ah, never once;
> For if doubt shook him, 'twas but a fleeting mood;
> Though others wavered, never wavered he.
> Though madness, like a flood, swept o'er the land,
> This way, now that; though love of pelf subdued
> The civic conscience, still he held his faith,
> Unfaltering, in man's true-heartedness,
> And in the final judgment of free men.

Judgments at the moment of bereavement by friends, associates, allies, and even enemies are understandably sentimental; the verdict of history is cooler because it is rendered later and, supposedly, impersonally. Because Grover lived and governed long before the advent of sound recording and motion pictures, with television and videotape in an even more distant future, the analysis and opinions of those who chose to write about him were gleaned from archives, whether found in the climate-controlled repositories of libraries and other collections, or extracted from sometimes dusty recollections of history's eyewitnesses looking backward through a prism, darkly.

The task was more challenging for the earliest biographers and historians because the subject of their quest had not cooperated. This lamentable fact was discovered by Professor Robert McElroy of Princeton as he set out to write what became a two-volume life of Grover. He found Cleveland's papers packed into rough wooden boxes, without systematic arrangement, the important and unimportant thrown together. Many of the most valuable manuscripts contained no title or other indication of the purpose for which they'd been prepared.

"In most cases, except personal letters," McElroy noted, "the very authorship of the manuscript would be in doubt but for the fact that all are written in 'copper plate,' as he called his own neat but distressingly illegible handwriting."

Practically every letter, message, proclamation, and executive order, even the publicity notices and the successive copies of addresses with revisions, had been done in Grover's hand.

Undaunted, McElroy provided the first fairly objective assessment of Grover's life and political career. At the end of the two volumes' combined total of 745 pages, he wrote, "Living, he dared to disregard party in the service of principle. Dying, he named no party as his heir. Dead, no party and no faction can fairly claim a monopoly of the glory with which the advancing years are steadily crowning his memory."

Nine years after McElroy's book appeared, Allan Nevins in *Grover Cleveland, A Study in Courage* surpassed the professor's text by twenty-one pages in a single volume. Yet even in that brief interval of "advancing years" between the works, the gleam of glory had dimmed, if only a little. Often sharply critical of Grover's personality, political philosophy, and programs, Nevins, as his subtitle advertises, came down on the side of Grover not only in worthiness as man, politician, and president, but in a greatness grounded in "typical rather than unusual qualities."

On pages 4 and 5, Nevins wrote of Grover:

He had no endowments that thousands of men do not have. He possessed honesty, courage, firmness, independence, and common sense. But he possessed them in a degree that others did not. His honesty was of the undeviating type which never compromised an inch; his courage was immense, rugged, unconquerable; his independence was elemental and self-assertive. Beneath all this was a virility or energy which enabled him to impose his qualities upon others in any crisis. Under storms that would have bent any man of lesser strength he ploughed straight forward, never flinching, always following the path that his conscience approved to the end. . . . It is as a strong man, a man of character, that Cleveland will live in memory. For all his shrewdness of judgment, he was never a great intellectual force. It was his personality, not his mind, that made so deep an impress upon his time.

Two prominent historians of the first half of the twentieth century who were not biographers of Grover Cleveland also found much to admire in him. Henry Steele Commager saw Grover alone in post–Civil War presidencies as having some suspicion of the significance and direction of the economic changes which were transforming the country and as daring to confront those individuals and groups who saw government as a way to enrich themselves. Writing in 1948, Richard Hofstadter found in him "the flower of American political culture in the Gilded Age" and "a reasonable facsimile of a major president between Lincoln and Theodore Roosevelt."

Arguably the harshest evaluation of Grover is found in Horace Samuel Merrill's 1957 book on Cleveland and the Democratic Party. Its general theme was that Grover was nothing more than a tool of so-called "Bourbon Democrats" who were businessmen supporting the status quo and opposed to social, economic, and governmental reforms.

In 1968 Rexford Guy Tugwell published a Cleveland biography asserting that Grover's "uncompromising honesty and integrity failed America in a time of crisis." A former member of Franklin D. Roosevelt's "brain trust," former governor of Puerto Rico, professor of political science at the University of Chicago, and scholar at the Center for the Study of Democratic Institutions, Tugwell wrote:

> Cleveland is the statesman in the public life of the United States who best represents the classic of tragedy defined by Aristotle: he was destroyed—or his power and influence were—by his own strength and virtue. . . . He would do nothing and would allow nothing to be done that he or any other might profit from. He would give no favor and accept none, except in the public interest. In the sense understood by all Americans, he was a man of conscience. . . . Above all, he was honest. That there was a higher honesty for governments and their Presidents he never comprehended.

This assertion that there were two standards of honesty—one for individuals and one for governments and presidents—seems astonishing, except that it was made by a New Deal liberal in a year when the very foundations of American government and society appeared to be staggering in the face of an onslaught of individuals and groups which claimed to trust no one over the age of thirty. Tugwell also faulted Grover for not being a visionary. He opined, "Democracies must have leaders who are the people's prophets and who act as their mentors. A prophet must see ahead and turn the people's minds to the future. A mentor Cleveland was—a stern and determined one. A prophet he was not."

This criticism of Grover was attacked two decades later by Richard E. Welch Jr. in *The Presidencies of Grover Cleveland*. He wrote, "Tugwell's censure appears to be not only harsh but essentially ahistorical. If Cleveland is to be damned, it cannot be for his failure to imitate Franklin Delano Roosevelt. Cleveland's record of presidential leadership must be evaluated within the context of the last decades of the nineteenth century, not by the criteria of the 1930s."

A suggestion to Grover that the people of the United States needed a prophet to lead and teach them, and that the person was himself, would have left him flabbergasted. He believed that the futures of individuals and nations were grounded in what *they* did in the present. "As thy days are, so shall thy strength be" was more than a slogan on his law-office wall.

The nine-year-old boy who'd written, "If we expect to be great and good men and be respected and esteemed by our friends we must improve our time when we are young," grew into a man who trusted that the people knew better where they ought to be in the future than could any man in the White House.

The role of a president was to see that government was not an obstacle and that those who governed understood that they were servants, not masters, and that public office is a public trust. The people supported the government—led it—not the other way around.

Rather than a prophesying and mentoring leader, Grover saw himself in the presidency as he had seen himself as mayor and governor—in the role of executive officer and administrator of a business. The business belonged to the people who'd elected him.

"One may regret Cleveland's failure to modernize the federal government or to attempt to make changes in the institutional structure of the presidential office," wrote Welch, "but the electorate in the Gilded Age made no demands that he do so. Grover Cleveland believed that there was little need for basic changes in the institutions of American politics. He advocated the reform of personal behavior, not the reform of the governmental structure."

When historian Arthur Schlesinger Sr. polled seventy-five historians and asked them to rate presidents for "greatness," Grover placed eighth in a field that then totaled thirty-three (counting Grover twice, of course). The ranking placed him in the "near great" category. A similar survey in 1982 by Robert K. Murray and Tim H. Blessing put him at seventeenth and "above average." As noted in the Prologue, Arthur Schlesinger Jr.'s 1996 poll placed Grover as "high average" with John Adams, Monroe, McKinley, Eisenhower, Kennedy, and Lyndon Johnson. In a 1997 book, *Rating the Presidents*, by William J. Ridings Jr. and Stuart B. McGiver, more than seven hundred historians and political scientists from every region of the nation graded Grover as follows:

Overall Ranking: 16

Leadership: 13

Accomplishments and Crisis Management: 17

Appointments: 17

Character and Integrity: 16

A unique evaluation of Grover was tendered by the United States Treasury. In honor of the president who fought to keep the country on the gold standard, it put Grover's portrait on currency. Never meant for public circulation and discontinued in 1934, it was a Federal Reserve note in the amount of $1,000.

Frances Cleveland remarried in 1913, becoming Mrs. Thomas J. Preston, the wife of a Princeton professor. She died in 1947. A hundred years after she had fulfilled her pledge that she and her husband would return to the White House to resume Grover's interrupted presidency, the esteem and legacy of her husband as president were either unknown or irrelevant to most Americans. The only people who cared were teachers of history and students required to take their courses, professional historians, political scientists, government buffs, and contestants on TV game shows. But that general ignorance or indifference quickly turned to fascination when Americans learned in 1998 that their current president was entangled in a sex scandal.

Suddenly, Grover Cleveland became a household name. Americans heard about the child he supposedly fathered "out of wedlock." In a country in which untold unmarried women and girls were having babies, the very phrase sounded quaintly anachronistic. While almost everyone in the country came to recognize the names of women with whom Clinton was alleged to have had affairs, the first being Gennifer Flowers, then Paula Jones, and then a White House intern named Monica Lewinsky, hardly any could have identified Maria Halpin.

What Americans learned was that in the handling of the somewhat similar sex scandals, Clinton had failed to measure up to Grover in one important aspect. In 1884 Grover had admitted the truth of his failing and ordered his campaign staff to do the same.

★   ★   ★

Had Grover been able to materialize in the era of Clinton, what might he have thought? It's more than likely that he would not have been surprised by the frenzied attention given to Clinton's women troubles and the press's obsession with them. He certainly would have marveled at—and been repelled by—the amazing new methods available to reporters to focus on both the public and private lives of a president—television, cable, talk radio, the Internet—and the extent to which private lives of all officials had become the public's business.

What of spinmeisters, pollsters, the use of focus groups to decide government policy, war rooms, dirty tricksters, private detectives hired to dig up negative information on opponents, paid political consultants, photo ops, press leaks? What about the parsing of words and twisting of the English language so that even the meaning of "is" could be questioned?

Grover also would have discovered about the Clinton era of politics and government and the press, as Gail Collins wrote in 1998 in *Scorpion Tongues: Gossip, Celebrity and American Politics*, that "once in office, it was natural that Clinton would become a trailblazer in eliminating the public's sense that there were certain things you didn't say about a president in public. His willingness to answer a question on an MTV forum about what kind of underwear he wore was the first stunning breach of the old propriety."

If Grover could rise from his grave in the old Princeton Cemetery to take a look around the United States nearly a hundred years after his death, he would not be surprised to find a president in the glare of sensation seekers. He would disapprove of a citizen asking such a question. And he would have been appalled that a president of the United States not only chose to answer it, but found it amusing to do so. In his beloved United States of America at the dawning of the third millennium, he would realize that he'd returned to life as a man in a fur coat in July.

Chronology

1837–1854

1837 Born in Caldwell, New Jersey, on March 18, named Stephen Grover.

1841 Family moved to Fayetteville, New York.

1850 Visited Uncle Lewis F. Allen in Buffalo, New York

When family moved to Clinton, attended Clinton Liberal Institute.

1852 Clerk in store of Deacon John McVicar, Fayetteville.

1853 Family moves to Holland Patent, New York.

His father, Richard, dies of peritonitis.

Appointed assistant teacher at New York Institution for the Blind, New York City.

1854 Returns to Holland Patent.

1855–1883

1855 Leaves Holland Patent for Cleveland, Ohio, but his uncle persuades him to remain in Buffalo and study law.

Appointed clerk in law firm of Rogers, Bowen and Rogers.

1859 Admitted to the New York State Bar.

1862 Elected ward supervisor.

1863 Appointed Erie County assistant district attorney, serves two years.

Name is first one drawn under Civil War Conscription Act of 1863, legally pays a substitute to serve for him.

1864 Birth of Frances Folsom, daughter of Grover's friend Oscar Folsom.

1865 Defeated in election for Erie County district attorney.

1866 Forms law partnership with Isaac K. Vanderpoel.

1870 Elected sheriff of Erie County for two-year term.

1872 Personally carries out execution by hanging of Patrick Morrissey, convicted of murdering his mother. Grover orders canvas put up to block public viewing.

1873 Hangs gambler Jack Gaffney for killing a man in a card game.

1874 Forms law partnership with Oscar Folsom and Wilson S. (Shan) Bissell.

1881 Elected mayor of Buffalo as a Democrat.

1882–1883 Earns reputation for honest government and is nicknamed "the veto mayor."

Mother, Ann, dies (July 19, 1882).

Nominated by Democrats for governor of New York (September 22).

Elected governor (November 7) with largest majority in state history.

1884

Inaugurated as governor (January 1).

Vetoes Five-cent Fare Bill; forms alliance with Republican Theodore Roosevelt.

Reform-minded Republicans bolt party after nomination of James G. Blaine for president; dissidents become known as Mugwumps.

Leading upstate Democrats ask Grover to be presidential candidate; he accepts and wins nomination (July 11).

Maria Halpin scandal; Grover admits fathering her son, orders campaign aides to "tell the truth."

Defends not serving in Civil War.

New York minister says Democrats are party of "Rum, Romanism, and Rebellion."

Grover's election as president confirmed after three days of doubts about vote.

FIRST TERM
1885

Sworn in as president (March 4).

Promotes civil service reform, asserts government posts will be filled on basis of ability, not party affiliation; defends gold standard; calls for repeal of the Tenure of Office Act, restricting presidential power to appoint and remove.

Youngest sister, Rose, fills role as White House hostess.

Vice President Thomas Hendricks dies (November 25).

1886–1889

Signs Presidential Succession Act, providing for heads of executive departments in order of department's creation to succeed to presidency in event of death, resignation, or removal of president and vice president (January 19).

Signs Dawes Act (Indian Emancipation Act) to disestablish reservations system and grant American citizenship to Indians (February 8).

Issues message to Congress on subject of labor, the first in history (April 22).

First of vetoes of special bills granting unwarranted military pensions (May 8).

Recommends Congress accept France's gift of Statue of Liberty (May 11).

Announces plans to marry Frances Folsom (May 25).

First wedding in history of White House (June 2).

Tenure of Office Act repealed (June–November).

Dedication of Statue of Liberty (October 28).

Samuel Gompers forms American Federation of Labor (December 8).

1887

Congress creates Interstate Commerce Commission; Grover approves (February 4).

Vetoes Dependent Pension Bill, which would have granted pensions to anyone who served at least ninety days in any war (February 11).

Vetoes Texas Seed Bill for relief of drought-stricken farmers (February 16).

Tenure of Office Act repealed (March 3).

Uproar over approval of return of Confederate battle flags (May 26–June 16) forces rescinding of order.

Tours states of the West and South (September 20–October 22).

Address to Congress deals only with repeal of protective tariff law.

1888–1889

Appoints Lucius Q. C. Lamar of Mississippi to Supreme Court (January 16).

Reveals revised civil service rules (February 2).

Appoints Melville W. Fuller as Chief Justice of the United States (April 30).

Department of Labor established (June 13).

Republicans nominate Benjamin Harrison for president (June 19–23).

Accepts presidential renomination by Democratic Party (September 8).

Signs Chinese Exclusion Act restricting Chinese immigration to U.S. (October 8).

Wins popular vote in election but loses to Harrison in electoral vote (November 6).

Signs bill creating Department of Agriculture (February 11).

Signs bill making states of territories of North and South Dakota, Montana, and Washington (February 22).

OUT OF OFFICE
1889

Benjamin Harrison inaugurated; Mrs. Cleveland tells White House staff Grover and she will be back as president and first lady in four years (March 4).

Grover and Frances settle in New York City, reside temporarily at Victoria Hotel; Grover joins law firm; Madison Avenue house is bought.

Supreme Court upholds constitutionality of Chinese Exclusion Act (May 13).

Clevelands spend summer at Buzzards Bay, Massachusetts, eventually buy a home which they name Gray Gables.

1890

Harrison signs Dependent Pension Act (which Grover had vetoed), Sherman Silver Purchase Act (mandating government purchase of all silver mined in the United States), and McKinley Tariff Act, raising rates.

Congressional elections give Democrats control of House of Representatives.

1891

Grover writes letter opposing silver coinage under Sherman Act (February 10).

Speeches signal Democrats that Grover is available again for president (April–May).

Ruth Cleveland (Baby Ruth) born (October 3).

Authorizes organization of a Cleveland presidential campaign (December 12).

1892

New York State Democrats hold "snap convention" in effort to block Cleveland's nomination; Grover wishes them "good weather" (February 22).

Populist Party of the U.S.A. organized in St. Louis (February 22).

Republicans renominate Harrison (June 7–10).

Democrats renominate Grover (June 21–23).

Populists nominate James Blair Weaver of Iowa (July 2–5).

Steel workers locked out of Andrew Carnegie's plant at Homestead, Pennsylvania, call for general strike; clash with Pinkerton men hired to keep plant running results in ten deaths; state militia breaks strike (July 2–November 20).

Presidential campaign is called quietest and cleanest in years (June – November).

Grover elected with 277 electoral votes to Harrison's 145 (November 8).

1893

Americans in Hawaii, led by planter Sanford B. Dole, depose Queen Liliuokalani and declare a republic (January 16).

President Harrison sends Treaty of Annexation of Hawaii to Senate (February 15).

SECOND TERM
1893

Grover inaugurated as only president elected to nonconsecutive terms (March 4).

Withdraws Hawaiian annexation treaty (March 9).

U.S. Treasury gold reserve falls below $100 million for first time (April 22).

Grover vows defense of gold standard (April 23).

Stock market crashes, beginning "the Great Panic" (May 4).

Malignant growth discovered on roof of Grover's mouth (June 18).

Grover calls special session of Congress for August 8 to deal with economic crisis through tariff reform and repeal of silver-purchase law (June 30).

Secret operation aboard the yacht *Oneida* in New York City's East River removes cancerous growth and a portion of Grover's jaw (July 1).

Congress begins debate on tariffs and silver (August 8); William Jennings Bryan delivers memorable speech in favor of silver (August 16); House votes to repeal silver clauses of Sherman Act (August 28).

Esther Cleveland born; first birth in White House (September 9).

Sherman Silver Purchase Act repealed (November 1).

1894

Treasury bonds offered for sale in effort to boost gold reserves (January 17).

Tariff revisions bill passes House of Representatives (February 1).

Jacob Coxey's "Army of the Commonwealth of Christ" leaves Massillon, Ohio, in march on Washington to demand government action to cure economic depression (March 25); their arrival on Capitol Hill (April 28) results in violence and arrest and conviction of Coxey for trespassing.

A strike by employees of the Pullman railway car company, led by Eugene Debs, president of the American Railway Union, spreads and halts rail service in the West; when rioting erupts, Attorney General Richard Olney recommends, and Grover concurs in, sending federal troops to Chicago; Debs and others are arrested and the strike is broken (May–July).

U.S. government recognizes Republic of Hawaii (August 9).

Wilson-Gorman Tariff Bill signed into law, including an income tax on stocks and bonds (August 28).

U.S. intervenes in boundary dispute between Venezuela and Great Britain; the issue eventually involves U.S. assertion of rights under the Monroe Doctrine; rather than go to war with the United States, Britain agrees to arbitration (December 1894–June 1897).

1895

Third Treasury bond sale to syndicate headed by J. P. Morgan restores depleted gold reserves and underpins the credit of the government; Morgan and associates realize a profit of $7 million (February 8–20).

Revolution begins in Cuba against Spanish rule (February 24).

Supreme Court nullifies income tax law (May 20).

Supreme Court upholds right of government to obtain injunctions to guarantee the general welfare, justifying the arrest of Eugene Debs (May 27).

Marion Cleveland born at Gray Gables (July 7).

1896

Utah admitted to statehood (January 4).

Fourth bond sale of $100 million announced (January 6); it results by month's end in restoration of gold reserve to a safe level ($124 million).

Republican National Convention nominates William McKinley (June 16–18).

Democratic nomination of William Jennings Bryan signals party's abandonment of the gold standard (July 7–11).

Disgruntled Democrats meet in Indianapolis and form "Gold Democrats" (August 7); their appeal to Grover to be presidential candidate is refused (September 3).

McKinley elected (November 3).

1897

Treaty of arbitration in the Venezuelan dispute signed by Great Britain and the United States (January 11).

Bill to ban illiterate immigrants vetoed (February 9).

McKinley inaugurated (March 4).

RETIREMENT
1897

Cleveland family settles in Princeton, New Jersey (March 18).

Richard Folsom Cleveland born, in new home called "Westland" (October 28).

1898–1901

U.S. battleship *Maine* blown up in Havana harbor (February 15, 1898).

War declared between United States and Spain (April 25, 1898).

Congress approves annexation of Hawaii (June 16, 1898).

Colonel Theodore Roosevelt leads his dismounted cavalrymen (Rough Riders) in decisive charge against Spanish fortifications atop San Juan Heights overlooking Santiago, Cuba, leading to Spain's surrender (July 1); Roosevelt returns home a hero (August) and is elected governor (November 1898).

Treaty between United States and Spain cedes Cuba, Puerto Rico, and the Philippines to American control (February 6, 1899).

Grover delivers two lectures at Princeton on "The Independence of the Executive" (April 9 and 10, 1900). The lectures and other writings on major issues of his administrations will be published as a book, *Presidential Problems*, in October 1904.

Democrats again nominate William Jennings Bryan (July 4, 1900).

President McKinley reelected, with Theodore Roosevelt as vice president (November 6, 1900); assassination of McKinley in September 1901 moves Roosevelt into the presidency (September 14).

Grover elected a trustee of Princeton University (October 15, 1901).

Roosevelt asks Grover to serve on a commission of arbitration in a coal strike by the United Mine Workers, but Grover eventually does not participate (October 4–6, 1901).

Grover speaks at Louisiana Purchase Exposition in St. Louis and receives a thunderous ovation (April 30, 1903).

Death of Baby Ruth at the age of twelve from diphtheria (January 7, 1904).

Grover declines to be nominated again for president (June 16, 1904).

Accepts post as trustee of Equitable Life Assurance Society (June 10, 1905) and later becomes head of "The Presidents' Association of Life Insurance Companies" (February 1907).

As a result of gastrointestinal disease complicated by kidney and heart problems, suffers a series of heart attacks and dies in his bed at Westland on June 24, 1908; buried at Princeton on June 26.

A Note on Sources

In setting out to write about Grover Cleveland nearly a century after his death, I had the advantage of having met the twenty-second and twenty-fourth president of the United States while writing about the life of a man of different physique, personality, and political party who through a series of remarkable events followed Grover's footsteps into the Executive Chamber in Albany and then to the White House—the irrepressible "Dude" and later "Rough Rider" named Theodore Roosevelt. You cannot deal with Teddy without encountering Grover almost every step of the way. Consequently, it seemed elementary that my telling of the story of Grover the Good would begin with both the ending of their association—TR at Grover's funeral—and its beginning in the capital of New York when the Dude and the Big One discerned mutual profit in not being enemies.

While I'd accumulated a great deal of information about Grover's relationship with TR as I wrote my two Roosevelt books, *Commissioner Roosevelt* and *Colonel Roosevelt*, I knew very little about Grover's life before he met TR and not much more of him outside that relationship—other than the facts everyone of my age had learned in school: he was fat, his naughty behavior which made him a bachelor father, the nonconsecutive terms as president, his wedding having been the first conducted in the White House, Baby Ruth, and her sister's unprecedented White House birth. I also knew Grover had gotten out of the Civil War by paying someone else to go for him, which I understood was not that big a deal.

As every Johnny-come-lately does in the writing of a biography of a president, I began my research into Grover by standing on the shoulders of extraordinary pioneers in the subject I'd dared to tackle. But what amazed me was how little had been written about Grover Cleveland, and how long it had been since the last book appeared dealing with his whole life in detail, rather than in the form of analyses of his politics and approach to governance. The most recent claim to "biography" had been Rexford Guy Tugwell's book in 1968. Before that, I had to go back to 1932's massive "life" by Allan Nevins, who is arguably the Cleveland touchstone because he produced not only the monumental *Grover Cleveland: A Study in Courage* but also a compendium of Grover's letters.

Yet even Mr. Nevins had enjoyed the benefits of the labors of a predecessor in Professor Robert McElroy's two-volume biography, published in 1923. And there were memoirs by George F. Parker and Richard Watson Gilder. In addition to these, there was Charles H. Armitage's trove of gems called *Grover Cleveland, as Buffalo Knew Him*, with its charming anecdotes of "Big Steve" Cleveland carousing in saloons while learning how to be a lawyer, not realizing he was laying a foundation for an astonishing ascent to the presidency without, I think, precedent or subsequent parallel. In reading accounts of Grover by people who'd known him, along with his letters and some retrospective essays, as well as a couple of collections of his speeches and official papers, I found myself wishing that Grover had not opted against writing an autobiography, as Roosevelt had done. It was sweet and even eloquent of Grover to tell a friend that the autobiography that counted was the one his wife and children had "written on their hearts." But a first-person, blow-by-blow, day-by-day telling of his story in his own words would have been nice.

As a lifelong journalist, I have always put a great deal of store in the value of old newspapers and magazines as a window into the past. As somebody once noted, "Journalism is history shot on the wing." Certainly, if what's being sought is the weather conditions, what someone was wearing, or the look of a setting, you can't beat the eyewitness accounts of the reporters who were there making notes for their stories. Fortunately, the 1880s and 1890s were a period rich in journalism which caught the details while providing the substance of events and controversies. Evidence of how ubiquitous the Fourth Estate was in Grover's time is found in his continuous complaining about its intrusion into his private life. I consulted the newspapers often.

Wherever possible in writing this book, I tried to cite such sources in the text. I count myself among authors who constitute what I suppose you could call "revisionists" on the use of footnotes. I agree with Theodore Roosevelt, who complimented an author for not cluttering his work with them. TR said, "I was delighted that you did not use footnotes. I believe they distract from the narrative." Amen.

Because I intended my treatment of the life and times of Grover Cleveland for a general readership, rather than for an audience of historians and scholastics, I did not wish to write a book that would pass what the late novelist John O'Hara called "the heft test," employed by people who believe a book isn't worth buying, or to be taken seriously, unless it's thick and heavy in the hand. Frankly, I wanted to publish a book which had a reasonable chance of being read by people like me who knew a bit about Grover Cleveland and wanted to learn more, without breaking an arm or falling asleep.

My purpose was not to stuff between the covers of this book mind-numbing details and minutiae, but to tell Grover's story as I came to understand and appreciate it—the tale of a man and president long ago who was intensely human, vulnerable, courageous, occasionally stupid in things he did, charming, romantic, sometimes infuriating; who could be petty at times and wonderfully magnanimous and gracious at others, and even funny.

What I discovered, too, in a man of his time is that Grover Cleveland is in many ways also a man for *our* day. He was, as President Clinton observed in citing a parallel between himself and Grover, a reformer, futurist, and vastly underappreciated leader. Ironically, Mr. Clinton's troubles while president prompted comparisons to Grover in which Mr. Clinton didn't fare well. It seems highly unlikely that a newspaper today would say of Mr. Clinton, as Joseph Pulitzer's *World* said of Grover in 1884, "He is honest. He is honest. He is honest. He is honest."

But the president was right in saying that Grover Cleveland has been underappreciated.

It's my hope that this book helps correct that misjudgment.

Bibliography

Armitage, Charles H. *Grover Cleveland, as Buffalo Knew Him*. Buffalo: The Buffalo Evening News, 1926.

Beer, Thomas. *The Mauve Decade*. New York: Carroll & Graf Publishers, Inc., 1997.

Boardman, Fon, Jr. *America and the Gilded Age*. New York: Henry Z. Walck, 1972.

Boller, Paul F., Jr. *Presidential Anecdotes*. New York: Oxford University Press, 1981.

Bremer, Howard F. *Grover Cleveland, 1837–1908*. Dobbs Ferry, N.Y., 1968.

Cleveland, Grover, edited by Albert Ellery Bergh. *Grover Cleveland: Addresses, State Papers and Letters*. New York: The Sun Dial Classics Co., 1909.

———. *Fishing and Shooting Sketches*. New York: Outing Publishing Co., 1906.

———. *Presidential Problems*. New York: The Century Co., 1904.

Collins, Gail. *Scorpion Tongues*. New York: William Morrow and Co., 1998.

Ford, Henry Jones. *The Cleveland Era*. New York: United States Publishers Association, 1919.

Garrison, Webb. *A Treasury of White House Tales*. Nashville: Rutledge Hill Press, 1989.

Gilder, Richard Watson. *Grover Cleveland: A Record of Friendship*. New York: The Century Co., 1910.

Gould, Lewis L. *The Presidency of Theodore Roosevelt*. Lawrence, Kansas: The University Press of Kansas, 1991.

Hollingsworth, J. Rogers. *The Whirligig of Politics: The Democracy of*

Cleveland and Bryan. Chicago and London: The University of Chicago Press, 1963.

Hudson, William. *Random Recollections of an Old Political Reporter*. New York: Cupples & Leon, 1911.

Hugins, Roland. *Grover Cleveland: A Study in Political Courage*. Washington, D.C.: The Anchor-Lee Publishing Co., 1922.

Lynch, Denis. *Grover Cleveland: A Man Four-Square*. New York: Horace Liveright, 1932.

McElroy, Robert. *Grover Cleveland, The Man and the Statesman*. New York and London: Harper and Brothers, 1923.

McMath, Robert C., Jr. *American Populism: A Social History 1877–1898*. New York: Hill and Wang, 1993.

Merrill, Horace Samuel. *Bourbon Leader: Grover Cleveland and the Democratic Party*. Boston: Little, Brown & Co., 1957.

Miller, Nathan. *Theodore Roosevelt: A Life*. New York: William Morrow and Co., 1992.

Morris, Edmund. *The Rise of Theodore Roosevelt*. New York: Coward, McCann, and Geohegan, 1979.

Nevins, Allan. *Grover Cleveland: A Study in Courage*. New York: Dodd, Mead & Co., 1932.

———. *Letters of Grover Cleveland*. New York: Houghton Mifflin Co., 1933.

Parker, George F. *Recollections of Grover Cleveland*. New York: The Century Co., 1909.

———. *The Writings and Speeches of Grover Cleveland*. New York: Cassell Publishing Co., 1909.

Ridings, William J., Jr., and Stuart B. McGiver. *Rating the Presidents*. New York: Carol Publishing Group, 1997.

Seale, William. *The President's House*. Washington, D.C.: White House Historical Association, with the National Geographic Society, 1986.

Tugwell, Rexford Guy. *Grover Cleveland*. Toronto, Ontario: The Macmillan Co., 1968.

Welch, Richard E., Jr. *The Presidencies of Grover Cleveland*. Lawrence, Kansas: The University Press of Kansas, 1988.

Williams, Jesse Lynch. *Mr. Cleveland: A Personal Impression*. New York: Dodd, Mead & Co., 1909.

Index

About the Author

A broadcast newsman for more than thirty years and a former professor of journalism and writing, H. Paul Jeffers has published forty books of fiction and nonfiction, including three on Theodore Roosevelt (*Commissioner Roosevelt, Colonel Roosevelt,* and *The Bully Pulpit*). His other histories are *Bloody Business: An Anecdotal History of Scotland Yard;* the story of the FBI's serial-killer unit, *Who Killed Precious?;* and the story of New York's famed '21' Club. He lives in New York City.